Sex Under the Swastika

Sex Under the Swastika

Erotica, Scandal and the Occult in Hitler's Third Reich

Tim Heath

First published in Great Britain in 2023 by
Pen & Sword History
An imprint of
Pen & Sword Books Ltd
Yorkshire – Philadelphia

Copyright © Tim Heath 2023

ISBN 978 1 52679 142 9

The right of Tim Heath to be identified as Author of this work has been asserted by him in accordance with the Copyright, Designs and Patents Act 1988.

A CIP catalogue record for this book is available from the British Library.

All rights reserved. No part of this book may be reproduced or transmitted in any form or by any means, electronic or mechanical including photocopying, recording or by any information storage and retrieval system, without permission from the Publisher in writing.

Typeset by Mac Style
Printed in the UK by CPI Group (UK) Ltd, Croydon, CR0 4YY.

Pen & Sword Books Limited incorporates the imprints of Atlas, Archaeology, Aviation, Discovery, Family History, Fiction, History, Maritime, Military, Military Classics, Politics, Select, Transport, True Crime, Air World, Frontline Publishing, Leo Cooper, Remember When, Seaforth Publishing, The Praetorian Press, Wharncliffe Local History, Wharncliffe Transport, Wharncliffe True Crime, White Owl and After the Battle.

For a complete list of Pen & Sword titles please contact

PEN & SWORD BOOKS LIMITED
47 Church Street, Barnsley, South Yorkshire, S70 2AS, England
E-mail: enquiries@pen-and-sword.co.uk
Website: www.pen-and-sword.co.uk

Or

PEN AND SWORD BOOKS
1950 Lawrence Rd, Havertown, PA 19083, USA
E-mail: Uspen-and-sword@casematepublishers.com
Website: www.penandswordbooks.com

'His skin wasn't soft in the slightest, it had the texture of some desert dwelling reptile, so much so that the nails of her fingers were unable to penetrate during their overly vigorous lovemaking; he traced the jagged edges of her mouth with his tongue, undecided upon this beautiful half-demon, half-angel whose belly he was laid upon; she struggled to break free of his restraints, like a rat in a trap whose only option to free itself was to gnaw through its own ensnared limb; he desired her, he teased her and she hated him for it.'

Alessa Goberg

Contents

Introduction		ix
Chapter 1	Sex Before the War	1
Chapter 2	Human Wreckage on the Moral High Road	18
Chapter 3	No Cow Without the Bull	26
Chapter 4	The *Sturmbannführer*'s Lolita	38
Chapter 5	Pariahs of Sodom	55
Chapter 6	A Lust for The Young	67
Chapter 7	Sex and School	86
Chapter 8	Virility and Velvet (The Martial Law Manual for Making Love)	92
Chapter 9	Orgasm and the Nazis	116
Chapter 10	Dressing Up	121
Chapter 11	The Pleasure and the Pain	127
Chapter 12	The Antichrist's Astrologer	139
Chapter 13	Sex on the Side	149
Chapter 14	Deutscher Militarbordelle	156
Chapter 15	Hermann Göring: Mr Toad of the Third Reich	165
Chapter 16	The Dr Goebbels Guide to Good Sex	169
Chapter 17	A Hard-on for Death	175
Chapter 18	The Man Who Made Love With His Boots On	181
Chapter 19	Rape and Sexual Abuse in the Concentration Camps	184

Chapter 20	*Lebensborn*: A Biological Call to Arms	190
Chapter 21	Sex in Psychological Warfare	197
Chapter 22	*Fit zum Ficken*! (Fit to Fuck!)	201
Chapter 23	Adolf and Eva: A Consummation of Death	212
Chapter 24	An Exclusive Club	226
Chapter 25	Pipistrelle Whispers	230
Chapter 26	Nazi Fetishism in the Twenty-first Century	237
Afterword		246
Bibliography		251
Acknowledgements		252

Introduction

'It wasn't the pigtail pulling, doggy-style sex on the straw of some deserted barn. The Nazi state wanted it cold, informal, orchestrated and biological, and in fitting with the hypocrisy of which it preached.'

Alessa Goberg

It can be said that Adolf Hitler's Third Reich, although pertaining to convey the racial and moral purity of its brand of Aryanism to the greater world, was a bloody, corrupt, nihilistic, fratricidal and purgatory regime, and that its sexual excesses compared favourably with those of the universally despised and feared Roman emperor, Caligula. Yet, today, attempts that are made within a literary context to explore both fact and rumour regarding the sexual morality of the period, particularly where Hitler's sexuality is concerned, are often met with fierce ridicule and condemnation from some modern historians. But why?

The objective of this work was to seek those who witnessed, either through first-hand experience, twitching curtains, a partially closed door, or private conversation, the innermost mechanics of Nazi sexuality. Since the end of the Second World War only a handful of historians have attempted any serious analysis of the Nazi perception of sex. Rumours of abuse, perversion, sadomasochism and sexual occult practices seem to have served only to muddy the waters further, making the separation of fact from fiction a difficult endeavour. To find the truth one must explore beneath those muddy waters, blurred even further by the passage of time, and challenge modern history's inability to see beyond the academically acceptable narratives of life under the Third Reich.

Sex Under the Swastika: Sex, Scandal and Erotica in Hitler's Third Reich aims to analyse the attitude toward sex from the pre-Nazi years of the Weimar Republic through to the Third Reich, with its contradictory, sometimes confusing, attitudes – not only to the perceived roles of males and females within the Reich, but with the act of sex itself.

Previously unpublished material from sources which include ordinary citizens, through to the sons and daughters of former SS staff, some of whom were on the personal staff of Adolf Hitler, Heinrich Himmler and Reinhard Heydrich, *Sex Under the Swastika* pulls back the clean white sheets to reveal the truth behind the sexual activities of one of the twentieth century's most evil empires.

Austrian-born Klara Busch, a close confidante of Eva Braun's youngest sister, Margarete, reveals what Margarete Braun has told her is a true account of the sexual relationship between Hitler and Eva. The story is documented here for the first time.

It is ironic that even within a totalitarian regime that professed the virtues of a national community, where strength, health, fitness and blood purity were core Nazi values, and every individual played their part, there was a furtive undercurrent, an almost parallel universe of necro-coital fixation, where those in power, together with their lapdogs and subordinates, were free to pursue affairs, engage in paedophilia, and indulge in every possible expression of lust, sexual excess and fetish, as they pleased.

Over the past thirty-six years I have researched primarily the social history aspects of Adolf Hitler's Third Reich, and I have been privy to all manner of previously unrecorded revelations. Some of these have been not only sexually explicit, but of such an abhorrent nature that I had absolutely no idea what could be done with them. But these disclosures kept creeping into the interviews I was conducting with a significant number of no-longer-young German men and women, over the years. It is these unsolicited revelations that prompted the idea of *Sex Under the Swastika* as a literary work. For me, personally, all the justification I required to produce the synopsis for this book was the full support of my publisher, Pen & Sword Books.

Despite the graphic and sometimes horrifying accounts recorded here, this volume is certainly not intended as some form of cheap humour and/or titillation. The subject of sex in Hitler's Third Reich is no laughing matter, as the reader of this book will discover.

Chapter 1

Sex Before the War

Well in advance of the opening salvo of the Second World War, Jews in German society were seen frequently as the perpetrators of the sexual immorality that seems to have defined Weimar social culture throughout its post-First World War existence. But of course, Jews were a convenient scapegoat and eventually bore all the blame and consequent wrath for every ill that had descended upon German society since 1918.

However, it is evident from stories of the burgeoning nightlife and social scene in Germany in the early 1900s that it was not just Jews participating in the pleasures of the flesh – and other excesses that church leaders would later proclaim as exclusively 'Jewish diseases'. It was quite the contrary. The world society of the 1900s by its very nature was a decadent culture. This is revealed all too clearly in the personal writings of Joshua H. Studding, the son of a wealthy American gold prospector. In 1910 Joshua was looking to invest in a friend's business venture in Berlin and gives the following detailed, explicit account of an evening out in that city:

> Despite the air of aristocratic respectability in this city I am amazed at the antics of young male and female socialites who I can only best describe as the privileged champagne brats of the city's elite. The young women in particular in their beautiful dresses appear the perfect hosts of the many cocktail parties one with money can be expected to attend; it is a small circle here and believe me you stand out. It was during the course of one such cocktail party I was introduced to the 21-year-old daughter of a city investor named Abbigail. Her evening dress was light to the point of near transparency, it was a hue of the colour of the pink champagne she was knocking back. Her pre-party manicure was flawless, her eyes lips and high cheekbones beautifully complemented and enhanced by the application of eye shadow, lipstick and rouge. Abbigail's English was not perfect, yet it was audible and easily understood. She made it clear that this was an

exclusive if Dionysian sect. Abbigail sits with me sipping from her glass and pointing out who was who in the room. Two particularly attractive young women enter the room, both wearing bejewelled tiaras. Abbigail explains they are not sisters as I had assumed them to be and that they were almost definitely lovers. The two girls remained detached from the rest of the clientele, totally engrossed within their own company. Occasionally they would glance about the room, offering the merest flicker of a smile, just enough to indicate some brief acknowledgement of the others in the room. I made repeated attempts at making eye contact with them but to no avail; they appeared to be interested only in each other. Abbigail began to tire at my obvious lack of interest in her; she jabbed me hard in the ribs with her elbow then muttered an expletive before snatching her glass and vanishing out of a door leaving me sitting by myself.

As the evening drew on the older guests began to leave for their homes and beds. Abbigail who much to my surprise returns to her seat beside me before leaning into my ear whispering, 'When the old farts have gone, we can all have some real fun.' There was no warning that this 'fun' might imply a heavy use not only of alcohol but drugs. By midnight, the curtains are drawn, shoes are kicked off and hair ornaments pulled out. Cocaine is brought in, and some indulge whilst others just watch. The drug fuels energy and sex drive simultaneously and it is not long before the remaining young couples begin to partner off and head for the bedrooms. Abbigail insists I go with her; she grabs me by the wrist pulling me along behind her like a teacher would a scorned child. As we enter the bedroom the door is locked and any notion of male domination during the act of making love is soon dispelled. My trousers are forcefully removed, cast aside along with our other items of clothing, her bed is firm yet comfortable as I find myself pinned to it. Her kisses are forceful, urgent, heavily moistened with her sweet champagne-perfumed saliva. Her tongue explores every contour of my bare torso as if an artist's brush. The feelings are delicious, the erotic anticipation building as her tongue reaches my groin. She gazes at me momentarily, her lips flicker a smile, the pupils of her eyes are fully dilated, more as a result of the drugs she has consumed; they possess a captivating beauty.

As she takes me fully into her mouth it is as much as I can do to contain myself. As her tongue dances about my glans, I find myself biting on my knuckles, the sensations are quite sweet if indescribably wonderful, she is an expert of her craft. Yet this is just the prelude; I orgasm hard into her mouth as she draws on me much as a thief syphoning out petrol from an automobile fuel tank. She has consumed the fluid within the blink of an eye and is soon lighting herself a cigarette. She kisses me on the lips and only now I can taste my own semen. She sits silently watching me as she smokes her cigarette which is clenched between her index and middle finger, her arm crooked in a movie star pose. I am feeling tired, yet we have not even made love yet. As I lie on her bed surveying her as she smokes, I feel myself becoming aroused a second time. No time is wasted as she extinguishes the cigarette and mounts me like a horse. I am ridden hard and rough and after what feels like an eternity, I feel her whole body go taut as pleasure rips through her. She draws a deep breath before moaning out loudly. I have yet to finish, as she sits astride me looking down at me; she smiles again before getting off me and assuming a kneeling position, beckoning me to finish off in her from behind. I have never done this position before. Within seconds I orgasm in her and roll off beside her.

Studding continued:

She lights another cigarette before remarking, 'I'm sorry about the rubbers [condoms] but the thought of having some screaming organism with a head the size of a medicine ball tearing its way out of my vagina fills me with absolute horror.'

Abigail then embarked on a short lecture on the virtues of the vagina but it is likely her words were being drowned out by the cacophony of Studding's own thoughts on the subject. He likened her vagina to the throat of a snake, capable of taking virtually anything she wished to insert within its warm, soft, tight confines, yet somehow of a less bony texture. By the witching hour, as announced by that simultaneous and precise din of chimes and gongs from almost every antique clock in the building, the cream had certainly begun to sour, the bacteria multiplying within. The mood was now decidedly pagan. Outside was an alcohol swamp, the air hot and moist and filled with egg-laying insects, while newly born larvae strove to break the surface film, struggling like fairies pinned by the throat to entomology boards. Studding's account continued:

With her ode to womanhood, pregnancy and the vagina over with, she [Abigail] extinguishes her cigarette before placing her head upon my chest; we both fall asleep quicker than what I had expected. During the night I am awoken by that searing sensation of having to piss quickly; my groin hurts, I get up to use the bathroom and after I look in the mirror, I pray that my shirt collar will hide the love bites I have been bequeathed this night. My mouth is dry, and I need a drink of water. I leave the bedroom for the darkened maze of corridors outside. Bumbling around in the darkness unsure of which door leads to a washroom, I walk in on a couple. He is lying face down, muffled moans of either pleasure or discomfort filling the room. She is stretched out upon his back and deeply engrossed in the process of pegging him. Neither is initially aware of my unintended intrusion; she is riding him in an almost ritualistic fashion, her thrusting forceful, almost spiteful. It gave one an uncomfortable feeling even if as an accidental casual observer. She is naked apart from a bay leaf crown perched on her head. She raises herself up like a serpent might before striking. Looking over her shoulder at me, she casually remarks, 'I can fuck you next if you'd like.'

I smile as I slowly back out of the room much like a cat retreating from a fight with a greater foe. When I return to bed Abbigail has kicked off the sheets; she lies on her back with one arm raised above her head, her legs apart. As I crawl in beside her I do so with all the stealth I can summon. I lie for a few minutes staring at her in the light of the moon, a bead of sweat runs down her torso into her navel.

By morning Abbigail is up and gone. Some of the girls and young males are slumped naked and hung over about the furniture like dirty washing hanging from a clothesline while the servants set about the unenviable task of cleaning vomit from the marbled floors, semen from the upholstery, and all before *mutti* and *vati* [mummy and daddy] arrive home for dinner. One poor young darling of a girl was slumped against a bedroom door, her head bowed against her knees, she looks up at me briefly as I walk past her. She had traces of white powder about her nostrils, the now-smudged red lipstick and dry beard of semen around her mouth indicated that even at this time of the morning she was still quite 'spunk drunk'.

Before I leave this opulent Babylon behind, I engage in brief conversation with another well-to-do young lady who rather surprisingly spills an incessant scathing narrative on her current boyfriend. She slumps half naked in a deep armchair, her half-closed eyelids shield her bloodshot eyes from the blinding rays of the morning sun; she sits there without a concern in the world and delights in exclaiming to me, 'My boyfriend, he is quite useless you know. Most young men with money are generally useless ... He is the proprietor of a bakery you know; people nickname it Bluebottle Bakery. He's not much use in the other department, either, though he is quite well endowed ... his dick reminds me of an enormous white salami. He also has a thing for sex in the wrong hole; you know, he keeps asking me to try it up the bum, as he calls it. I find the whole idea quite disturbing and can only imagine the discomfort that might be involved. Another thing, the thought of his sea-monkeys oozing from my anus and trickling down the insides of my thighs as a brown stain afterwards is just totally disgusting.'

For a moment she returns to her former state of silence, her complexion beneath her foundation must be turning to a shade of pale as the distinctive sound of vomit hurtling up her throat breaks the quiet. I help her to her feet with an urgency of getting her to the bathroom before she vomits. We get halfway across the hall when it happens, that horrible retching followed by the sound of vomit splashing against the cool marble floor ... the vomit looked like a mixture of champagne, blood and semen. I guide her to the nearest bathroom and leave her there embracing the lavatory bowl.

The reference to 'sea-monkeys' as a term for seminal fluid in this narrative, is also somewhat interesting, if a little puzzling. Sea-monkeys, the child's novelty aquarium pets as we know them today, were not developed in the USA until 1957. It is certainly an odd coincidence, but one wonders if the name may have been taken from a conversation with this mysterious young socialite at some later date? Or whether Studding himself had some later affiliation with Harold von Braunhut, the man responsible for gifting this cryptobiotic pet to the masses? Either way, it is clear that the girls who so willingly brushed lips with the young Studding were aware that the young male eclectics of a post-bagel America required very little effort where the production of a hard-on was concerned Studding continues:

Again, I was quite shocked at the antics of this place, yet whilst I had enjoyed its hospitality and the copious warmth of my hosts, the fact that the young girls by now were mostly hung over from their alcohol abuse of the previous evening, [but] were still quite lucid [meant] no doubt that most were still riding upon a cocaine high of sorts. Had I told mother or father about this encounter, independent young man or not, I feel they would have killed me, somehow imagining that their son was now riddled with clap [VD] and hiding a secret drug and alcohol addiction, along with a possible love child. No amount of reassurance would have convinced them to the contrary, so it is just as well that they will never know.

Studding's recollections conjure mental visions on a par with Emperor Caligula's palace – minus the sadism – where nymphs were plucked from warm rose petalled pools before being taken to bed for sex. Yet this was more of a Château de Brat, where the sexual debris of discarded clothes and underwear somehow led to an alternate reality within high society, where the air was permeated with a scent reminiscent of mouldy ocean creatures. As the girls purged their bodies of the poison from the night before, by way of vomiting, one could be excused for wondering if they were just vomiting, or ridding themselves of the excess juices they used to paralyze their prey? When daylight arrived, they cowered from its rays, rather like vampires who, having had their fill of the blood of their sexual partners, could retreat to the graves of their privileged existences, content in the knowledge that there would always be more willing victims, ready to be seduced by a glass of fine champagne and a pretty face.

The open use of cocaine should also come as no surprise, even in the early years of the twentieth century. The abuse of cocaine has long been associated with the alchemy of the Pandora's box of sex and has served to supercharge the sexual appetites of the world elite. Behind the locked doors of tall opulent homes ringed with gargoyles an 'anything goes' culture existed for those with money, particularly the privileged brats of businessmen, politicians and diplomats, and the world outside seemed oblivious. Occasionally, if one was persistent enough, one might catch a glimpse through the dirty, milky glass of an ill-lit basement the confused patination of a couple making love, blurred, indistinguishable, cartoonlike and racing to orgasm before being discovered. This was 'pie-'n-custard' spread across the sheets, as opposed to the caviar on low-carb, low-salt wafers being served on the upper floors to 'The Board of Polygyny' and its fawns.

Despite Studding having spent the night with Abbigail it was the two tiara-wearing girls who appeared to have made the biggest impression on him, even though neither showed any interest in him. Did he somehow reminisce upon their memory as he too lay in the warm comfort of his bed, slowly becoming erect the more he thought of them? Did he somehow envisage them as 'those coldsore Valentines' engaged in the consumption of some exclusive insect caviar-savouring those sweet secretions of the ants before double-dildoing each other in the privacy of their room? Their badly decaying opera masks, not-so-seraphic nature, half-smiles, bright colours and perfumed piss with which to defend their otherwise lost integrities, he imagined them kissing passionately, rubbing coldsores, their red lipstick smudging about their faces, abandoning all that was considered godly in the eyes of their prudish church-enslaved elders, hastily making their way to a bed of nails in a room freshly stocked by the thorn florist herself. Once inside they kissed, they bit, they chewed in celebration of their emancipation and the fact that their wombs would now forever remain void from what they felt was the filth of manhood. The friction of vulva against vulva, sparks illuminate a cobalt murk, fingers claw at the stars and their moans become deafening. In the wake of their pleasure there may be that ritual sharing of a cigarette, the settling of the senses prior to peaceful slumber. They would extinguish the lights before falling blissfully asleep in one another's arms.

If we believe that sex was any different anywhere else in the world at that time, then we are fooling ourselves. America, France, Italy and Russia were much the same. In the United States of America, the 'cat houses' were always full; the professions of sex and vice were (and still are) among the oldest professions in the world.

In Germany Berlin traditionally had always been the epicentre of recreational decadence. In the many bars, brothels and dance clubs, from the elite establishments to the dives, people of all social backgrounds indulged in relative freedom. The young women in particular wore clothes which some considered risqué, drank heavily and chain-smoked. At the cabaret venues couples pursued each other with the vigour of toads, and many a young woman or man would end up losing her or his virginity in some dark corner of the establishment after closing. There was an alternative club and social scene frequented by those who understood they were different in their sexual preferences. Under the Weimar society, which came about in the wake of Germany's defeat in the First World War, this alternative or sub-cultural social scene seems to have thrived, relatively unhindered despite Germany being fraught with social, economic and political problems.

Yet, just two years after the end of the First World War, the emergence of the Nazi Party became the seed for Germany's destruction. It would take some fifteen years before this fledgling political faction possessed sufficient power to enforce its own sets of ideals upon Germany's people and its ancient culture. In the meantime, many Germans, both young and old, enjoyed a bittersweet good time. People were still having sex and sex in some cases could be exploited for profit. Of course, there were girls who liked girls, and men who liked men, and it seems that both often frequented the same clubs in what may have been a subconscious form of social solidarity. Homosexual or gay people rarely frequented the clubs where heterosexual couples mingled. There was much hatred toward anyone considered 'queer' at that time, yet there was this alternative scene where people who were gay, were happy to comply with the other's boundaries and basic rules, and could avoid conflict. Basically, this meant keeping to yourself or to your own group. As a result, many gay men found sanctuary in clubs that catered for lesbians, while many lesbians felt a greater sense of security in frequenting clubs that catered for gay males.

It is no surprise that lesbians were fascinated by the way gay men loved one another, as much as the gay men were fascinated by the antics of the lesbians. There was of course a time when many heterosexual men found the merest hint of two males having sex with one another quite repulsive, yet times have changed. However, one of the few things that has remained unchanged within the male sexual psyche, is the fascination with two women having sex with one another. In fact, two females having sex has been a predominant male sexual fantasy for centuries, and this preoccupation continues today.

Tula Kubiczek, the 19-year-old daughter of Latvian immigrants who had settled in Berlin, understood from an early age that she was different from the other girls with whom she mixed:

> I always preferred the company of girls to boys, yet that, at a young age, was not something considered out of the normal. Girls liked to play with dolls and their dolls' houses, while the boys would rather play with mud, tin cars and guns. Which girl owned the biggest doll house became almost status-like in our part of Berlin. We were neither rich nor poor, but my father was a great woodsman and was able to build me a wonderful doll's house which was the envy of my other female friends. As we grew older the dolls' houses were soon substituted for the pursuit of boys, only I never developed that supposedly normal attraction toward boys. There was nothing within me that made me feel excited when I saw a handsome boy; it just wasn't there for me. I had girls that I used to play with as a child that at one point I felt attracted to.
>
> Whilst this was before the Nazis came along, you could not reveal such things to your parents; they would have never accepted it. Whilst society knew it was there and tolerated it behind closed doors, it was not considered something any normal, well-brought-up girl should do. It was nothing to laugh about as it was a serious problem and considered a sin as bad as, if not worse, than a female having a child out of wedlock. I went

out with boys more as a cover than anything; I didn't enjoy the company of males at all and did not enjoy them kissing or pawing me either. It was only when I left home and began working and earning my independence that I felt I could finally break my emotional chains. Berlin had many popular nightspots. If you went to each one and sat there with a drink you would soon know if you were in the right one for your sexual orientation.

I recall finding the one club and while I did not find a suitor straight away, I found the clientele charming, well dressed, well mannered and with no drunkenness or violence. Some of the girls were dressed in tuxedos and had short haircuts, some were very manly yet others very feminine. This small club was similar to the one just a block away which was known as the *Zur Katzenmutter* [The Mother Cat], only that place was frequented mainly by soldiers. It was more for the gay males than the lesbian females yet going there was an interesting experience. The last time I went there I saw men wearing makeup kissing quite openly, yet at a discreet distance from the other patrons. It just felt like how freedom should feel; there was no lewdness about it at all, not in my opinion.

For me my most memorable evening was spent at a club called The Dorian Gray. This club used to have a special night for women only. I was not just looking for sex or a lover, I was looking for a partner. I knew in my mind what type of girl I was looking for; I wanted a girl who was soft, feminine and sensual, not butch and brutish as some lesbian women were. I didn't wish to be in a relationship with a woman who was trying her best to be a man minus the penis. I was approached by a few girls who made their interest in me clear over a period of time; they were nice but none of them was what I was particularly looking for personality-wise. I almost gave up at one point, until I was approached by a girl I guessed was around the same age as me. She was pretty, meticulously clean and wore nice clothes, and I could tell she was as much an amateur at this female dating game as me. She stuttered badly as she introduced herself, clearly very nervous. She told me her name was Gerda and asked me if she could share my table with me and maybe a drink. I held my hand out to her to introduce myself and told her, 'Please sit down, I would be delighted.' So, she shook my hand then sat opposite me.

We drank wine and talked for the next three hours solid. One of the first things I noticed about Gerda were her eyes. She had such beautiful hazel eyes, they were quite mesmerizing, the kind of eyes that drew you in. I also liked her hands; her fingernails were not long like most women at the time, yet not bitten to their quick like some I had seen; they were clean and well-manicured. As we talked, I studied every contour of her face, her mouth, eyes, hair, ears, everything. I was surprised to learn that she was a year my senior, a working girl with her own apartment in the city too. She spoke a little of her parents telling me how they had almost driven her mad with requests for her to bring a man home to meet them soon.

She took a huge gulp of wine, lit up a cigarette and said, 'Fucking men; I'd rather die than have to live out my life with a fucking man, have to cook, clean and screw to order, and have to deal with kids into the bargain. No, I can't see myself consigned to the licking of cashmere pears [testicles] until death frees me. Oh no, fuck that.' We both laughed and at that point, with the ice broken by our laughter, we both leaned forward and kissed. It was merely a peck, but [it was] the moment when we confirmed that yes, we were both comfortable with each other.

Shortly after our kiss a drunken young male staggered over to our table and introduced himself as Luc. He told us he was from Belgium and asked us if we would both like to go home with him where he could entertain us both at the same time. We laughed at him, then he looked over his shoulder to make sure no one was looking before getting his semi-hard manhood out to show us. This only made us shriek even more with laughter. Despite Luc's unorthodox introduction he became a friend of ours through our visits to the club as he was always in there and we nicknamed him 'The Bruges Banana'; this nickname should be more or less self-explanatory. We were the only two females left in the premises at closing time. As we threw on our coats our hearts were pounding in our chests. Which one of us would be brave enough to make that move, that point at which all couples arrive in any relationship. Admittedly the question of, 'Would you like to come back to mine for coffee?' usually only came after a period of familiarization.

We walked out of the club to the jangle of keys locking the door behind us and I turned to Gerda, asking her, 'Would you like to have some coffee at mine?' She smiled broadly, replying, 'Yes of course.' For many couples the question of an invite to one's home for coffee was a test of receptivity, an invitation for intimacy to take place, a kind of sub-conscious signal that you were somehow receptive to being mated. Yes, it was very exciting. We walked off down the street shyly at first but were soon arm-in-arm on a journey that would take us thirty-five minutes to my doorstep. When we arrived at my apartment, I was shaking with excitement. I could barely get the keys in the door, I was so excited at what might happen once we were on the other side, alone. As we went through the door, we took off our coats, hanging them on the pegs the other side of the hall and kicked off our shoes. I went into the kitchen to put water on for the coffee while Gerda walked around studying the photos on my wall and perusing the ornaments on my shelves. She picked up a photo of me as a young girl, and told me I was still as pretty as in that photo. The water on the stove seemed to take an age to boil; I could have quite easily skipped the coffee for whatever else was going to happen next. After making coffee I brought the cups into the living room. As a single girl I had just the one sofa, so we had no choice but to sit beside one another. We both took a sip of our coffee then Gerda asked me if I minded if she smoked; I told her I didn't mind as I smoked occasionally myself. She then offered me one of her cigarettes. I took one from her cigarette case placing it between my lips and she leaned forward with her lighter and lit it for me. We both drew heavily on our cigarettes and sat silently blowing smoke rings, more as a distraction from our nervousness than any serious attempt at creating halos for ourselves. I think in all respects we were two girls beyond any form of salvation; no doubt we would be condemned to burn in hell for the so-called abhorrent emotions that raged within our bodies.

Gerda broke the ice by asking me if I had ever been in a relationship with a girl before. I had to admit to her that no, I hadn't, that she would be my first. As she leaned toward the coffee table, stubbing out her cigarette, she looked at me smiling, I felt obliged to follow suit stubbing out half of my cigarette as if somehow following her lead. We both reclined back into the sofa, Gerda then turned to me and cupping my face in her hands she began kissing me on the lips, only this time it was different. Prising my mouth apart with hers, her tongue flickered wildly, serpent-like, in and out of my mouth as we shared that first passionate kiss, that physical milestone which has to be broken by all lovers prior to any physical union. Girls used to say if you allowed your lover's tongue to enter your mouth it was a sign that you were ready to take things further.

I responded, and our tongues wrestled within one another's mouths. I found myself gulping down her saliva; it tasted of the mix of red wine and tobacco, yet it was not unpleasant; it was still sweet, clean and distinctly female in flavour. We were suddenly all over each other like a rash on a baby's arse. As we kissed, we unbuttoned one another's blouses, pulling them off the shoulders and arms and casting them aside. I felt the sensation of her taut nipples against mine. I was moistening rapidly as I felt her soft mouth against my neck. I placed my hands around the back of her head, pulling her against me, beckoning for her to deliver a love bite to my neck. We were both flushed with ecstasy and as she bit my neck I fell under her spell. Like a spider might seek the dark sanctuary of some darkened corner of the room, her fingers slowly made their way up my skirt and between my thighs where she massaged me into a lather. It was at that point she whispered, 'Can we go into the bedroom?' I got up and took her by the hand, leading her into my bedroom, closing the door behind us. She did things to me no one else had ever done before; it was obvious that she knew what she was doing.

There are seven erogenous zones about the human body, the mouth, ears, neck, armpits, chest, groin and feet. All seven have the capability of making a woman orgasm provided that the attraction is there and if stimulated in the correct fashion. Gerda kissed me from head to toe then performed cunnilingus on me, before mounting me in much the same way that a man might. Placing one of my ankles on her shoulder she began gentle yet firm rhythmic thrusts against me.-it felt like at any moment my whole body was going to explode, this tingling sensation suddenly began to build, and I couldn't help but gasp like a fish suddenly finding itself out of the water. Gerda looked down at me reassuringly and whispered, 'It's okay, you are going to have an orgasm.' I had heard about orgasms many times in girlie conversations in the past, yet here I was on the verge of one myself, for the first time, but with another girl, a girl I had never known up until this evening. I could feel my whole body becoming taut like the sail of a yacht in a gale, the tingling sensation becoming how I could only best describe as being beautifully unbearable. I began to utter expletives I had never used before or ever imagined myself ever using. Then it was like a release of butterflies that flew through my whole body, a pulsating series of the most wonderful feelings between my legs. Gerda continued for some minutes until she too reached the point of no return; she threw back her head gasping out loudly before collapsing on top of me.

We were both very tired by now, the perspiration on our bodies suddenly made us both shiver; giggling like a pair of kids we kissed passionately again, before pulling the blankets over ourselves. We fell asleep within a few minutes with our bodies entwined. As dawn began to break, we had sex again. Afterwards we lay in each other's arms, the blankets of the bed tangled around us. We lay there talking for around an hour before going back to sleep again. When we woke again it was 10.30 in the morning and I recall the sunlight straining through the curtains. Gerda stretched out her arms as she yawned before making some half-hearted attempt at getting out of the bed. She sat up on the edge of the bed, stretching again and complaining at how quickly the weekend was almost over. We shared a breakfast of toast together and drank cups of coffee. Gerda finally left my apartment at midday. It was a Sunday and she had to visit her parents. She promised to come and see me again early evening on the Tuesday.

From there we enjoyed a romance that lasted for over six months where most weekends we went out to the clubs we used to frequent when we were single. We would dance, drink and socialize and go back to one another's places on weekends. We never decided to share an apartment and just after six months had passed, we separated. It was perfectly amicable. The thing was neither of us wanted to settle down just yet. When we were out with each other we would both look at other girls and think to ourselves,

'Hmm, I wonder what she would be like', and things that many young people today would think. We were very attracted to one another but at the same time we were not in love anymore if that makes sense. We remained friends and were still a shoulder to cry on when we needed one, but both of us wanted to experience sex and love with other girls. Neither of us had yet found our soulmate.

For young gay males entering the heady Weimar social scene there was also a degree of freedom which many used to their advantage. There were bars and small clubs which soon became the favoured haunt not only of young gay males, but lesbians and straight women too. In these establishments alcohol was consumed and cross-dressing and dancing with the same sex occurred, yet with a degree of control. Unlike in modern society, the gay men, rather than having sex in the club's toilet cubicles, either sought somewhere private outside or, if one or the other had an apartment, they would go back there. The clubs were merely focal points, places where drinks could be enjoyed and people could meet, socialize and dance; they were not brothels and rooms were not provided for the purposes of having sex. Many of the clubs frequented by young gay men rather surprisingly soon became the haunts of soldiers. Johannes Kriebst wrote of one such experience in one of Berlin's notorious gay haunts:

> For those of us who come here there is liberation. Throughout the week we work, we fit in, and we conform for the sake of our society around us. On a weekend we can be ourselves and among those who understand what we are and how we feel. In the clubs we can talk with one another, we can kiss one another, dance with one another and there is not one person to object. Sometimes there is the odd jealous fight, the combatants often get thrown out onto the street where it ends as abruptly as it started. Most of us range in age from 17 to our mid-20s, yet we get the older military-type men coming in here.
> They will sit drinking their beer staring at you like an owl might a mouse in the forest. They think that in uniform they have more chance of finding a partner while at the same time showing that they have money in their pockets. They attempt to buy you; they don't understand that we are only here to enjoy ourselves, not always here for their sexual convenience or looking to fuck or be fucked, that we are human beings maybe searching for love instead of lust or just a quick orgasm. Some of these soldiers are clearly drunk and they have probably already been in other clubs and by this time they are desperate.

We notice some boys leave with them, maybe these boys will get payment for sex, I don't know, and I'd never ask them. I've heard stories of young men being lured back to the barracks by these soldiers with the promises of money and beer only to end up being raped multiple times. I never wanted to find out the truth behind the rumours, so I kept away from the soldiers. Besides, as I have said, most were much older men and older men were not what I was looking for. There was this horrible presumption, even during the relatively relaxed period of Weimar society toward gay men, that we were dirty and promiscuous. You couldn't go out on the streets like today and protest, as you'd get arrested. There were still constraints, still hatred toward us, so we kept quiet, keeping ourselves to ourselves.

For heterosexuals the Berlin club scene and its nightlife attracted young men and women in much the same way an electric bug trap attracts airborne creatures to a fiery demise. The end of the working week for many was on a Friday, thus the Friday night culture began, with society looking forward to two days of family time, recreation, and for the young, outright fun. For some citizens, the working week was not over until Saturday afternoon, and for them Saturday night held much the same delectation as it does today. Young people went out to dances and, if they had reached the age of consent, 16, they could drink, smoke and, if they wanted, they could have sex. Whether a girl instigated or agreed to having sex with a boyfriend was entirely dependent upon individual upbringing.

The bands at these dances played mostly American-style jazz music and so it is perhaps important to note at this point that many of the bands that supplied the music for these establishments were of African American origin. Quite the opposite of being ostracized, in Weimar society they proved very popular with the ladies and as a result many mixed-race relationships began, many ending in marriage. Charlotte Antoinette Bonn, a young French journalist, recalled the African American musicians:

> Far from being viewed as the lowly subjects of some far-off primitive kingdom the name of which is seemingly impossible to pronounce, here both the men and women find them attractive and interesting. They have the most wonderful manners, and it is intriguing to see at the end of many an evening them escorting well-to-do white ladies back to their hotel rooms. Some will undoubtedly be staying for the night.

The above piece certainly paints an endearing vision of the Weimar era, the carefree attitude, its decadence and its relative tolerance, all of which would vanish under the nightmare of National Socialism.

However, young girls in early 1930s Germany were subject to strict parental control. Some were not permitted to attend even local church hall dances without a chaperone present to oversee the proceedings. In many cases this would be the matriarch of the girl's family, usually a grandmother, who would accompany the girl to a dance. The grandmother had the right to terminate the evening at any moment she felt the girl might be behaving in an improper manner. The rules were pretty draconian; the girl often had to wear a full-length dress (no skirts) to prevent any young male seeing her legs. There could be no kissing and definitely no groping or hands on bottoms. In many respects it is no surprise that many teenage girls in Germany welcomed the freedoms that the later League of German Girls, the Bund Deutscher Mädel (BDM) – the girls' section of the Hitler Youth, allowed them. But in the pre-Nazi era, for many young German girls, it was all about behaving as a young lady should, finding suitable husband material, and, if you happened to marry, only then was sexual intercourse allowed to take place. Of course, there were always the mavericks who devised clever distractions to escape the gaze of their chaperones, as Greta Streibaum recalled:

> Early on a Saturday evening I could attend our local dance along with my friends. The dances were held at the local church hall. Some of the girls who were older, like 17 or 18, were able to have more freedom than us younger ones, aged from 14 to 16. We had to endure chaperones. In my case the chaperone was either my father, brother, mother or grandmother. I actually preferred it when my grandmother came to keep an eye on me. She would sit and watch me dance either on my own, with my friends or a boy and after half an hour she would fall asleep. There was a local boy I quite liked, and he liked me and while it was very risky, we took advantage of the situation on more than one occasion. My friends would watch my grandmother in case she woke up while me and the boy would run outside around the back by some trees. It was at that spot in the trees that I had my very first proper kiss, snogging they later called it. That's all we really did as there was no time for anything else to happen; it was too risky to disappear for long so that was it. I know a few of the older girls who went into those same trees and lost their virginity there; one of them was made pregnant from her first time with a local boy. She was forced to marry and

that was that, her youth over before it had really begun. I was much like any normal girl; I was both curious yet scared of the idea of having sex. As I grew older and my shackles were released. I still did not wish to end up with an unwanted pregnancy, so I was very careful, yet others were not as cautious as me. I waited until I was married and that was the way I was brought up by my parents.

For young people within the higher echelons of their society there were no such moral boundaries. Herbert Lange, a 21-year-old junior accountant at a city bank in Berlin, has written extensively of the early to mid-Weimar years, at the height of the German depression, as follows:

I count myself among the lucky ones. I still have a job here at the bank, the bank is power and it is well paid and as I live by myself, I have few outgoings to worry over. There are new people in town grabbing the headlines [a possible reference to Hitler and the Nazis] and the banks are just holding on, as there is rumour that political change will bring about a relief from this misery. I still socialize and frequent those clubs that are still open. Many have now closed and are bankrupt, as few have the money to socialize. It's an odd time to be young; when you go out you can never be certain a girl wants you for you as the person you are, or for the money in your pocket. Only the daughters of the wealthy locals can indulge in the luxury of drinking wine now.

Things at this time are a tawdry repetition in the social context. I go into a club in which there is barely a handful of females. I get talking to a wealthy divorcee from Sweden about the rights and wrongs of the world, we drink far too much, and I accompany her home and there is no question of whether I will be joining her in her bed for the night. She is neither attractive nor unattractive in a strange way, too old for me at 55, yet I am full of curiosity and excited. When undressed her physique was far from a montage of erotic perfection. An unflattering lifebuoy of fat hung low about her abdomen, no doubt the scourge of multiple childbirths. There was little in the way of pre-coital formality … as she lay down on the bed her sexual orifice resembled the arse end of a chicken, the part where the stuffing is pushed in. For a moment there was this awkward pause in the proceedings. I thought of poor, young Winky about to be thrust into some unimaginable inflamed tunnel. I rode her well … when she threw me over onto my back, her face contorted like some insect. I envisioned her leaning down over me before tearing off my lips with her mandibles.

Afterwards I lay awake unable to sleep. I felt slightly disgusted with myself. In the event, I left at 4 in the morning, having not slept at all.

Once home I washed myself in the sink before getting into my own bed, my head was hurting, and as much as I tried to get some sleep I couldn't. I told myself, 'Never again Herbert!'

The whole social aesthetic in Germany had been crushed beneath the German depression; the good times were over, many of the clubs and nightspots which once were full, particularly on weekends, had either gone bankrupt or closed due to lack of business. Many of Germany's citizens were now unemployed, families were losing children to disease and malnutrition, and naturally many began to blame the Weimar government for its past weakness. There was this anger, a brooding resentment, that the Weimar regime had somehow enslaved the German people to the wealthy Jews of the world elite, that the Treaty of Versailles of 1919 had been engineered specifically to destroy Germany. It became common to witness gangs brawling on the streets, the violence always politically and sometimes racially motivated. This dire economic situation became just one of the components that propelled Adolf Hitler and his Nazi Party to absolute power in Germany. When Germany finally began to recover from the global depression in 1935, the Nazi Party claimed the credit. It is true that the Nazis appeared at first to breathe new life into a country that had been hit particularly hard. Yet, when Germany emerged from that darkness would her social fabric remain the same as that of the old Weimar government? Would sex and attitudes toward sex in Adolf Hitler's Third Reich be any different form how things had been in the past? This book demonstrates that the Nazi views on sex were a confused miasma of contradiction.

Chapter 2

Human Wreckage on the Moral High Road

With the achievement of absolute power in August 1934, Adolf Hitler and his cohorts within the Nazi Party's inner circle set out on the moral high road in a drive toward cleansing Germany of what it termed its Weimar-influenced excesses. This drive became a mission that left the alleged moral high roads, envisaged by Hitler for his Third Reich, littered with human wreckage. Persecution flowed as freely as a venom through the veins of the entire German nation. While traditionally Jews of course were the focal point of Nazi hatred, homosexuals and lesbians also became implicated among the reasons for Germany's ill fortunes and moral decline. By casting these aspersions, the Nazis were attempting to create a veneer of courage and rectitude, intending to promote strong traditional family values along the lines of work, church and home, thus espousing a stronger, healthier future German Reich. Of course, the reality was very different from the moral perspective being advocated. Whilst Jews, Bolsheviks, homosexuals and lesbians were collectively portrayed as the enemies of the new German Aryan ideology, the Nazis by their very nature were responsible for the creation of a sexual dark age which would last until the end of the Second World War, in 1945. The infrastructure of the Third Reich, like a spiderweb, was vast and complex. The power bestowed upon its local and distant subordinates was ripe for exploitation and abuse, and there were those who would take full advantage of this chaotic governmental structure, not only to settle old scores and inform on others, but to also indulge in their own sordid behaviour, of which we will learn more, later. Hitler was keen to portray Nazi society as a healthy, clean, moral, family-orientated heterosexual community. As with Jews and Bolsheviks, homosexuals and lesbians could have no place in Nazi society, and it was obvious that those who chose to remain in Germany would soon be subject to the scrutiny of the state.

Measures were rapidly implemented in a concerted effort to round up anyone considered to be sexually deviant, i.e., homosexual or lesbian. Under Hitler the society at large was obliged to inform on anyone suspected of being morally corrupt. Many of the nightclubs frequented by homosexuals and lesbians throughout the Weimar years were liquidated, along with any other establishments thought to have been operating as proverbial dens of ill repute. The owners of these clubs faced severe penalties, and some were sent to prison following trials by puppet courts, on the grounds of aiding and abetting indecent behaviour. Early in the tenure of the Nazis those who were able to flee Germany did so; those who, for whatever reason, were unable to leave Germany and start new lives in a different country, faced a dangerously uncertain future and were likely forced to live a lie in order to survive.

Tula Kubiczek sat down to write a letter to her close friend just prior to Christmas 1935. She penned the letter but never sent it, and this among other items of her personal writings survived the war, later to be donated to a historical archive in Latvia. In her letter Tula wrote:

> There are those in our neighbourhood who know me well, yet I was always discreet regarding my lifestyle and choice of romantic partners, yet I am still very frightened. The focus of Nazi hate is mainly toward Jews, yet I have had male friends who have been arrested by the police; once in the cells they have been beaten up even tortured as the police want them to admit that they are homosexual. The strong ones withstood the beatings and torture finally convincing the police that whoever informed on them was lying. Others were not so lucky and broke quickly as they were stripped naked, kicked and beaten about their cells. I know of three young men I was once on first name terms with – they were Friedrich, Hans and Joachim. All three have vanished and where they have gone, I don't know. I dare not even ask around about them. As much as it flies in the face of everything that I believe in, in terms of my social freedom I am going to have to live a lie, maybe even marry a man, have children, all the usual shit we women are expected to do. The police have not been and questioned me yet, but they must have their suspicions of a young woman who is living alone and unmarried. There are those who might yet inform on me; it is the constant fear that is so unbearable, the fact that our lives have now been taken away from us. We can no longer live as we want but how we are told. I might not be able to write to you again for a very long time, but give

my heartfelt regards to Mirka, Jaki and Marcin, send them all of my love and I will write to you again when I am able.
All my Love,
Your Best Friend,
Tula XX

On the other hand, Hilde Gabel tells us that Hitler's moral crusade had little effect upon her sexual lifestyle:

> I was bisexual, and I enjoyed having sex with both men and women. During the years of Weimar Germany nobody really cared, everyone was doing it. The moment Hitler, that ferret with a toothache, swindled his way to power, that's when it all changed for girls such as me. I was not a Hitler voter like so many women of my generation were. I could see his ideas would conflict with mine, so I didn't vote for Hitler. Before the Nazis were in power a girl could go out and drink and if she wanted to, she could spend the night in her own bed, [or] a man's or a girl's, it didn't matter at all. It wasn't as if I wasn't discreet about my sex life, because I was.
>
> If I chose to go home with a girl, we would leave a club or bar separately, either meeting up at my residence or hers, whichever was the best option for privacy at that time. It was the same with any male I would go out with. With the males I generally made them wait until I had been out with them for a few weeks before agreeing to sleep with them and I always insisted on them using birth control. With girls it was all very different; I found them more exciting and the sex with girls was a more fulfilling experience as they knew exactly how to pleasure you without any of the fumbling around. For me it was far more natural. The only quarrels you had was deciding who was going to brew the coffee in the morning when you both woke up.
>
> The art of seduction is natural within a woman, it's in her body from birth, yet it develops and manifests in her teens as much as her breasts ripen like fruit in the summertime, it is a gift all women have. Yes, I found a regular girlfriend, whose name was Anna, after a night out in Berlin's bars and clubs where we drank, danced and had a great time and then decided whose house we would go to. Once we had shut the door behind us, we would run up the stairs to bed. Anna wasn't like me as she preferred women only and I remember her once, sitting on the edge of the bed, pulling off her heels and stockings and saying, 'I could never stomach having sex with a man ever again. For one thing, men are about as romantic as extracting haemorrhoids from someone's anus with your teeth!'
>
> When Hitler climbed upon his little pedestal and began his work of cleaning up Germany of its immoral past, we too had to change. It wasn't

change through choice; it was a matter of survival. The last time I met with Anna we both understood it would probably be for the last time; it was just too dangerous. The funny thing was in the morning she made the coffee without protesting that I should make it, she came and snuggled up beside me in bed and told me, 'It's easy for you; all you need to do is get yourself a soldier boyfriend.' When I asked her why, she said, 'Well, with the way things are looking, if you start dating a soldier he is going to soon be at war. Hitler doesn't want peace, he wants war, so a soldier boy will be away from home much of the time and at least that way you have some peace to yourself.' I laughed it off at the time but ironically that is exactly what happened. As we lay in bed cuddling, we discussed Hitler. Anna said, 'I envisage his house as being decorated with wallpaper made from human skin, you know, possibly decorated with shrunken heads and things like that. He's weird, in my opinion, yet our women are fixated with the beast. These women who profess their undying devotion to the man are the types who couldn't smell a rat if you shoved a dead one up their noses.' She then remarked, 'All this talk about Hitler has put me into faecal labour; I have to go and take a shit now.'

Yes, I missed not being able to see Anna anymore, but I had some fine memories. Our country had changed so much by the late 1930s. All the fun had somehow been drained from our society in order to fall into line with the Hitler way of thinking. Hitler's new morality where Jews, political opposites, homosexuals and lesbians would form the base ingredient of the tarmac that would be spread over the roads to places like Auschwitz.

Peter Bachmann-Barwald wrote of the complexities he faced as a young gay male who had once enjoyed Berlin's club scene. The steadily flourishing resentment toward homosexual men in Germany soon incited a frightening level of violence and many gay men lived in fear. In 1936, in a diary entry, Peter wrote boldly about his thoughts and fears, recalling:

One is forced to assume a false identity in much the same way as a mannequin in a tailor's shop. One feels a constant sense of dread, of being under suspicion, hunted even. My mother is the most concerned as she always knew her boy was different to the others. Only a mother knows her son so intuitively. She is so frightened of the authorities learning that I prefer the company of males to females that in our debates over the question she begs me, 'For god's sake, can't you just marry a girl and try your best?' There is little guarantee that such a ruse would work; it's not that I lack the ability to care for a female as a partner, it is more that I could not love a female partner. I would be living a lie and subjecting a decent human being to a life of torment. Being a homosexual beneath this regime which professes a hard veneer of such masculinity toward the outside world leaves only one choice and that is to leave the country. In doing so I will be leaving everything and everyone I know behind. I will also probably be leaving my family in danger as the authorities will want to know why I have gone and where I have gone. It would be classed if nothing else as some great disloyalty to the state. I am torn between my fear and the feeling of total selfishness that I am putting my own flesh and blood at such risk under this awful regime. If I were discovered, I would be thrown into a cell as if a common criminal and treated as some incurable disease awaiting a cure. The Nazis have a cure for everyone they regard as an abhorrence to their Aryan culture – it's called a rifle and a bullet. People vanish here all the time, shots ring out in the middle of the night, no one dares to question as most are too afraid to ask. It is a shrinking society, where the walls are constantly moving in, death constantly breathing down one's neck everywhere you go. Only last week I was informed through quiet whispered conversation that Ferdinand, a young man whose company I had enjoyed on several occasions, has gone. When I asked, 'Where has he gone?' I was told the police took him away and he has not returned home. They told his family he was guilty of committing offences against the Reich. His parents turned to their local church for help but the doors were slammed in their faces.

The fate of Peter Bachmann-Barwald remains unclear. There are several conflicting stories including one which stated that he died in 1940, but no circumstances of his death are available.

Kirsten Eckermann, whom I have interviewed on numerous occasions, for *Hitler's Girls: Doves Amongst Eagles* and *In Hitler's Shadow: Post-War Germany and the Girls of the BDM*, recalled how the question of one's morality was discussed in school lessons:

Yes, they'd tell us that the Weimar era had caused German society to degenerate, that it was a Jewish product and had permitted our society to go the way of the Jew, the criminal and the sexually immoral. We, as the new generation under Adolf Hitler, had a duty to ensure that this would never be allowed to happen again. We had to understand how poor morality corrupts then destroys a society. Those that went about seeking casual sexual relations, it was said, were spreaders of disease and moral corruption and it was our personal duty to our Führer Adolf Hitler to report anyone indulging in any activity considered to have been an offence against the Nazi morality doctrine.

Our school head teacher was quite firm and explicit with us, as 14-year-old girls, that 'One only breeds within the sanctity of marriage, never outside this valued National Socialist institution.' The object of breeding, as she constantly referred to it, was for the production of fine healthy German children, and this could only be achieved through marriage with pure German males with untainted Germanic bloodlines.

Many people have asked me what was the age of consent for girls to have sex in Nazi Germany. This is not as clear-cut as many would think. Most girls in Nazi Germany had sex later than girls do today. Our parents didn't want us having sex as young teenagers, though there were those who did with their boyfriends. With Hitler in power the minimum age at which a girl was permitted to have sex with a male was 16. This was in the hope that it would encourage teenagers to reproduce sooner rather than later, while at their optimum fitness, to enable the state to have a constantly available source of manpower later. It was merely a call to fill the gene pool more quickly, if you understand me.

Our head teacher also told us that lesbians were the scourge of womanhood; that lesbian women sought to pervert innocent girls to their own ways and use them for their own gratification and perversion. Lesbianism was considered the single greatest threat in our German female community, the proverbial fox in the hen house, and if we had even the slightest doubt about any girl's or woman's sexual orientation in this respect then we should report it immediately, even if one of these girls were our closest friend. That is what they preached, and they were deadly serious about the threat of lesbianism within the BDM, the Hitler Youth organization for girls.

I thought to myself, 'How could anyone inform on family or friends in this way and live with themselves afterwards?' Of course, there were girls I knew who had grown closer to one another than they should have; you could just tell they were perhaps more than friends, but they had little chance to become lovers under the strict circumstances. I would never have informed on them, and I took no notice of the little signs that I personally saw. You could say the two in question were very touchy-feely with one another, any excuse to be physical with one another and they would take it [she laughs]. But no, it didn't bother me at all. They were my friends, after all.

When asked about sex education in the Nazi school system, Kirsten recalled:

There was no sex education, not as there is today in school. The Nazis used natural processes such as how insects pollinated flowers and things like that to try and explain the reproduction process. This of course was ridiculous, as you could not apply this to human reproduction and some girls had no idea at all how babies were made or even what menstruation was all about. This is how moral they were trying to be, and it was just stupid. Girls have to be educated on all aspects of womanhood if they are to develop into normal healthy adults. There were mothers who sat their daughters down when they came of age and taught them all about menstruation and the birds and the bees, and some had elder sisters who would tell them. In the BDM there was always some girl who knew more than the others and in private moments, which were few, we would discuss sex and babies and things as girls still do today. There were some girls who had no idea that the man had to penetrate the woman during sex. The one girl argued with me, and she said to me, 'No, no, no, Kirsten. The boy just sprinkles his semen onto the woman's vagina, as frogs do when they mate with each other.'

I couldn't help but laugh at her, in fact soon we were all rolling around laughing. The thought of us all thrashing around wildly in waters polluted with seminal fluid was just too much. [She laughs for some minutes] We would have to sit these girls down and say to them, 'Look you have three holes: one for pee, one for poo, and one where the willy goes when you make babies.' We would tell them, 'Don't you dare tell anyone we have told you this.'

In a sense we had to educate ourselves as much as we could, and we did over our formative years of youth, despite Hitler and the Nazis and the Hitler Youth babbling on about the immorality of the lesser races, and how the Nazis were clearing the human wreckage from the moral high ground. The Nazis were a contradiction along with their teachers, their police, their Burgermeisters, Gauleiters, shopkeepers, soldiers, the lot of them. Few practised what they preached, yet we were constantly told we were the moral conscience of the Third Reich. They wanted us to be these quiet submissive mules and walk into marriage not necessarily out of love, but for this moral duty to Hitler, get pregnant, have a baby, then get pregnant again, then get a mother's cross, then get pregnant again and again and all this running around after a husband. The mere thought of which was enough to make you want to commit suicide.

Andrea Brecht, a young wife and mother of two children from Berlin, at that time, recalled that even married heterosexual couples had an obligation to adhere to the moral principles of the new ruling Nazi Party:

It was the summer of 1938, and I was 20 years old, and had two children over the two years before. The first child was a straightforward birth but the second was a nightmare, long and painful, and I was glad when it was finally over. I was having coffee with my friend Helena one afternoon in one of the city cafés and I told her about my neighbour who had just given birth to her sixth child. My neighbour seemed to delight in the whole 'I have more babies than you' ethos. She would stand there with her latest sprog in her arms, beaming with national pride and she would say, 'You have much catching up to do, dear Andrea.' I said to Helena, 'I'm so fucking sick of all this duty and morality shit and I'm beginning to feel like a cow in a concrete meadow and all this is making me feel a lesser woman.' Helena sensed I was a little melancholy, smiled at me and retorted, 'You are certainly no lesser woman, Andrea; imagine that neighbour of yours, imagine her poor husband when he slides his dick into her, and it feels like his dick is inside a bucket!'

I almost spat out my coffee all over her, as I burst out laughing. Helena had forgotten one little thing though, that we were out in public, one had to be careful what one said in public. The state didn't approve of its females swearing or talking about sex, especially in such public surroundings as a café. Helena nervously looked over each shoulder before continuing to laugh. I lit a cigarette and mumbled, 'It's much too late to make a moral citizen out of me.' Even when I got home later, I couldn't help laughing to myself at what Helena had said, and how would I ever keep a straight face when I saw my neighbour again?

I remember my first communion and my parents reminding me afterwards to honour my communion and be a good servant to God; it was more like an exorcism. I felt trapped from that moment onwards. Trapped within the dull, incessant demands of the male-oriented world about me. It would be a world of cooking, cleaning and having to face the constant demands for sex on top of it all. The thought of growing old and still having to conform to this way of life was enough to conjure despair within my mind.

Andrea Brecht was by no means alone in her fears. Privately, women throughout the Reich felt much the same and were party to the same resentments. They were unanimous in their loathing of what the Nazi state had created for them as a community of women. Yet, in part, they too had to accept responsibility for having allowed the monster in their midst to aspire to heights which allowed him, in turn, to remove many of their freedoms.

Chapter 3

No Cow Without the Bull

There was no great, fundamental change in the way that either single or married couples had sex in Third Reich Nazi Germany, although the Nazi authorities went to considerable lengths to encourage young girls to set aside any career ambitions, and to get married and have children instead. The act of procreation, to produce children for the new Germany was defined by the Nazi education system more as a moral duty than the pursuit of mutual pleasure between a man and a woman. Newly married couples, in particular, were lectured as to the importance of their biological duties to the Reich. The Nazis evinced a near pathological obsession with ensuring a healthy bloodline for what was to be a new master race, one that would take control of Europe and beyond, and strongly encouraged young married couples to have large families. A form of competitive babymaking game was initiated in many communities throughout Germany, played between young women eager to please their Führer.

A series of awards known as the *Ehrenkreuz der Deutschen Mutter* (Cross of Honour of the German Mother) were instituted by decree on 16 December 1938, as a means of recognizing the efforts of German women to produce children for the Reich. The crosses were designed by architect and sculptor, Franz Berberich, based in Munich. They were all of the same design – a slender, elongated Iron Cross, similar in design to the Marian Cross of the Teutonic Knights. The cross was enamelled in translucent blue with an opaque white border. Resting on the central starburst rays was a metal roundel bearing the inscription, *'Der Deutschen Mutter'* (To the German Mother). The roundel enclosed a white enamel circle with a a black enamel swastika at its centre. The reverse of the decoration bore two official styles. The first version of the award, in early 1939, bore on its reverse the inscription *'Das Kind adelt die Mutter'* (The Child ennobles the Mother) on the reverse. This inscription was replaced on all Mother's Crosses produced from late 1939 to 1945, with the date of the decree, '16 December 1938'. Directly beneath the reverse inscription on both the early and later versions was the inscribed facsimile signature of Adolf Hitler. The award was designed to be worn around the neck, suspended from a blue and white ribbon of 60–70 centimetres in length. A Mother's Cross was awarded annually, on the second Sunday in May (Mothering Sunday or Mother's Day) to those women who qualified, and was also extended to include other national occasions of celebration in Germany.

The first awards were conferred upon their recipients subject to the statutory legislation in May 1939. There was a great sense of pride among women who earned one of these decorations, which was divided into three separate classes. The lowest was Third Class and constituted a cross fashioned from bronze. The bronze award was given to all eligible mothers with four or five children. The Second Class award was fashioned in silver, and was presented to eligible mothers with six or seven children. Finally, the premier version of this award, First Class, was fashioned in gold and was awarded to all eligible mothers with eight or more children. The award of a First Class gold Mother's Cross conveyed not only a huge sense of social prestige in Nazi female society, but on occasion it also earned recipients afternoon tea with Adolf Hitler himself.

Despite these eloquent awards and the high esteem conferred by the Nazi Party on German mothers, there was a sense among many young, married German women that the Nazi state was intruding directly into their sex lives. Katherina Briedenich, a 19-year-old woman from Bremen, recalled:

> There was immense pressure placed on young women to get married. This pressure came from both within the home and within the community. Prior to the Hitler government it was not like that, there were slightly more freedoms; there was no outright urgency, yet the Nazis were obsessed with the marriage ethos, that being married and having children was the path to greatness, and the primary role of the German woman was to be somehow owned by a man and in the place where she belonged. So, yes, I married even though I did not think of myself as being ready for marriage. I was in my last year as a teenage girl and because my father, mother, grandparents, aunts and uncles were all pressuring me and my boyfriend to marry and start a family, we felt we had to get on with it and do it. We

were happy, but it was just a bit too soon, I felt. Once we had married the second wave of pressure was put upon us, as a young healthy couple, to begin a family. The state even interfered in these personal matters by the way – they advised you on how a woman could best be impregnated by her partner.

Now I never knew a great deal about sex at that time. My mother never really talked to me about sex and sex outside marriage was not considered something a proper young girl should do; that was my parents' attitude to it. Of course, I discovered much about sex from other girls, mostly my close friends. So, marriage was for many young women their first experience of what this slightly intimidating thing called consummation was all about. Yes, we all knew that to have children this barrier of losing one's virginity was crucial. I knew girls who had had sex and they told me all sorts of things; some said it was painful the first time, while others said it was not. I guessed on the night of my marriage I was going to find out for myself what it was like.

Just prior to our wedding I was visited one morning by a kind of what would best be termed today as a female health inspector. She was a stern-faced middle-aged woman obviously keen to preach the virtues of National Socialist womanhood and she emphasized to me the importance of having children. Such a conversation happened now so long ago, but I can remember as if it were yesterday what she told me, and when she left, I wrote it all down. We sat in my parents living room alone and she said to me:

> Fraulein Briedenich, you are of course aware of how important childbearing is to our Führer and the German Reich. When you engage in the act of intercourse you are gifting yourself biologically, not only to your Führer but your country's future and its ability to expand and to grow beyond the shackles that our enemies imposed upon us. The act of conception is not one to be taken lightly; on the contrary it is one of the greatest duties a German woman can perform for both Führer and fatherland. There are many ways by which a woman can conceive a child, yet some have been proved more successful than others. On your wedding night when you consummate the joyous occasion that is your marriage, allow your man to control you fully. You can do this best by lying on your back and allowing him to draw your legs back and apart. He should place your ankles upon each shoulder. In this way, when he has had his pleasure, every ounce of that precious German seed will remain un-spilled and within you. It may not be very comfortable for you, as you will need to hold this position as if you were statues for a few minutes or so afterwards. This is the surest, most efficient way that

you can conceive a child on your first time. Your husband to be should already be aware of this, but if he is not then you can discreetly direct him.

The conversation between Katherina and this stern-faced medical/political entity of the Nazi state left her feeling like a toy, an object, as opposed to a human being with feelings and desires. She continued:

So, those were the instructions, my manual for my first night of marriage and losing my virginity. I was not shocked by what she told me; if you didn't know, then you had to be educated. There was no mention of love, pleasure or orgasms, just this duty to the Führer and the German Reich. It was very cold and formal, and I wondered at the time how many other young girls would be subject to such a pre-marital briefing as this? This woman also mentioned to me that should I fall pregnant I should avoid penetrative sex with my husband until the baby was safely born. She told me the baby could be harmed if we had sex during pregnancy, which of course is rubbish, but that's what I was told. Once the baby was born, it would then be up to me when I felt comfortable enough to resume having intercourse, that there was no particular waiting time; I could start the process of trying for more babies again after a few weeks or so. When I look back, what did this woman really know?

In the event I married Paulus Retschildt who, at 21, was two years my senior, in a church of our local community. On our wedding day we both felt thrilled and while Paulus was excited about our wedding night, I was dreading it. We had been dating for around a year and I did love Paulus but my perception of what was love, as a 19-year-old, changed as I grew older. We had come close to having full sex on several occasions, but I stopped it for fear of what my parents would do to me if they found out I had defied the rules of our house. On our wedding night there were no such barriers and when the moment arrived, it is something I can remember very clearly. We had both drunk a lot, me in particular, as it deadened my nerves. Paulus did the traditional thing and carried me up the stairs to the hotel room we had been booked into. I couldn't stop giggling at first despite my nerves; we began kissing and within minutes my wedding dress was discarded on the floor, my stockings torn off in the haste and my red lipstick smeared about my face. My head was pounding as Paulus lay between my thighs, kissing my neck and breasts and telling me how beautiful I was. I felt shudders of excitement, sensing that I was becoming as aroused as he was, and receptive to him. I could feel his penis brushing the inside of my thighs and droplets of pre-cum which were creating snail trails upon my skin. I asked Paulus, 'Are you ready?' as I wanted to get this part over with, unsure as to whether it would be a positive or negative experience for me. I was well oiled and ready to receive him, but I held onto the shaft of his penis like a farmer would the neck of a chicken, determined there would be no hard-painful thrusts. The minute he began to enter me there was some pain and I recall looking down and thinking, 'My god! That's not even all the way inside me yet!' He was patient, taking his time with me. He would go so far inside me then stop if it became uncomfortable. After doing this for some thirty minutes or so he was able to fully penetrate. Once he was fully inside me, it actually felt very nice and the fact that Paulus was careful with me made it quite wonderful.

I ignored the instructions the Nazi nurse gave me, we did it in the normal missionary fashion as I felt we needed to develop before experimenting with gymnastic lovemaking positions. Afterwards we both went to sleep, and I can now look back as any other normal woman and think to myself, 'Well, that wasn't too bad, was it?'

In the morning despite the fact we both woke late with dry mouths, throbbing heads, and had ignored our morning call for breakfast, we made love for what was our second time. Well, it was my second time, but I could not be sure that Paulus was being totally honest with me when he said he had been a virgin before our marriage. The alcohol-driven fucking of the night before had been somewhat clumsy and pause laden, but this time we were both perfectly sober, both perfectly aware there was this consideration between us and a natural progression toward the pursuit of passion. Paulus was very considerate; I sensed this was not new ground for him as he pulled one of my pillows from under my head and placed it at the small of my back. Before I could even ask, 'What are you doing?' he had pulled my legs up and placed each of my ankles over each of his shoulders. He then leaned forward and right down so as he could kiss my lips. It was nice as we could look into one another's eyes and see the pleasure we were giving to each other. This position was what they called the 'Baby Making Position' and Paulus asked me if it was okay, was I comfortable, did my legs hurt. As we stared into each other's eyes it felt very erotic. I could feel his hardened shaft which seemed to get sandwiched between the cheeks of my backside. I reached down with my hand and guided him easily inside me. I could tell from the look on his face and the noise he was making that this position was highly pleasurable for him. I too found it immensely satisfying and was soon crying out like a whore. I could never have imagined myself doing that before. Had my parents heard the filth spilling from my mouth they would have hung their heads in shame at their slut of a daughter. I was amazed at my own passionate aggression during this act of lovemaking. I gripped the cheeks of his arse with my fingers and dug my nails into the soft heaving flesh. I think it must have hurt as he pulled my hands away by the wrists and pinned me down so I could do nothing at all. Even though this was pure passion, that animalistic side of me came through again. I stared up at Paulus with almost contempt at him dominating me in this way; like some restrained animal I found myself repeating 'Fuck me, fuck me harder.' My vocalization may have tipped him over the edge. I watched as his facial expression changed, an agony of ecstasy, then an explosion deep within. His moans of delight were muted by the fact that he had his mouth around my neck; it was like a lion with a zebra, only a pleasurable bite that sent shivers through my whole body. As we held this position, I felt the familiar tingling sensation build. God, it felt nice, it was really very nice, and a feeling of warmth came over me afterwards. Paulus released his grip on my wrists, and we kissed for some minutes holding the position. I could feel his warm semen and I wondered if I might conceive through these first two bouts of our sexual union. As we lay panting like two greyhounds at the end of a race, I lit a cigarette and reflected on what we had just done. For a girl with limited sexual knowledge, it wasn't so bad. Though I did hope I wouldn't become pregnant too quickly, as I just wanted to enjoy this physical side of our marriage for the moment without the constraints of children.

Yet, we had to have children, as the state required us to have them. A young married woman without a child in Nazi Germany stood out as much as a leper would in a beauty pageant. Yet at the same time I felt I had torn up *The Martial Law Manual for Making Love*. I was content that the sexual side of our marriage would never be a robotic, dull or repetitive process, nor one where male domination had to be adhered to.

Not all youthful marriages were the domestic nirvana that many young women were led to believe, under the Nazis. For some young women marriage became a convention which forced them to have sex at the will of their husbands; some even became subject to what today's society would term sexual abuse.

Berta Littmann celebrated her twentieth birthday in October 1934. Berta came from a middle-class family who had lived in several of Germany's major cities over a period of fifteen years. Her father, Arnold, came from a military background, had served in the German armed forces, and by 1934 had become a reservist. Arnold Littmann was described by his daughter as being a very strict disciplinarian with a regimented attitude to almost every aspect of daily life. Berta recorded many of her memories before her passing and the following material came to me via her great-granddaughter, Celina Falk, who now resides in the USA. Berta's memoirs were mostly in the form of handwritten essays and required translation, which Celina very kindly did for me and then sent me the transcripts. In all they make for some sad reading. Berta's words are honest, explicit and reminiscent of a life trapped behind closed doors, within a marriage which soon turned abusive. Berta begins with meeting a young man whom, her father had insisted, would be a good match for her: honest, conscientious, smart and hardworking, 'a man's man', as he always called him.

> My father always taught us girls of the family to aspire to be like our mother. He always referred to mother as a 'good woman'. Our mother never went anywhere without father; he would insist wherever possible on going everywhere with her. As a young girl this was something we never questioned as we knew no other way. Our father's view was that a woman's place was in the home, that a woman shouldn't go out unaccompanied, wherever possible, whether that was a potential suitor or a husband. It was in Christmas 1934 when my father introduced me to a young man who was four years older than me, at 24. My father, who was a staunch National Socialist and member of the Nazi Party, assured me this young man would make a great husband for me.
>
> That first meeting was spent innocently talking about things, we talked about politics, the future and places we would like to visit in the world; just normal, if slightly nervous, conversation in many respects. I had had boyfriends in the past, but my father had never approved of any of them, telling me they were wasters and drifters. One was an aspiring artist my father had accused of being a Jew, which was of course totally wrong. I was forbidden to see him again and I had to accept that living under my fathers' roof. I couldn't afford to rent anywhere of my own as much as I had dreamed of leaving home and doing so. It was never a good idea to argue with my father as he would think nothing of hitting you with his belt, something he had done frequently in the past. He was very strict with us all and if we displeased him, we were given the belt across our backsides.
>
> I began seeing this young man whose name was Peter Rath and we struck up quite a friendship and all appeared normal. Rath was very intelligent for such a young man. He had been through university studying engineering and had gained his degree. He had joined the new German Army (the Heer) as soon as the Nazis had gained a foothold, and he believed Hitler was the right man to lead our country. Rath was an attractive man with dark hair, brown eyes and chiselled cheekbones. He was strong and participated in physical exercise most days. I noticed other

girls would stare at him when we went out walking, as he always liked to wear his uniform. In some ways I should have noticed that there was this arrogance lurking beneath the smile, but I was young, and I didn't see this as others may have done.

We were at a café one afternoon enjoying some coffee when some lads who knew Rath began to make fun of him. They were calling him things like 'show-off' and 'fat head' nothing really bad, but his reaction was almost psychotic, and it was frightening. He got up and chased the two young men off and I went after him, shouting for him to just leave them alone, they are being stupid. He cornered the two of them up a side street and began punching them both in their faces and shouting at them, 'You dare to call me a show-off and fat head! If I see you both around here again, I will fuck your arses for you both.' At that he allowed them to flee. The two boys ran off with blood pouring from their noses and their clothing in disarray. Rath was breathing heavily from exertion yet at the same time he was smiling while wiping the blood off his knuckles. We returned to our seats at the café and Rath had a smile on his face all the time, as he kept saying how he had just given those two idiots a beating. It wasn't my idea of a pleasant afternoon, and he was not really someone I cared to develop a relationship with.

When I returned home later, I told my parents what had happened and that I was going to break up with Rath as I felt uneasy with the way that he seemed to enjoy violence. My father argued, 'No, you will do no such thing; it is a pity that there are not more young German men like Rath who are willing to stand up for himself and this great country of ours.' He went on and on, berating me for wanting to be in the company of dreamers as opposed to realists. I reminded father that Hitler had been one of his so-called dreamers, that Hitler had once aspired to become an artist. My father then went on to say, 'Yes, that is true, we all know that story, but he came to his senses to rescue Germany from the very people you wish to spend your time with.' I couldn't win with father, and mother wouldn't become involved in any arguments, always preferring to leave the room when he went on one of his tirades.

I met Rath again and asked him if he would mind not getting involved in any more fights, at least when in my company, as I didn't like it. He appeared hurt at my suggestion but agreed to my demand. We would go out to the theatre, cinema and see musicals together and things seemed to be how I had thought they should be. We shared kisses which he gained much pleasure from and as our relationship progressed Rath suggested we go for walks in the forest like other couples would, so we could have some privacy. So, we went for walks in the forest which were mostly very pleasant. We would pack a picnic and blanket and head out along the woodland trails to find a quiet spot. I had no intention of having sexual intercourse before marriage, despite the fact that Rath tried a few times to initiate lovemaking. I pushed him off and told him I was not that kind of girl. I wasn't totally cold with him and offered him hand relief which he seemed to enjoy very much. He would offer to do the same for me, but I told him no. I didn't think I was being unfair or prudish, as they say; I was just trying to maintain my own perceptions of how a proper romance should evolve. It shouldn't be exclusively about the sex; there have to be romantic times and love and spending time together. Rath felt that me giving him hand relief was somewhat demeaning for him as an Aryan male. He didn't think it right that in a sense I was in control of him when pleasuring him with my hand. He would argue that as much as he enjoyed it, it felt wrong.

My father was eager for me and Rath to marry so Rath proposed to me during the winter of 1934, while we were out walking. A family meeting was arranged with Rath's parents, and we all sat down to tea one Sunday afternoon. Everyone sat around our table and thrashed out the details of my future, or so it felt. The wedding was set for the summer of the following year and the parents shook hands with one another. It was like the signing of a contract, that is how it all felt to me. Rath was overjoyed that finally I was going to become his wife. I felt that marriage would be a blessing to us both, that we would share good times and any troubles, and overcome them as a couple should. I hadn't realized what a charade Rath really was in the emotional sense. Behind the smiles and cordiality lurked a beast that would only reveal its true extent after we had married.

The marriage ceremony itself was very pleasant and to all present appeared like any other happy day where two people joined together to share the rest of their lives. Rath was the perfect gentleman throughout the proceedings and while I was very nervous about our wedding night, I felt at ease with the fact that I would be losing my virginity that night and soon afterwards maybe becoming a mother. As the day drew toward night everyone had drunk a lot of beer and wine. Rath had not drunk as much as the other men, including my father, and I thought he might have taken this opportunity to let himself go a little, but no he didn't.

We said our farewells to our guests and retired to our room for the evening around 11 pm. Rath closed the door, locking it behind us, and took off his uniform, carefully folding it and putting it away in a suitcase. This was the first time I had seen Rath in nothing other than his underwear, and marvelled at his well-defined muscular physique. I sat on the edge of the bed feeling slightly awkward when Rath insisted I take off my dress so he could see my body. I stood up and slowly removed the wedding dress, peeling it off like some second skin before hanging it up on the bedroom door. I then sat down on the edge of the bed. Rath walked over to me and began kissing me, removing my bra as he did so. I was feeling very nervous at this point but just closed my eyes, lay back on the bed, and tried to enjoy the experience. Rath slowly worked his way down from my mouth to my breasts, he began sucking on me like some hungry infant and I had to tell him it felt uncomfortable and not to use so much force. He continued as if he hadn't heard me, so I told him again, 'Please don't do that so hard, it is hurting me.' Again, he said nothing continuing to suck hard on my nipples, so I tried to move his head away with my hands. I didn't use much force I just wanted him to stop sucking on my breasts. With not so much as a word he grabbed both my wrists in his one hand, holding me down so I could not stop him. With his free hand he actually ripped my underwear off, and he said to me, 'I have waited a long time to fuck you, Berta.' I pleaded with him to be gentle and not be rough as I had not made love before. I felt him put a finger inside me which hurt a little and despite my complaints of it hurting me, he continued. Then he began saying to me, 'I am going to fuck you now, Berta, fuck you hard like a man should fuck his virgin wife.' He repositioned himself and pushed himself into me in one forceful thrust which really hurt. The pain was so bad I actually started punching him, but he quickly held me down again. As he began thrusting, he was saying all these things like 'You are very hot down there' and 'Your hole has the grip of a fist'. Thankfully it was over very quickly, and he rolled off me and I went to the bathroom where I shut the door and cried for some minutes, more from the humiliation than any pain. There was a little blood coming from me and I washed this away. I looked at myself in the mirror and thought, 'Berta, what have you done, you silly fool?' When I came out of the bathroom Rath was laying on the bed, smoking a cigar. I told him, 'You hurt me, why did you do that?' He shrugged it off and said, 'It always hurts for a woman on her first time; it's nothing and you'll be fine next time.' Then he just pulled the sheets over himself and went to sleep, without even a kiss. I got into bed and tried to sleep but I couldn't. The day had gone well up until this point and I just hoped it would get better over the next few days when things had settled down.

The problem with Rath was that it never did settle down. I soon began to understand I was the wife of a sexual bully, a man who couldn't orgasm in a woman without first inflicting pain and humiliation on her. The honeymoon was hardly sweet as honey. Over the seven days we were away, it was just him having sex with me at every possible chance. We had barely unpacked in our room at Havel when he pounced on me, and it felt more and more like rape than making love. He took off my clothes before stripping off himself, manhandling me onto the bed like some naughty child. He told me, 'I want you to be my dog, now kneel down like a dog.'

He demanded I give him oral sex which I was not comfortable in doing but I did it to stop him becoming angry with me. I knew if I refused, he would get violent. It was not a pleasant experience, and I didn't appreciate the taste as some women may have done. I wasn't even sure if I was doing it properly and all the time, he was saying, 'Use your lips and your tongue only and keep your teeth out of the way.' He refused to lie down as I gave him oral sex; he couldn't bear the thought of any woman having power over him and insisted on standing before me as I knelt down on the bed. It was all about him being in control all the time. When he had had enough of oral sex, he told me to move over into the middle of the bed and kneel down like a dog. As I was kneeling down, he was already behind me positioning himself between my legs, holding me hard by my hips and telling me to spread my thighs as wide as possible and, 'Keep your arse up so I can fuck you properly, fuck you like a dog does his bitch.' These are the kind of things he would say to me; it was never romantic or loving, ever. As he took me from behind, he would be squeezing my breasts with his hands then he would use his hands to massage me, trying to make me orgasm as he would say. I used to pretend to moan out with pleasure hoping this would calm him down, but it never did.

Before sex he would always make me wear my hair in two plaits as many girls and women did in Germany at the time. Whenever he took me from behind, he would grab my plaits in his hands and pull my head back as far as he could and put his fingers in my mouth. In his view this was pleasurable and quite normal and a woman should enjoy being taken this way. It was like this most days. Sometimes he would demand sex three or four times during the day. I was hoping I would fall pregnant and maybe that might stop him desiring me so much.

Eventually I did fall pregnant and for a while Rath seemed to change his ways and be gentle during sex, but this was a short-lived period. When I gave birth to a baby boy it was wonderful. I thought now that Rath had the son he had always wanted he would change. Sadly, this was not the case and he wanted to have intercourse with me almost right after I had given birth. I told him I couldn't do this that I needed to wait for a month before I could have intercourse again. This was of course advice I had taken from a physician after I had given birth. Over the weeks afterwards I was tired from caring for the baby, my body felt like a deflated tyre; the last thing on my mind at the end of each day was having sex, I just didn't want it. Three weeks later Rath began raping me. I say rape as the sex was not consensual. I told him no, I didn't want to have sex with him yet, so he would force me.

Rath received his call-up in 1936 and he and thousands of other members of the German military were called to barracks. He didn't say much about what was happening, but he said he would be 'going to a war'. I actually felt happiness at the thought of him going away and it was soon revealed he was going to Spain to aid General Franco's fascists with something called the Condor Legion. When Rath left for Spain, for the first time I saw real concern, fear and perhaps a little sadness in his face. He kissed me on the lips and then kissed our baby boy and he said to me, 'I will be back very soon; I will write to you both.' He never said, 'I love you'; no, he stopped short of saying that.

That was the last time I saw Rath. He was one of the German casualties of the fighting. I received notice that he had died of wounds in a bombing or something. I wasn't sad at receiving the news of his untimely death at the hands of the Republicans, but I did not rejoice either. I felt nothing at all, I was emotionally numb. My parents and his parents were horrified by my lack of sadness. I should have been the perfect widow, beside myself with grief, but no, I was not, I was in many ways happy.

I refused to go back to my parents' house to live as I didn't want my son to grow up anything like my father, or his father, for that matter. My sisters were not too happy about me not coming back home either, but when I talked with them about what happened they began to understand. I wanted to bring my boy up as a decent human being, I wasn't interested in getting involved with another man, I had had enough of men. I recall one night Rath had taken me by force on our bed, as usual forcing me into a kneeling position where he could pull my hair back and put his fingers in my mouth and down my throat to the point I could barely breathe. He said, 'My dear Berta, you can't ever have the cow without the bull.' What he meant by that I don't know, and I don't care.

As Rath's death was in the service of his country, me and my baby son were quite well looked after. I was happy that way and made up my mind I would not marry again.

I did remarry some years later and married a lovely man I can be proud to have called my husband. He was kind and loving and a totally selfless human being in every respect. I tried to make peace with my father, in particular, yet both my parents refused to attend my second wedding ceremony. In their eyes it was a betrayal of some sort. We spoke but things were never the same between us, which is sad, as they missed out. I don't think for one moment I was the only one who had experienced the things I did. Back then it was not the right thing to speak out, so you had to keep these things to yourself. My experiences, far from making me a weakling, actually made me a stronger woman and these attributes I was determined to pass onto my children.

Chapter 4

The *Sturmbannführer*'s Lolita

I was a child, a girl whose only misfortune in this life was being born in the year 1928, as Germany and the world around me slipped into a severe economic and social depression. This was much as a result of the Wall Street Crash which occurred in the United States of America. The fallout of this unfortunate event had widespread repercussions, which were felt all over the world, but more so in Germany which was suffering the effects of losing the First World War. I began to understand later on, as I grew older in what would be Nazi Germany, was the fact that I was born to a loving working-class mother and father, who were left with two choices in their lives, in two years or so after my birth – either give me up or starve. My parents made what must have been a very difficult decision to place me in the care of an orphanage run by a group of nuns of a Catholic order. It was this place that I would call home until I was old enough to make my own way in the world, or someone adopted me.

Sadly, at that time my world was being distorted as if it were a piece of plastic in a fire. National Socialism was rising throughout Germany under the enigmatic leadership of Adolf Hitler, a stern-faced man with a Charlie Chaplin-style moustache and an immense oratory gift. As a young child the name Hitler was heard frequently, it was part of my existence; as with the other girls we faced a daily chore of prayers and teaching which included that of National Socialism. Even the religious orders could not operate outside the scrutiny of the Nazi state. Many supported the Nazis provided they were left to get on with things as they had done before Hitler came to power.

The meals we received barely filled our grumbling stomachs, and we were constantly hungry. In the orphanage there was little by way of compassion. There was no one to cuddle or console you when you felt frightened or sad about something. The nuns were cold, bald, faceless, religious bureaucrats, devoid more of warmth than maybe death itself. If they felt you had been disrespectful in any little way they would scold and beat you to rid you of the devil or cleanse you of your sins, and they would deprive you of the very few treats you did receive, as extra punishment. The literature we were allowed was that of a theological nature, but we also read books which explained the ethos of Nazism. There were no fairytale books, no psychological means of escape from them; you never dared to dream, sleep was a void of blackness, never a theatre of dreams as such, just a bodily function which served exclusively to rid one's eyes of their daily fatigue. We slept in dormitories, huge draughty rooms with their cold stone floors with three rows of beds. We wore these long white gowns which were buttoned at the neck, it was forbidden for girls to show any of their legs or body, full stop. Only your head, hands and feet were visible once you put those things on. Each of our beds had a mattress filled with horsehair, we had woollen blankets and a single pillow which was about as comfortable as a sack of cement. We were consigned to these hovels from 8 pm of an evening until 6 am following morning. At bedtime there could be no talking or reading, you were expected to nourish your soul. There were girls who were friends who would try and sneak into one another's beds for comfort. If they were caught doing this, they were given a right thrashing in front of us all. It was considered infantile and unclean, even though we were just children seeking comfort. All you could do was rest, as the nuns used to say, 'Ready to serve the almighty another day.' Each day began the same as the last, with oatmeal, usually, followed later by a lunch of stew and hard black rye bread. In the evening we gathered at our tables again for another meal. This was what the characters of me and the other girls were built upon.

In some ways as a teenager, I blamed the nuns for extinguishing the fire of my youth, the ability to stand up and question, to say, 'Yes, this is correct' or 'No, that course of action is wrong.' They broke us emotionally, made us these submissive docile creatures that would be easy prey in the world we were to enter later. The rule of survival under the order was to comply with them as you would any authority, survive, get through it, get out and, with a bit of luck, live your own life. In the winter it was even more unbearable, the building was cold with the embrace of a grave. Night-time was even worse, when the temperature dropped further.

When I was 8 years old, in 1936, I recall that winter when the first snows arrived. We were allowed out to play for a while, but we did not have proper winter coats or boots to wear. I recall how many children fell ill over the weeks that followed. They had to separate us from the sick children, and I remember that this period was the first time I saw members of the German Army. The army had arrived with extra supplies, including a little coal, blankets, boots and clothing, all of which had been donated to us under the Winter Relief Fund instituted by Adolf Hitler the Führer, or leader of Germany. Of the eight children who fell ill during that winter, six of them died. The help for them came far too late. I lay in my bed the one night thinking about them, how they would not be around to smell the spring air or enjoy another glorious summer like the last one.

What had happened here was considered embarrassing to the local Nazi authorities. In a short period of time, it seemed the nuns were no longer in charge of us, not in the same context as they were over the years previous. I recall a local Gauleiter coming to visit. We were having breakfast when he arrived and when he saw us seated at these long tables with bowls of oatmeal and cups of goat's milk, he went berserk. He shouted out, 'What is going on in this place? Prisoners in our jails are fed better than the tripe these children are being fed!' The head of the order, a surly, pale-faced woman, dropped to her knees and began to weep and offer her hands up in prayer. The Gauleiter continued his verbal torrent and ended it with the words, 'Fucking hell!' You have to remember this was a religious order and blasphemy of any type under the roof of this order was considered very bad. He didn't seem to care at all and before he left, he shouted again, 'I am going to sort this out, this is disgraceful.' His outburst had a profound effect upon the order, and it slowly changed. After a few weeks we were sent out to attend normal schooling and many couples began to visit the order. Stern efforts were being made to ensure all of us German children were placed in good homes as fast as possible. It all happened overnight, and it was from this that the whispers of how the Führer had saved us and made our lives better began to emanate. In a sense this was correct. Had it not been for Hitler we would have been under that miserable order well into our teens when we would have been finally permitted to leave.

I was adopted when I was 9 years old by a couple who originally came from Bavaria. Their names were Ernst and Gretl Vogel. The Vogels had been to see me on a few occasions to ascertain my attitude and emotional stability. My adoptive father was a medical psychologist, perfectly qualified to assess me as a prospective daughter. My adoptive mother had been a nurse and as expected was a kindly soul whom I warmed to very quickly. I had never learned the identity of my true parents and all I had ever known about them was that they were working-class Germans who had to make difficult decisions in difficult times. I never even discovered their names or what they looked like. I was now part of a new family who had taken me out of the order and into their home. The day I left with them is one I will always remember – as I left with absolutely nothing, I had not even a teddy bear or toy to my name, I had nothing at all. I was able to say goodbye to the remaining girls whom I knew as friends, I told them I would see them again someday, but the reality was I would never see many of them again in my life.

My adoptive parents owned a substantial home in the suburbs of the city of Heidelberg. As my new parents drove up a tree-lined lane this large old house came into view and I asked them, 'Is this home?' to which they replied, 'Yes, it is my dear.' They rarely ever called me by my birth name, which was Ursula, instead they always called me 'my dear'. I was always their dear. As we pulled up outside this house which to me looked like a mansion from one of those old Frankenstein horror films, I felt a slight pang of nervousness. I think both my new parents noticed this and offered me reassurance. Two small dogs ran out of the front door as we got out of the car. Running after the dogs were three other children – two boys named Max and Willi, and a girl named Heidi. These were the Vogels' natural children, my new brothers and sister. The two Dachshunds were adorable little yappers which I came to love dearly and who shared my bed some evenings.

I was shown to my room. I had never had a room of my own in my life and this was luxurious. The bed had a thick quilted covering and sumptuous fluffy white pillows. On the shelves in the bedroom sat numerous toys such as teddy bears and soldiers with tin drums. It was beautiful and I was filled with excitement at this spectacle. Outside my bedroom window loomed the heavy imposing branches of an old oak tree which my father explained was home to an owl which frequented the outer branches on warm summer evenings. He pointed to the hole in the oak where the bird spent the daylight hours and the branches where it would sit of an evening. My father remarked, 'Owls kick up a right row you know, keep you awake they will some nights. If they get too much just shoo them off.' There was also a small bookcase stacked with books – these books were ones I had always wanted to read, fairytales, myths and legends.

I was told, 'Everything in this room is yours now, you are part of our family, and you shall be treated as such. As you will see there are clothes in your drawers and shoes and boots for your feet.' My mother asked me to remove the dreadfully worn-out T-bar sandals I was wearing so I took them off and handed them to her and tried on the shoes and boots which had been left in my room for me. We still had to get to know each other but we had got off to a good start and I was happy to refer to this warm, pleasant couple as 'mother and father'. I was told the routine of the house by my brothers and sister and how I must help out with chores when asked to do so. I was also told of the local school I was to attend from the Monday morning. Afterwards I was told to come down and join my new family for dinner in the dining room. Heidi excitedly took my hand and led the way downstairs to the dining room.

As I entered the dining room and pulled out a chair from the long highly polished dark wood table, I sat down and looked around the room. On the walls were many photographs of smiling couples and their children, obviously my new relatives. As my eyes scanned the room one huge oil painting dominated the central open fireplace. Either side of the fireplace on the mantle was a brass shell casing. The huge oil painting was that of Adolf Hitler in military uniform. I looked hard at the almost steel expression, those piercing eyes which captivated the masses wherever he went. I was mesmerized by the painting until my parents came into the room and placed dishes upon the table followed by a glass water jug.

That night I ate like a queen, it was the best I had eaten in a long time – meat, roasted potatoes, vegetables and gravy. This was followed by a traditional German strudel dessert with crème fraîche. After this meal I felt quite sleepy and after falling asleep several times in the living room I was taken up the stairs to bed by my mother. She carefully undressed me and helped me into a beautiful pink silk nightgown and I climbed wearily into the blissful comfort and warmth of my bed. No sooner had my head hit the soft white pillow than I was fast asleep. Before I drifted off to sleep, I was aware of both my father and mother standing over me and my two brothers peering from either side of them at me. I heard mother say, 'Look at that child, isn't she just so perfect, so beautiful?' The next morning, I remember was Sunday. Heidi came running into my room to wake me up for church that morning. The Vogels always attended church and my going was no exception to the rule. Church was always boring, and I secretly loathed having to go. I felt I had spent most of my life in the church.

Once the morning service was over, we walked back home and then we children were permitted to play in the extensive garden at the rear of the house. We had a swing there and we could climb the trees and in summer pick fruit off them. We played in the garden up until lunch and then again in the afternoon. At 6 pm on a Sunday we had to all have a bath and wash our hair ready for school on the Monday. My first day at my new school was uneventful; I had two older brothers and a very feisty younger sister to look after me. They went everywhere with me in the playground, the other children were curious as to where I had come from and asked many questions as children often do. The Vogels were supportive of National Socialism and Hitler, and we were expected to join the Hitler Youth movement which we did. Our parents bought us each a uniform and everything we needed. We were also given private tuition on the new political theory. Our father was not convinced the school we attended was thorough enough in this field of education. He wanted us to understand we had what we had because of Hitler. He wanted us to grasp the politics and not feel sad that what he termed as 'the other races' had to perish in order for Germany and its people to thrive. So, we attended the Hitler Youth and began our indoctrination into National Socialism, but otherwise we were just normal children.

My first introduction to the man the Vogels always called 'The Sturmbannführer' [SS equivalent of Major], a Major Gerhard Ziegler, who came around a month after I had joined the Vogel family. Ziegler was an ambitious young soldier then and one who rapidly rose through the ranks of the German armed forces due to exemplary conduct and his combat record. Ziegler had fought in Spain, Poland and France with distinction, being awarded the Iron Cross, both first and second classes, and later the German Cross in Gold, which he was particularly proud of and always wore on his grey tunic. Ziegler always cut a very handsome figure, wearing his uniform with his clean-shaven face, high cheekbones, short cropped blond hair and blue eyes. Yes, I recognized even at a young age that he was a very good-looking young man indeed, a very aesthetic Nazi.

Ziegler was very fatherly to the other Vogel children yet with me he was different. He made great efforts to make me feel special. Some days I remember he would take me out in his truck with him. Apparently, it was against the rules to have child passengers in any military vehicle without there being a very good reason. I remember the one occasion Ziegler asked me, 'Do you like it? Riding along in my truck?' I told him, 'Yes, I do.' He then said, 'That's good as you are riding in the front, only Jews ride in the back you know.' I smiled at him, the impact of his remark not really registering within my child's mindset. As I grew older and joined the Nazi girls league, the Jungmädelbund, Ziegler's interest in me intensified. If he took me out in his truck, I had to be wearing my Jungmädelbund uniform of white blouse, black tie and dark skirt. When I was 13 years of age the whole dynamic of the relationship between me and this Major Ziegler changed irrevocably.

The Vogels suspected nothing of the man they had known for years, who was considered almost a part of their family. Me going off in his truck with him became commonplace, but it was always me on my own, neither Heidi nor anyone else ever accompanied us, which struck me as being odd. Heidi and my brothers used to get a little jealous at times, but their petulance was always quelled by my father's promise of giving them other treats. Nobody suspected anything about Ziegler, that he may have been developing some unhealthy infatuation with me. I began to feel a little uneasy whenever we went out in his truck. I just felt there were other intentions, though, at that time, he gave me no reason to suspect anything sinister. On our usual truck rides we would often go to a depot where a few supplies were unloaded and then take a leisurely drive back and I would be dropped off at home.

On one occasion in the late summer Ziegler insisted we stop, as he wanted to take some photographs as souvenirs. He pulled the truck over, parking up by some fields where there were cattle quietly grazing and a river flowing through a meadow. It was a hot day, and the fresh air was nice and he wanted to go and walk beside the river with me, so I agreed. We jumped out of the truck and climbed over a rickety wooden fence which ran the length of the field. As our feet touched the soft meadow grass there was this air of freedom about us, it was intoxicating, and we walked toward the river which weaved its way snakelike through the greenery of the meadow toward some woods. Ziegler then said to me, 'Go on, just paddle in the water and I will take some photographs of you.' I sat down on the riverbank and took off my shoes and socks and stepped into the cool water which felt so refreshing on this hot summer's afternoon. Ziegler clicked away with his camera shouting out to me, 'Hold up your head and smile.' It was 'Stand like this' and 'Stand like that' while he just photographed me. When I got out of the water, he then asked me to lie down on my side. He placed his cap on the ground a few yards away and I asked him what he was doing. He then placed his camera on top of his cap, peered through the lens and said, 'That's it, I've got it.' He then moved a switch on the camera which he said would set the self-timing mechanism. He set this switch then leapt over to where I was lying on my side, and he lay down and cuddled up behind me putting his right arm across my waist and shouting, 'Smile!' There was the brief noise of a clockwork motor in operation within the camera, before the sound of the shutter clicking. As soon as the photograph was taken, I quickly got up feeling a little embarrassed. Ziegler was just saying, 'That will be a beautiful photo.' As I put my socks and shoes back on Ziegler continued to take photographs of me, running around me, from different angles. It just felt so weird.

After he had used up almost his entire roll of film, taking photographs of me, we walked a little way along the riverbank. It was here right at this moment he attempted to make that first physical connection between the two of us, by asking me if I would hold his hand. I nervously replied to his request by saying, 'I'm not a child – I don't need anyone to hold my hand.' He replied with a smile, 'I know you're not a child, I just want to hold your hand that's all, nothing else.' Before I could say anything more, he took hold of my hand, stroking his thumb up and down mine as we walked along the riverbank. It was shortly after he stopped me, held me by my shoulders and said to me, 'You really are beautiful, do you know that? I could walk with you like this forever.' I was very nervous about all of this and looked down at the ground. He then stroked the side of my face with his knuckles and then lifted my chin with his fingers, before leaning forward and kissing me full on the lips. I was speechless and couldn't have said anything had I wanted to. It was then he said to me, 'Let this be our little secret, my dear Ursula, we could both be in serious trouble if anyone found out. You probably more so than me, but we won't let that happen, will we?' I nodded to him in agreement as I was still quite shocked.

At that we walked back across the meadow, climbed the wooden fence and jumped back into the truck. I sat silently deep in thought as we made the short journey back home. When we arrived, Ziegler accompanied me inside and was invited in for tea and drinks. As we sat at the dining room table Ziegler barely took his eyes off me and smiled throughout the proceedings until it was time for him to leave. I wanted to tell my parents, but something told me if I had done so they'd never believe me and I might end up back at the order with those dreadful black crows. I dreaded that more than Ziegler's infatuation, so I kept quiet. It was a heavy burden for a young girl to have to shoulder, to have no one to talk with about it.

In our girls' Hitler Youth, they would all talk about boys, and our duty as future mothers. There were girls who could not wait to grow up and marry a soldier or a fighter pilot. One of them had seen me with Ziegler in his truck and remarked, 'What a handsome young man he is; you are very lucky to be such good friends with him.' During the evenings I would often lie awake examining my feelings: what did I feel? I only felt a sense of emotional numbness. I thought Ziegler was good-looking and I liked him as he was so kind to me; was it really such a bad thing that he had kissed me? My emotions and conscience wrestled with one another until I fell asleep. I was woken sometime later by the screech of the two resident owls who sat out on the tree branch outside my open window. I got out of my bed and looked out the window for a few minutes until the birds flew off into the night sky. I stared at the moon and felt the warm breeze caress my face before getting back into bed. I thought of many things as I drifted off to sleep. I thought of the grassy meadow and the river, the cows who idly chewed the sweet grasses which flourished there beside those cool waters, and I thought of Ziegler. His face even haunted my dreams. Was there no escape from this Ziegler, I asked myself.

This is how it all started. I fought with my emotions, trying hard not to develop feelings for this man much older than me, but it wasn't easy, I was young, stupid and naïve. Over the weeks that followed the photographs and the kiss in the meadow, things developed further. Ziegler would call at the Vogels, usually on a Sunday afternoon, and take me out either in his truck or a car he would borrow from one of his men. He would always take me to that same meadow, and we would walk holding hands. The way he held my hand even began to change. At first, he held my hand much like a mother or father would hold the hand of a son or daughter, just in the normal way. It soon progressed to him sliding his fingers between mine, so our fingers were interlocked. I didn't really like this at first as again it just felt wrong to me. On the fourth occasion the kiss he gave me was different from the previous three. I remember him instructing me, saying, 'This is how a proper couple should kiss one another.'

He tilted my head to the side, told me to close my eyes and open my mouth. Before I knew what was happening, he was kissing me passionately in a way that sent shivers down my spine. I should have stopped things there, but I felt powerless and very nervous to resist what he was doing to me. I felt the trembling fingers of his left hand as they unbuttoned my blouse. I tried to pull away and tell him 'No', but he held me so tight against his body with his right hand that I could do nothing. I could have shouted out, but I didn't. As we continued kissing his left hand caressed my breasts; his hands felt clammy against my skin. He pulled me down to the ground, unbuttoned his trousers and then took my hand and pushed it down into his underwear. I asked him, 'What are you doing?' He just replied, 'Shhhh, hold it like this.' I took hold of the rigid shaft of flesh and simulated the back-and-forth motions he was instructing me to do. All the time he held onto me, kissing and caressing me, like a human toad. His kissing became more aggressive and his breathing heavier. I had never done anything like this before and wondered what was going to happen next. I did not have to wait very long to find out. I felt his body go very tense as if he was about to have a seizure, and then he let out a gasp which sounded a mixture of agony and ecstasy. I felt warm fluid on my hand, and I immediately pulled away and jumped up. I thought it was blood or something. I wiped my hand against the grass asking him, 'What is that, what is it?' He lay there staring at me, smiling, and just replied, 'That's what happens when a man blows his load.' That's how he explained the function that was the male orgasm. I had just experienced it for the first time, and I found it unpleasant. He thought it was all very amusing before getting up off the grass brushing himself down and doing up his trousers. He kissed me again and said to me, 'This is our little secret,' again. On the drive back home, he stopped off at some shops and bought me sweets. He made me feel special as I could see the other women who passed us by in the shop looking at him, 'giving him the eye' as they call it. All the women fancied him, and it made me feel special being in his company.

As we drove back through the town, I sat in the passenger seat eating sweets and feeling confused about the events of the last couple of hours. I would say I was quite mature for a girl of my age, in the physical sense, but mentally I was just a child really. This routine of him picking me up on a Sunday afternoon continued through to the wintertime. By this time, I had begun to believe that Ziegler really did love me, that to him I was very special. He bought me nice things and the Vogels never suspected a thing as he bought nice things for their natural children too. As winter arrived it was far too cold to go into the meadow and he began taking me to this apartment in Heidelberg city. I am not sure whose apartment it was, but I sensed it was not his own property and that maybe he was renting it, or it belonged to one of his acquaintances, I wasn't sure.

The apartment was located on the Hauptstrasse, situated above two large shops and this building still stands today. It was tastefully furnished, had a large open fire, with a piano in front of some doors to a balcony which overlooked the city street. I recall the first time I was taken to this apartment, Ziegler fumbled with the keys for some minutes until finding the right one, another thing that made me feel that this was not a property he had visited frequently. We walked inside and he closed and locked the heavy oak door behind us, then went over to the piano and began to play some Bach. I was very impressed with his skills on the piano, and he told me, 'Maybe I can teach you to play.' He told me to come and sit beside him then began showing me some tunes that beginners often started with, promising to build my repertoire over the coming months and years. It was here, at this apartment in Heidelberg, that I was initiated into Ziegler's iniquitous world. It was at that apartment that Ziegler took my virginity, at the age of 14. For most of the visits to the apartment it was a routine of slowly convincing me to take off my clothes and join him on this huge ornate double bed, where he began to pleasure me using his fingers. I believed he loved me, and I thought that I loved him and that by doing what he wanted some day we could even be married, when I was old enough.

I remember the Sunday afternoon he took my innocence from me; every girl can remember her first time, whether it is a good memory or a bad one. I remember that it hurt at first and that he gained more pleasure from the experience than I did. It wasn't that he was rough with me or anything; he would take his time and if he couldn't penetrate me, he would wait a little while then try again when he felt I was ready. He was the master, and I was the student; I was completely under his thumb in every respect. After a few times it grew in intensity and was much more pleasurable. Ziegler always wore birth control as he was paranoid about getting me pregnant, yet this fear never prevented him from producing an erection every time I was alone with him. Ziegler delighted in teaching me what he called 'the art of love'. When it came to oral sex, I was revolted by the idea of it, yet I did it because I wanted him to love me, and I wanted to keep him happy. To this day I am still revolted at the thought of a man ejaculating in my mouth, the salty-tasting fluid with the thick consistency of raw egg whites. It always made me retch and I spat it out onto the sheets which was the only thing he would complain about afterwards as he cleaned it off with a wet towel. I admit that the first time he performed oral sex upon me I found it a highly pleasurable experience, much more pleasurable for me than the act of lovemaking. Ziegler was obviously very experienced with a varied sexual repertoire. He enjoyed doing a lot of things that appeared odd to me. He used to like sucking my toes as he made love to me. I found this act annoying as it tickled greatly but he insisted on doing it. He would tell me to stop squirming around like a silly child and relax and enjoy the sensations. Then he would insist I turn around so as I was facing away from him. I didn't like this method of sex at all which he crudely referred to as 'dog fucking'. I certainly didn't want to think of myself as being a dog. In fact, he did everything with me, including these weird positions which required great physical dexterity that often left me with aching limbs. He also enjoyed what he used to call 'riding the horse' where he would lie back, allowing me to sit astride him, allowing me to dictate the pace as we had sex. This whole thing became a weekly routine, Ziegler collecting me from home and taking me to this apartment, telling my father he was giving me piano tuition.

My whole world changed in mid-1942. At the time I thought of it all as a total emotional disaster, yet as I grew older and today, I can count it as a blessing. It was at around this time that Ziegler visited and he didn't take me to the apartment for the usual 'piano lessons'. He came into the house sombre faced, and I could tell something was very wrong with him. My father asked him to join us in the living room and once we had all sat down my father poured Ziegler a large glass of brandy. Ziegler sat stony-faced for a moment before announcing he was leaving Heidelberg for the front, as part of the reinforcements being sent into Russia. Ziegler explained that more and more Wehrmacht forces were required in Russia in order to defeat of Stalin's Red Army. All of us, apart from my father, began to cry tears of sadness at this terrible news. It felt as if someone had stuck a knife in my stomach and I felt sick at the thought of him having to leave. All kinds of horrible thoughts went through my mind, 'Would he get badly wounded?' and 'Would he ever return to Heidelberg again?' My parents knew how fond I had grown of Ziegler, in ignorance of course of what had really been going on. As Ziegler left, I walked with him out to his car, and I asked for a few minutes to talk to him alone. I told him I would wait for him to return home as I cried in his arms. It was then he held my face in his hands for the last time, telling me, 'My dearest Ursula, I love you so much and I will come back for you I promise.' Then he said to me, 'Just promise me one thing: that you will never let another man steal your heart from mine.' I gave him my word that I wouldn't. He looked to see if anyone was watching before kissing me on the lips. He then removed his German Cross in Gold badge from his tunic and placed it in the palm of my hand. He said, 'Here take this, whenever you look at it you will think of me.' I told him I couldn't take it from him, yet he insisted, saying he would have it back when he returned. He then got into his car and I stood watching as he drove off. The remainder of that day was a nightmare, my emotions were in turmoil, and I couldn't stop crying. Even that night, I cried, so much so my parents nearly took me to see the doctor in the city. I didn't want to see any doctor for fear they might discover what had really been happening between me and Ziegler. I had to force my sadness and despair to the back of my mind.

As the weeks and months went by, we received no letters from Ziegler. He had promised he would write but we received no word from him at all. Boys in our neighbourhood used to try becoming friendly with me but I resisted all their attempts at being romantic. I had made a promise to Ziegler, and I was not going to break it. As a result, the boys would call me names, things like 'Ice Girl', 'Cold Beauty', or 'Frigid Fraulein'. Three years passed by with no word from Ziegler. My father would say, 'I fear that good young man has met with a terrible fate.' I felt sad when father used to say these things, but I had to face up to the reality that Ziegler was very probably dead.

With the arrival of American forces in Heidelberg and the war over, there was still no sign of Ziegler. I used to walk into the town asking around to see if anyone had any information. Nobody knew anything and after a while I gave up and started to get on with a more normal life. Then in 1948 while out shopping in Heidelberg I saw a man I knew had been one of Ziegler's colleagues. I had to run to catch up with him, weaving in and out of the crowd of people. I was almost out of breath when I managed to stop him and ask him, 'Do you know what happened to Major Gerhard Ziegler? He was a friend of mine.' The man replied, 'Major Ziegler is fine, Fraulein, and he is currently living in Wilhelmshaven. I can give you his address if you want it.' I was very excited and stood impatiently as the man wrote down Ziegler's address on a piece of paper that he had to procure from a nearby bakery shop. He handed it to me and said, 'Here, this is where you will find him. Give him my regards when you do.' I asked, 'What name do I tell him?' 'Kristoff Wyborny is my name; tell him Kristoff asked about him.' I walked home feeling quite elated at this piece of news and decided I would travel to Wilhelmshaven the following weekend. I didn't really think much about why he had not written or got in touch, but felt I might surprise him if I visited him. I was now 19 years old, and Ziegler had not seen me for many years, I hoped he would be very pleased.

I planned to catch trains all the way to Wilhelmshaven and maybe stay over there for a couple of days. With everything planned, I left early on the Saturday morning, not telling my parents the whole story of why I was going to Wilhelmshaven. They just assumed I had maybe found an admirer there; either way they did not ask too many questions. I boarded the first train to my destination and sat staring out of the window, reminiscing back to the last time I had been with Ziegler in the Hamburg apartment. My mind soon became engrossed in erotic thoughts and memories. I had all these romantic notions of meeting him; he would be thrilled and whisk me off in his arms to marry me. Sadly, this was not going to be the case.

After the long journey, I was feeling quite tired and when I arrived in Wilhelmshaven, I just wanted to get a coffee and find somewhere to stay for a couple of nights. It was not difficult to find places to stay and I found a room available through a friendly local couple who lived near the harbour. I unpacked my things and decided I would go to see Ziegler the following morning after a decent night's sleep. The next morning, I was up early as I didn't sleep as well as I had thought I would. My thoughts were consumed with passion; I felt aroused and hot for most of the night, and it was torture. I washed and dressed and had breakfast with the kindly couple and their pet dog, Alfred, who ate more of my breakfast than I did. I was excited and didn't feel that hungry and was eager to go to see Ziegler.

As I left the house overlooking the harbour the sun was climbing high into the cloudless sky and it was already getting warm. I felt invigorated by the scent of the ocean carried on the warm breeze, feeling it was in every sense a perfect day. As I approached Ziegler's address, I could clearly see a man wearing brown shorts and a white sports vest using a lawnmower in the front garden. For a moment I stopped walking, waiting for the man, who had his back to me, to turn around with the mower, so as I could see if it was Ziegler or not. As he turned around, I could clearly see that it was Gerhard Ziegler.

Excitedly I ran up to the white wooden picket fence which bordered his garden and shouted, 'Major Ziegler, it's me Ursula!' Ziegler looked as if he had seen a ghost. He stopped in his tracks, quickly looked around to see if anyone was looking, then he came over to me and he said, 'Excuse me, Fraulein, I am Gerhard Ziegler but I do not recall who you are.' I said to him, 'Don't be silly, of course you know who I am. I am Ursula from Heidelberg. I lived with the Vogel family; they were your good friends there.' Again, he looked about to see if anyone was looking before staring into my eyes, those same eyes that had stared so deeply into mine as he made love to me when I was just 14 years old. He shrugged his shoulders at me replying, 'No, no, you must be mistaken. I know no Vogel family in Heidelberg, and I don't know any girl named Ursula. I'm sorry but you must have me confused with someone else.' At that a woman peered out of the front door of his house and shouted, 'Is everything okay?' He shouted back, 'Yes, it's okay, this young lady is looking for someone, that's all.' As the woman peered out of the door two little children barged through the gap, shouting, 'Daddy! Daddy!' They ran down the path and hugged

Ziegler's legs as if they were the stumps of some fallen oak. He then said, 'I am sorry, I can't help you any further; I hope you find who you are searching for.' He then turned away, took his children by the hand and took them back inside the house, promising to get them ice cream. He didn't even look back at me.

I turned away and began walking back to the harbour. I uttered the expletive, 'Fucking bastard,' repeatedly, as I walked in the hot sunshine. He knew full well who I was – and here he was, a married man with children. Had he been married while he was screwing me in his apartment in Heidelberg? I just wanted to find out more about him now. As I walked along the harbour, I suddenly realized I had Ziegler's German Cross in Gold in my coat pocket. I had intended giving it back to him but under the circumstances I hadn't. I took it out of my pocket and marvelled at what a pretty jewel this was. I stopped for a moment, wiped the tears from my eyes, then I tossed it into the harbour where it probably still lies to this day.

I stayed in Wilhelmshaven until the Monday morning. The stay was pleasant, and I became good friends with the people whose hospitality I enjoyed while there. I became particularly fond of their little dog, Alfred. When I arrived back at the Harbour House, as I nicknamed it, the couple could see I was upset. I had cried on the walk back and had sworn to myself so many times that I thought God himself might strike me down where I stood. The middle-aged couple asked me what was wrong but I told them it was a long story and maybe something best kept to myself at this time. I never did tell them about this Ziegler; I felt slightly ashamed, embarrassed and stupid and I decided he was not worth it anymore.

When I returned to Heidelberg one of the first things I wanted to do was find out who owned the apartment that Ziegler had taken me to, for sex, while he was staying in the city. Finding the records was not that difficult and, as I had expected, the apartment had belonged to a Jewish family who had been living in the city up until 1936 when they had left. The apartment was then taken over by the man whose two shops were situated below. He said the apartment had been gifted to him as the family was never going to return to Germany. I laughed at him loudly and said, 'Gifted? You mean they have probably been murdered?' He avoided my question, so I then asked him if he had known a Major Gerhard Ziegler. At this point his facial expression became troubled, concerned, and he asked me if I was from the police or something. I told him, 'No, I am not from the police. I am simply searching for some answers to some questions.' He insisted, 'No, I don't know of any Major Ziegler. The man who was renting this apartment was a Leutnant Heinz Webbel.' He then fetched the contract signed by this man Webbel, who had vacated the apartment around the same time Ziegler had left for frontline service. I asked where this Leutnant Webbel could be found, only to be told he was dead now, and hadn't settled his account prior to leaving either. I was then asked if I were interested in renting the apartment cheap, to which I replied, 'No thank you. I would only ever have the most awful of memories if I chose to live in this place.' I got up, shook the man's hand, thanked him for his time, before leaving the building.

With hindsight, I had been used and abused by that man and I still have the feeling that I was probably not the only teenage girl he had seduced. I kept this from my family to spare them any distress or feelings of guilt. I did confide in my sister Heidi many years later about what had gone on with Gerhard Ziegler. She found it all very hard to believe at first but after some time of thinking about it all, she recalled how it was always me that he took out and not her or the two boys. I recall Heidi's shock at the story I told her; she sat there and just said, 'That dirty, filthy swine.' She even insisted we both go back to Wilhelmshaven, to confront Ziegler in front of his wife. I told her we couldn't do that as there were children involved. I didn't wish to ruin their lives in order to gain revenge on their father. It wasn't something that damaged me or ruined my life. I was still young, and I had recovered from it.

I had boyfriends like any other young girl, and I married when I felt I had met the right one. What I had learned were the basic mechanics of how abusers of young people operate, and I was very protective of my own children as a result.

I have always wondered how many others like me there must have been. There must have been thousands more; I couldn't have been the only one who went through such experiences. Men like Ziegler were protected by powerful people, they had allies in high places. Had I tried to make him pay for what he did with me back then, I know I would have failed. Even in postwar Germany, had I tried to make Ziegler pay, they would have called me a liar, said I must have led him on, that I was a slut or something. I had to let it go, learn to live with it and ensure my own children never fell victim to creatures like Ziegler

Chapter 5

Pariahs of Sodom

Both the Catholic and Protestant orders in Germany were well aware that from the moment Adolf Hitler seized absolute power in Germany, they would be in very precarious positions. Aware of the Führer's leanings toward atheism, coupled with the fact that the Nazi elite comprised many anti-religious radicals, the Protestant Church in particular openly colluded with the Nazi government, in a cohesive effort to rid Germany of everything they termed immoral influences. In the German elections in 1933 the percentage of German Catholics who voted for the Nazi Party was lower than the national average. The Catholic Church expressed its opposition toward the Nazi Party, yet under pressure from the state, the Catholic-aligned Centre Party capitulated in 1933.

Article 24 of the party platform of the Nationalsozialistische Deutsche Arbeiterpartei (*NSDAP*) called for the conditional tolerance of Christian denominations. The 1933 *Reichskonkordat*, a treaty negotiated between the Vatican and Nazi Germany, was signed on 20 July 1933 by Cardinal Secretary of State, Eugenio Pacelli (who later became Pope Pius XII). While this treaty purportedly guaranteed religious freedom for Catholics in Nazi Germany, many traditional Nazis remained essentially hostile toward those of the Catholic faith. Adolf Hitler often signed treaties he had no intention whatsoever of honouring, but signed merely as a temporary remedy to a particular problem. Hitler himself was among several key Nazis who had been raised in the Catholic faith, but who became hostile toward all religions in general, in adulthood.

The hierarchy of the Protestant Church in particular cooperated fully with the Nazis in their programme of religious condemnation and the persecution not only of Jehovah's Witnesses, homosexuals, lesbians and prostitutes, but also Jews. Hans Kerrl was appointed to the post of Minister for Church Affairs in Nazi Germany and envisaged the creation of what he termed a 'Positive Christianity'. In effect, this was an alternative Christian faith within an already existing Christian faith, but it was a uniquely Nazified version of the existing religion – which rejected its Jewish origins, together with the Old Testament, insisting that true Christianity was a battle against Jewry, with Jesus Christ depicted as an Aryan. In brief, the aim, as with the Nazi ethos, was to transform the subjective consciousness of all the peoples of the German Reich, and their attitudes, values and mentalities, into a single-minded, fully obedient 'national community'. To accomplish this, all class, religious and regional alliances would have to be abolished in favour of the establishment of a unified Protestant Reich Church from Germany's twenty-eight existing Protestant Churches. This was an overly ambitious undertaking which did not enjoy the success that the Nazis envisaged.

The attitudes and subsequent actions of churchgoers in Third Reich society were shaped and defined by many factors. Many were already disillusioned prior to the Hitler government. There had been a general backlash against the Weimar Republic and its excesses plus the political, economic and social changes it had brought about in Germany throughout the 1920s. In general, anti-communism, nationalism and the hatred of homosexuals, lesbians and Jews were already rife, and these philosophies or groups were blamed for many of Germany's ills through this time. Both the Nazi state and the Protestant Church worked together to capitalize on this resentment. From the Nazi perspective one could say that these actions were purely for political gain, but where the Protestant Church was concerned it was more about survival. By colluding with the Nazis and distorting the traditional beliefs of the Protestant faith to conform with the views of their new masters, some people in the religious order were free to continue with their activities, as they had done before, and also enjoyed a degree of protection from the regime itself. Despite the support the Protestant Church may have given to the Nazis, the long-term plan of the Reich, was to abolish all religion.

The increasing hostility toward Catholicism in Germany from 1933 onwards, meant that the Catholic press, schools and associated youth organizations were closed down. Property and assets were seized and around one-third of the Catholic clergy faced reprisals by the authorities. Catholic lay leaders were targeted for elimination during the Night of the Long Knives. Yet despite the Church hierarchy endeavouring to cooperate with the Nazi government, the encyclical distributed by Pope

Pius XI in 1937, *Mit Brennender Sorge*, accused the Nazi government of hostility toward the Church.

Despite this Nazi hostility toward the Church and religion, away from the big towns and cities in the quiet, rural areas the Church was still viewed as being the beating heart of the community. Although the activities of churches in the rural districts of Germany were heavily curtailed and subject to the scrutiny of the state, bribery, corruption and sexual abuse flourished. An internal investigation by the Catholic Church itself revealed that between the years 1946 and 2014, some 1,670 of its clerics, mostly priests, were implicated in the sexual abuse of young males. The figures prior to 1946, during the years of the Second World War, are a proverbial grey area. Throughout thirty-six years of my own research and interviews with both German males and females, the unwanted sexual advances of certain individuals within the Church arose frequently within conversation. The truth is that the abuse of young boys and girls in Nazi Germany, under the auspices of the Church, was far more widespread than was initially thought.

The greatest problem within this area of research is finding victims who are willing to talk. Most of the people who were happy to speak were discovered accidentally, through discussion of their lives in Nazi Germany and having been forced to join the Hitler Youth movements. Convents and children's orphanages in Nazi Germany were also rife with all manner of abuse, physical and sexual, both traditionally managed by the religious orders. Over the years I had become good friends with Theresa Moelle and had met and interviewed her on many occasions prior to her death. Theresa was raised in an orphanage outside Berlin until her adoption by Walter and Greta Moelle, whose surname she took as her own. Theresa's perspective on her upbringing within what she called 'The Order' was not a happy view at all. Our several conversations produced the following recollection:

> I never knew who my real parents were, and I had no desire to learn who they were as I grew older. In my view, as a child, I was unwanted, unloved and rejected by the very people who should have loved and raised me in a home I could call my own, just like other children. Back then, even in Germany, if you were unwanted, you were simply dumped with that dreadful religious order. As I grew older, they made you pray for your

own salvation and made you pray each day for sins you had never even committed. How could I as a baby or young child even know what sins were? But that is what they were like.

If you displeased any of the sisters in even the slightest way, they would take you into a room, strip you naked and beat you. They often did this with a leather strap while they forced you to kneel down and pray as they hit you with the strap. It was both humiliating and painful and I was not the only girl who was beaten in this manner. As it was a Christian order, they sometimes made you kneel before the effigy of Christ on the cross to beg for his forgiveness.

There were never any cuddles, kisses or bedtime assertions of 'I love you'. There was nothing at all but pain, a sense of loss and the heartache of knowing you were unwanted. I recall, before the Moelles came and adopted me when I was around 8 years old, there were certain nuns who, despite the rules of their religion, touched me sexually. They would make me strip naked and then they would examine my body. They would force me to lie down and examine me between my legs too. They would tell me they were looking for the devil's marks upon my body. There was nothing I or the others could do about it. As a child you could never question this, and to us their abuse was normal. We thought it was the kind of thing which happened in every home; we knew nothing else.

I interviewed a man named Arnold Hilbe who recalled how the Church had close contact with the young people of his community and described how susceptible they were to abuse by the clergy:

> It was easy for them; firstly, the church and local priest had much influence over people of the local communities and the local people looked up to them. If they had any problems, they could go to the local priest for guidance and moral support and he would help them. The problem was there were always deviants amongst them, as there is in all areas of human society. I joined the Hitler Youth movement when I was around 11 years old. Hitler was an atheist and didn't trust the Church, yet he understood he had to tolerate it, that the Church was a vital part of German society at the time. Although much of the activities of the Church were reduced in our community after Hitler, it still operated.
>
> We once had a priest named Theodore Goddet; he was truly a compassionate man, he did not have a bad bone in him and was not anti-Jewish, he didn't agree with hatred against any areas of the human race, he was not supportive of the violence which National Socialism espoused in many young people and we liked him a lot. He was replaced in 1936 with this other devil. I say devil as that is just what he was. He was a man who

used the Church to protect himself; he was one of those who liked boys and used everything within his powers to gain close access to us children. His idea of tea at the vicarage was merely grooming. I was invited, as were other boys, to discuss our beliefs privately with him, so he could get to know us as individuals; that was the pretence with which he operated and gained our trust. Of course, my parents encouraged me to go and sit and talk with him about things, yet they didn't know what went on on as I could never bring myself to tell them.

I was threatened with the usual warnings of, 'Nobody will listen to you' and 'You could get into serious trouble if anyone finds out'. So, you stayed silent, out of fear. The first few times I attended his little talks his wife was never far away. She would be washing or preparing things in her kitchen. As time went by his meetings were conducted while it was just me and him in this huge old house, alone. I never suspected anything at first, I trusted him and sensed nothing. Talks which began in his living room soon changed to an upstairs office-like room he had. It was there he first started talking about sexual things; did I know this, or did I know about that. Had I ever seen a man's penis before, would I like to see a man's penis? He would ask me to sit beside him and he would place his hand on me inappropriately. On one occasion he unzipped himself and took out his penis and asked me to just hold it in my hand. I did as he asked me to and I felt quite scared, like I had no other choice. I wanted to run but I would never have found my way out of that house alone; it was a maze of dark rooms and passageways. Then he asked me to make these movements up and down. I knew what all this was and that it was all wrong, but could do nothing. After a couple of minutes, he stood up and asked me to follow him to the bathroom which I did. It was in there that he asked me to masturbate him over the toilet. All of the time he was groaning with pleasure remarking at how wonderful my soft hands felt around his penis compared to his old hands. When he had finished, he insisted I wash my hands thoroughly and he flushed the toilet and then we went back downstairs. He gave me a glass of water, told me what a good boy I was and reminded me again that if I spoke with anyone at all about what had happened, both me and my family would be in big trouble with the authorities.

This went on for a few years. As I got older, he seemed to lose interest in me and began to focus on other younger boys. I was basically too old for him and he wanted someone younger. I can't say it damaged me as I never let it get inside my head, but it made me aware that there were some very bad people within the Church.

The Church organized all sorts of things in our community, including markets, dances and other events that children attended. This was where they focused on certain individuals to test whether they were quiet types or likely to kick up a fuss over anything they might do or say. I knew of other victims of this man; many of us got together after the war to form an action group. The problem was this was years later, and he was dead by that time and there were still those who thought he was this wonderful man. No one would have taken any notice of us.

Through Arnold I was able to make contact with other men who as boys had been in the same Hitler Youth group. The scale of abuse was shocking for such a small community. There were at least eight of Arnold's friends, including three girls, who had experienced abuse or unwanted sexual attention at the hands of this individual. While most still stand by their decision never to reveal what had happened to them, two of Arnold's friends did agree to come forward and talk about their experiences. Both of them wished to remain anonymous which, under the circumstances, is quite understandable. The first friend, another male from the same village as Arnold, recalled:

Nobody suspected men of the cloth; they were seen as people beyond vice and any worldly perversion, but these people were among the worst. As Arnold has explained, our local member of the clergy did things of an improper nature with him, and he did with me too. With me it was much the same as with Arnold. As boys we would never have dared to speak about it as we would have been labelled as homos; it would have mattered not to the other boys that we had been preyed upon; we would have been labelled the same as him, that is for sure and why we have kept it quiet all these years. It's not something any man can talk about easily, is it?

My dealings with this individual were much like Arnold's. I would go to visit his home usually on a Wednesday evening to discuss religion and its place within the Nazi community. He was all for the Nazified version of Christianity, not the traditional version my parents had embraced. Parents were powerless to intervene in religious matters of the state, as much as they were with political ones. What the Nazis believed in you had to follow. This man was supposed to be schooling me in the new Christian philosophy. Boys and girls visiting his home for this purpose would have been nothing out of the normal back then. It went from lectures on how treacherous all Jewry was and that God had created the Nazis to rid the world of the curse of Jewry, and that destroying them was not seen as evil but a divine act, a necessary course of action and retribution for the sins of Jewry.

To me it was all hogwash, religious talk that I was not particularly interested in listening to. This occurred for several sessions until he asked me to go into his library with him where I was shown books not on religion but ancient artworks mostly featuring nude males. I was asked how these artworks made me feel. Did they excite me in any way? I couldn't answer him; as a 12-year-old such things didn't really interest me. It went from looking at these books to me looking at the books while he stood behind me. It got to the stage where he would rub himself against me and touch me inappropriately. I gained absolutely nothing from this. I was just a boy and he was taking advantage of me through his role as one of our community leaders. This kind of abuse went on for three months until, as suddenly as it had begun it stopped, and he went on to other boys as he had got what he had wanted from me.

He had tried to get me to remove my underwear so he could do more, but I told him 'No' despite the threats he made to me. I often think to myself: what if he had raped me? What would I have done and how would I ever have dealt with it? He's dead now and God will have been his judge; he wouldn't have gotten away with it, if there is any truth in heaven. I can take some comfort from that, but it still makes me angry when I think back about it. My parents never knew about it. I don't know how they would have reacted had I told them, I really don't know. In all honesty I don't think even in old age they would have believed it; that was the big problem with sexual abuse and the Church. They had money and treasures that they could bribe unscrupulous Nazi officials with, people just like them, really, who would keep quiet for a fee.

The second of Arnold's friends was female. This had surprised even Arnold, who had believed this predatory priest was interested only in young boys. The woman in question is now 88 years of age, but still lives in the same community. This is what she recalled:

Today some of them [the deniers] would say I've lost my marbles, that I have gone senile and am telling you lies. My memory is as sharp as it was yesterday, and I am certainly no senile old woman. There were others who suffered this man's attention; me and Arnold were not the only ones. What made this man the devil in a dog collar, you might ask?

For one thing you do not expect your local priest to insist on kissing you passionately like a man would his wife, and this man had a wife too. As he kissed me his hands would be all over me; it was horrible and that is what I remember most – his hands were sweaty yet cold. He would put his hands inside my dress and up my skirt, telling me that it would feel nice, yet it didn't feel nice to me at all. When he got you inside his house and you were all alone with him, knowing what was going to happen and that you had no control over it, was frightening, but he would give me sweets to try and make me feel more comfortable, make me feel special, as there was a war going on and sweets were not that common at the time. He would tell me if you let me do this, I will make sure your family is well looked after and receive some extra food. All the kinds of things a child would want to hear.

The things he wanted me to do were just masturbation mostly and kissing him. After the war this man seemed to almost melt away; he should have faced the courts for what he had done but it's all too late for that now. Do I have any grudges? No, I don't bear any grudges; he's dead now and I think he died of an illness if I remember correctly. He didn't live to be as old as what I am now and, unlike Arnold, I did tell my parents what happened after the war, safely in the knowledge that the Nazis had been defeated and I could not be harmed for telling my parents. I think there were certain Nazis in our community who knew what he was doing and accepted bribes to keep quiet about it. I would imagine that some of them too were abusers, as these people rarely operate alone.

My parents were very upset about it; my father naturally wanted to go and kill this man. My mother had to physically restrain him, and I remember her shouting at him, 'If you go and do that who will look after us while you are in prison?' I think that was the only thing which prevented my father from killing him, I think he would have done it too. My mother took me to see a doctor who checked me; the doctor assured my mother that I had not been raped. I think my mother just wanted to be sure he hadn't harmed me physically.

Today there are no scars upon my body, no sweaty handprints, nothing. Today only the memory is left; they were bad times for many people with the war going on and all the hatred thrown in with it. I'm still here, I lived, and I went on to marry, have children and live my life to the full after Hitler. No one, not even he or Hitler, could have taken that away from me. I gain comfort from thinking like this, but I have never attended church since my marriage and the only time I will ever set foot in one again is when they carry my coffin into one to bury me.

Melitta Kramer and her younger brother, Balthasar, also have recollections of the inappropriate behaviour of the supposed pillar of their little countryside community. Melitta recalls:

This man was vile; he was a devil hiding behind the Church. It seemed that these men, although representing the old excesses that were said to have been partially responsible for nearly destroying Germany, enjoyed a high degree of protection to get up to things they shouldn't have.

When we first moved into our new village after leaving our old home in the city of Bremen, it all felt like a breath of fresh air, a new start in an idyllic surrounding. The local people greeted us and made us feel welcome and the local priest came to visit us in our home, to introduce himself and convince our parents that we should attend meetings with him as did the other local children. Mother and father thought nothing of it, other than a kindly old representative of God trying to welcome us into what was a quiet country community. Yes, we went to his house with the other children which was not a problem. Yet, during Christmas of 1942 this man revealed what he really was.

Christmas is the greatest celebration of all in Germany, on a traditional level. The Church organized plays for the local community, the local girls and boys would dress up and play the various parts, all quite normal. On the runup to our Christmas holidays we went to this priest's home for what he insisted were dress fittings, to check that the clothes we were to wear for our plays would not be ill-fitting for us. The boys all had theirs checked and were fine and they left without waiting for me, so I went to follow them when this man called me back. 'You have not tried this on yet my dear young Fraulein. Please come back and try it on as we need to make sure it fits you.' I went back and went into the small room where robes were hung up in the church and he came in and closed the door behind him. He handed me this white flowing dress with a black sash-type belt and a rural crown which he said his wife had made specially. This rural or countryside crown was formed out of twigs, with dried painted leaves weaved into the twigs. I was in the process of pulling the dress on over my clothes when he stopped me. He told me, 'You have to take off those clothes of yours first; you cannot try on this dress over your other clothes, it may not fit you, and what a disaster that would be – you are the angel of the performance.' For a moment I just stood looking at him nervously, I did not want to take off my dress with him watching me. I took off the dress as quickly as I could and hurriedly put the play costume on. I just wanted to do this and get out, so I told him, 'There you are, it fits me' and I was going to take it off and put my normal clothes back on when he stopped me. 'But you are not wearing the crown, you must try that on too; please try on the crown.' So, I put this crown on my head so it sat just above my ears. He stood back and said, 'Oh yes, that is beautiful, Fraulein Kramer,' and he stood there clapping at me.

I took the crown off and placed it back in the box and was just pulling the costume over my head when I became very frightened. I was aware of him suddenly grabbing me as my arms were up in the air. I couldn't move my arms and I couldn't see; he had me in a kind of bearhug. I could feel his breathing through the material, and I said to him, 'Will you please let me go. What are you doing?' He replied that he was just trying to help me and yet he was holding me against his body really hard. He put his one hand on my bottom, and it was at that point that I became both angry and frightened and I did the only thing I could think of doing and I kicked him in his shin as hard as I could. When he let me go, I told him I would tell my parents what he had done, and I ran away. He followed, making sure no one else was around before stopping me and warning me, 'If you tell anyone about this there will be serious trouble. Do you know the people I have as friends? You don't know, do you? If you say anything you will be sorry, not just you, Fraulein Kramer, but your family too. If you are wise you will put this misunderstanding out of your pretty little head, and we will say nothing more of it and all will be well.' I was dropped from the play shortly afterwards in favour of what he called a 'prettier maiden'.

I kept quiet for many years about it all. When I finally did tell my mother and father, they were horrified about it. The priest who had done this to me vanished after the war. I don't know where he went and maybe he had people after him, I would not have been surprised as I was not the only one he tried to meddle with; he had tried to meddle with my younger brother too.

Melitta's brother, Balthasar, recalled his own experiences with this individual.

No one would have thought ill of this man at all. He came across as pleasant, kind and warm to everyone. If anyone died in our community, he would visit the family and offer sympathy and help with everything. In that respect he was very kind indeed, but there was this darker side to this man and he was not all what he seemed to be. If you found yourself alone with him, which I did on more than one occasion, his demeanour would change. He would look about himself to make sure no one was looking and he would touch me between the legs, but make a joke of it, as if it were nothing. He was careful in only doing this to very young boys, not the older ones. The older boys would have caused too much fuss, so he targeted the younger ones, as is often the case with these kinds of people. In a way we had to just put up with him, avoid getting in situations where we would be alone with him.

All the local kids thought he was odd, a bit queer as they used to say, but their parents would scold them for being disrespectful if they heard them saying this about him. I remember after that war, when we could begin to talk more freely again, one of the boys, a good friend of mine, told me he had caught this priest wanking himself. Of course, he was an older boy, and this man was fearful my friend would tell all his friends what he had seen, so he offered him some money to keep quiet. My friend told me: 'Yes, I took the money off him, I didn't like the man at all, and it was pleasant to see him have to squirm. His threats didn't sit with me. I wasn't afraid of him at all and I was prepared to call his bluff. I would take money off him and share it with my friends. I know it was wrong as I was blackmailing him. I didn't know what he had been doing at that time, but I understood he was not what he was portraying himself to be. He was definitely weird, in the sexually deviant sense. Looking back, I wish I had just given him a beating, dirty old bastard.'

The sad thing is the Church is full of deviants like him, protected within the whole organization. Under the Nazis they continued with their undercurrent of vice while bribing Nazi officials by giving them money, gold or other valuables. Yes, many Nazi officials feathered their nests with bribes from the Church in Germany. Many made enough money to escape from Germany after the war and live in luxury elsewhere. It is all so wrong.

The above material is not intended as an attempt to demonize the Church or any other religious faith, but to to demonstrate that sexual deviance was endemic within the Church in Germany at that time, even under the totalitarian rule of Nazi Germany. The Church itself has had this problem firmly rooted within its foundations for centuries, but the Nazi state in many aspects made it easier for those with ill intent to operate above the normally accepted laws of the land. Corruption, blackmail and bribery was the very currency of Nazism, as it is within many dictatorships. The saddest thing of all is that so many young people fell victim to unscrupulous characters within the Church, under the Hitler regime. There was sexual abuse and there was rape, but many of the victims are now well into old age and refuse to speak about what happened to them. I can only commend the above contributors who found the courage to speak of their experiences, even after the passing of all these years.

Not all the men and women involved with the Church in Nazi Germany were evil, but there were many pariahs of Sodom, and they profited in many ways from the Nazi reign of terror. Of course, there are those today who, when reading accounts such as those presented above, will doubt that the interviewees were telling the truth. To those people I will say this: while I have never in my life experienced actual physical sexual abuse, I myself, as an 8-year-old, experienced what today we know as 'sexual grooming'. I count myself lucky; I told my parents what was happening and my father dealt with the individual attempting to groom me. Not every child is so fortunate; not every child has the confidence to inform their parents or to seek help in such situations. The disease that is sexual predation on the young is a widespread social scourge; it's always been there, and sadly it always will be.

In previous chapters paedophilia, as we understand the term today, has already begun to make an appearance. A typical example of this is the account given by the child adoptee, Ursula Vogel. In the following chapter I aim to provide a more in-depth analysis of what is without doubt one of the vilest lusts to permeate the greater human community, specifically, in this case, within the context of Nazi Germany.

Chapter 6

A Lust for The Young

For centuries there was no clear distinction between adult men who sought sex with other adult men, and adult men who sought sex with young boys, or girls. Paedophilia is a relatively modern term for what is a centuries-old scourge on society. Paedophilia is by no means a modern menace; past civilizations, particularly those of ancient Greece and Rome, were known to have practised sex and sexual intercourse with children, the very act that defines paedophilia in the world today. Paedophilia is often wrongly viewed as something of an exclusively male-oriented sexual perversion, as opposed to a female one, yet there have been and are female predators, as much as there have been and are male predators.

I refer to paedophilia as a sexual perversion because that's exactly what it is. Labelling this behaviour as an 'illness' or 'disease' appears very conveniently to remove culpability from the perpetrator. In my opinion, paedophilia is not an illness; it is a perversion, although the *Diagnostic and Statistical Manual of Mental Disorders* (2013; *DSM-5*), refers to it as a psychosexual disorder and has replaced the term '*paedophilia*' with '*paedophilic disorder*'. In any event, the individual who chooses to prey upon a child makes a conscious decision to do so, fully aware of what he or she is doing. One of the interviewees for this book described it perfectly, saying, 'It was more like the interaction between acid and skin.'

Sexual grooming is a commonly used term today; it describes behaviour by the sexual predator (male or female) to test both the reaction and receptivity of the potential child victim. This behaviour has not changed over the ages. Paedophiles are highly cunning yet dangerous creatures who rely on the innocence and naïvety of young children in order to gain their trust. The reader may ask of me at this point, 'What does he know? He's not a criminal psychologist.' I speak merely from the experience of having been sexually groomed at the age of 8 years old. Fortunately, I came to no harm as I told my parents and my father went and confronted the culprit himself. That is how it was back in the 1970s and I was not the only one to have experienced grooming from this loathsome individual. Many in the community were aware of this person's deviance but it was a case of, 'It's no one else's business, not even the local police.' Back then no one was interested, and many perpetrators got away with it.

Victorian and Edwardian England are two very good examples of eras in which children were sexualized for commercial purposes, or so it might seem. Children were sexualized in photographic portraits, many examples of which were printed on postcards. Many of these images portray young undeveloped girls in provocative poses, often with their chests partially or fully exposed. Today such sexualized images would be rightly, totally unacceptable. Yet what was the real intent and purpose behind these images, and why were they deemed permissible by a society whose moral principles were such that even the merest sight of a bare ankle in the street would be enough to cause immense consternation? The reality is it wasn't art, as many would espouse, and that some people became aroused by these images. Most societies which proclaim to be the living embodiment of health, hygiene and moral decency are often among the worst.

This brings us to the point in question with Nazi Germany. Was paedophilia as rife under the Nazis, as it undoubtedly was elsewhere in the world at the time? Was naturism (nudism) in some cases used merely as a cover for the iniquitous pursuits of camera-toting dirty old men in long grey raincoats? The answers to these questions are a mixture of both yes and no, as we will learn in this chapter.

At the 1936 Nuremberg Nazi Party Rally both the girls and boys of the Hitler Youth were displayed as one of Nazi Germany's greatest future assets. The new youth of Hitler's Germany were perceived as its future, its lifeblood and its foundation. While the Nazi Party itself may have had the best of intentions for its fledgling brood as the future bearers of the proposed thousand-year Reich, other people with far less honourable intentions were also present at these rallies.

Klara Wyborny, a 15-year-old former member of the Berlin BDM, recalled an experience which took place during the 1936 rally at Nuremberg, an experience which left her feeling frightened, humiliated and concerned for her safety. Klara bravely related what had happened to her during an interview conducted during the course of writing my earlier books:

I was very excited about Nuremberg at the time. I was just a 15-year-old girl and, yes, I was probably too naïve at the time to recognize the evil brought about by the entire Nazi regime. I was present at Nuremberg, as all the girls of the Hitler Youth (and boys) were obliged to attend in uniform, wherever possible. It was known as the Rally of Honour that year and it represented the restoration of honour to the German people. Of course, my mother and father travelled with me to Nuremberg, and I was with them when not participating in any of the parade events, yet they were not with me all of the time – it would have been impossible for them.

The atmosphere there was like electricity, you could feel it in the air; it was a mixture of both excitement and apprehension. There were photographers everywhere you looked, from all over Germany. Many were press photographers yet there were many from abroad, including freelance operators. I had been taking part in a gymnastics sporting routine with the girls of my Hitler Youth group and as we walked off the field there were many men with cameras asking us to stand and pose for photographs for their newspapers. There was one who pushed through all the others saying he was with the *Volkischer Beobachter* (*People's Observer*). This was a big Nazi newspaper at that time. The man was tall and balding, and I would say he was in his fifties. He had this camera around his neck and politely asked if he could take some photographs of me for the newspaper. I had no initial suspicions about him at all; he seemed genuine and did not appear creepy or threatening at all – he certainly did not come across as a 'bogeyman'. We were always lectured at school and in the BDM that the Jew was the bogeyman, who'd drag you up a dark alley and defile you. He convinced me to go with him as he had found a better setting with which to shoot some photographs and asked if I minded going with him. I told him I didn't and foolishly I went with him. It was only a short distance away and there was this stream which ran between a small wood, and once in this wood, no one would have seen anything.

I could hear the crowds cheering and clapping as another event at the rally began; the chance of anyone wandering over to where we were, were very slim. He probably knew that and this was the likely reason he chose that spot for his so-called photographs. He didn't appear nervous or anything and began taking pictures of me, first just me standing, then he asked me to remove my gym shoes and socks and step into the stream and splash water up into the air, which I did. I only began to feel uncomfortable when he asked me to lie down, place my arms behind my head and pretend I was sunbathing. I did as he asked, and he knelt down beside me to take the photographs. Although I felt uncomfortable with what he was doing he had done nothing wrong up until the moment where he sat astride me and, as he did, he removed his camera from around his neck, putting it down by his side. He put one of his hands over my mouth and told me that if I created any fuss that I would end up in some very serious trouble. He pointed to his Nazi Party pin on his lapel, telling me that people like Goebbels and Göring were among his friends and that if I ever told anyone about this no one would believe me, and me and my family would be in big trouble.

At that point, yes, I was very scared and afraid of what he intended to do with me. I couldn't get up as he was sitting on my stomach. I complained that he was squashing me and that I couldn't breathe with him on top of me like this, and he shuffled himself back. I had pulled my knees up together and he was leaning back against them. Then he leant forward pushing his one hand up beneath my sports vest. With his other hand he unzipped himself and took out his penis and began to pleasure himself while running his other hand over my breasts. At one point he lay down on me and while holding my wrists down he rubbed himself against me, so his penis was against my stomach. He tried to kiss me, but I turned my head from side to side to stop him from doing so. His thrusting motions hurt as he was a big, heavy man, and he was thrusting against me quite hard. It must have been ten minutes or so he was doing this when he let out a stifled series of grunts and held himself up off me. I felt splashes of warm fluid over my stomach and knew very well what it was. The look on his face was one of gratification and enjoyment.

He then got up off me, fastened his trousers, picked up his camera and warned me again about saying anything to anyone about this. He peered out from the trees to make sure the coast was clear then off he went like a fox from a chicken house. I lay there for a few minutes, too scared to move, before getting up and washing his semen from my torso in the stream. I put my shoes back on and made my way from out of the trees; all the time I was looking around to see if he was still lurking nearby, but I never saw him again.

I didn't tell anyone, not even my parents, as I doubt they would have even believed me had I told them what happened. I never spoke about it because I knew there would be accusations that I was telling lies, that such things did not happen under dear Adolf Hitler. Do you know what that feels like, for some old man to do that to you and not be able to do anything about it, or go to anyone for help or advice?

He didn't rape me and I'm thankful for that, but he could have raped me easily had he wanted to, as he was bigger and stronger than me; he was a man, and we were always being told men are stronger than women. It made me very wary in future and maybe that was one good thing – it would never happen again because I was now aware of the modus operandi of these dirty old men.

Kirsten Eckermann, one of the first of the former BDM girls with whom I spoke recalled the unhealthy interest of a particular BDM leader toward some of the girls under her charge:

> It was in my first full year with the BDM after Jungmädelbund which was the junior version of the girls' Hitler Youth, the entry level, if you like, which you had to join at the age of 10. I was 14 years old and we had this one leader who was much older than all of us; she was around 19 years of age and had risen through the ranks rapidly, being a committed National Socialist with a wealthy father. As a child, which at 14 is what you are, you are just a child, you tend not to be fully aware of your own sexuality, or how you may appear attractive to an older member of either the same or opposite sex. I am sure she was one of those women [a lesbian], as there were just certain things she did that I felt were inappropriate. In the girls' Hitler Youth nakedness was embraced as a form of naturism, nothing to be ashamed of and perfectly natural. Yet, when we were naked this leader would look at us intensely and you could almost read what she was thinking from her facial expressions. When she was around it just made me in particular feel very uneasy, though at the time as a youngster I could not have explained to you why. I once bruised my leg; it was nothing much at all, just a bruise, yet she insisted that she examine my leg. She took me inside her tent and ordered me to remove my shoes and socks so she could have a look. She didn't really say much, she just started massaging the calf muscle of my leg and worked her fingers down to my foot. She appeared more interested in my foot than the bruise on my leg. As she ran her fingers around my foot it made me jump as I was ticklish, but she remained impassive asking me to keep still and stop jumping around. She remarked what beautiful feet I had, then she moved her fingers higher and higher up my leg. I looked at her and was about to ask her 'What are you doing?' when she said, 'Shhhh, be quiet.' She continued her massaging routine and worked up between my thighs which made me flinch violently. I felt one of her fingers brushing my private parts and I tried to move back, away from her. She then asked, 'Does this not feel good to you, girl?' I told her, 'No, it doesn't.' She looked into my eyes with a scowl on her face; for a second, I felt her nails digging into the flesh of my thighs, hurting me to the point where I cried out, 'Ow! Stop it! It hurts!' before she said to me, 'That is all now, now get out of here.' I put my socks and shoes back on and was very glad to get back with the other girls and away from her.
>
> The only person I later talked about this with was my close friend Anna [Anna Dann]. If I had gone to the police or something and told them about it there is every chance, I would have been blamed for it. The Nazis made it easy for us to be abused and exploited, but some of our so-called

leaders were of the opinion that 'You are ours, and we can do what we want with you'.

Engela Losch experienced the darker aspects of the new regime in Germany under Hitler and the National Socialists. She told me how something as innocent as violin or piano tuition could expose young girls, in particular, to old men who lusted after children:

> We lived in the village of Ramsau in Upper Bavaria when I was 10 years of age and it was in the August of 1943. Ramsau was a quiet community where everyone knew each other very well. We even felt somewhat detached from the war which was going on, like we were separate from it all. Of course, girls and boys could not avoid Hitler Youth membership as it was compulsory; we had no choice at all and our parents had little influence on these matters. I recall all had been relatively carefree up until this Nazi 'administrator' as he was known came to live just outside of the village. He expressed concern that the girls and boys of the future Reich were too immersed in country dancing and their local culture and needed to embrace the wider picture of Nazi arts and culture. I recall how he was particularly interested in music and his skill with musical instruments such as the violin and the piano mesmerized us. We all wanted to be able to play musical instruments like he did.
>
> My parents had bought me a violin two years previously yet my progress with the instrument had been sluggish. When this man encouraged girls and boys to be taught by him, we, including our parents, felt it was a good idea. I will not mention this man's name here but when I first began violin lessons with him, you could see from his home that he was very high up the Hitler ladder. He must have been very good at whatever tasks he had done in Berlin and other areas where he had worked since the start of the war. He never took groups at his home for tuition, always just one pupil at a time, which I never thought anything of and neither did any of the others. I started going to his home every Sunday evening for violin tuition which lasted for one hour.
>
> I remember my first lesson with him very well. As I walked through the front door of his house, I was amazed by the paintings hanging on the wall and the antiques which decorated the rooms. He led the way down a long hall to a study on the right and once inside it was comfortable with a chair, table, sofa and large desk. There were these French doors which opened up onto an ornate stone balcony. He opened these as it was quite a warm evening, being summer, and then closed the curtains which hung in front of them. There were two pairs of curtains, a thick heavy pair of

drapes like the ones you would see in a castle, then a thick black pair to ensure no light could be seen from outside. I was asked to take the chair in front of the desk while he sat on the sofa. He then asked me to play some pieces which I had learned so he could assess my level of skill with the instrument. I played him three pieces and he was not impressed with any. He basically told me I was at the lowest novice level with the instrument and he told me he had a lot of work to do. He would demonstrate and his playing was beautiful, and I was very impressed by his skill and wished I could play half as well as he could. So, these lessons started off being just normal pupil and teacher music lessons, nothing to be alarmed about other than a few nerves. My playing improved greatly under his tuition and soon my parents were congratulating him on making their daughter a musician at last.

It was around five months after my first lesson that I discovered this man was not the man I thought he was.

Most predatory behaviour of a sexual nature begins with the perpetrator becoming familiar with his victim's likes, dislikes, fears and dreams. Engela Losch had dreams of aspiring to the level of an orchestral violinist. Her tutor would tell her, 'You are good, but you are not that good. I can help you achieve your dreams. There are special things you could do for me if I am to do special things for you.' These cryptic assertions to the young Engela exacerbated the emotional dilemma which she was so desperately trying to overcome. She continues:

I desperately wanted to be someone. I think all young people think they are going to be famous for something, and I really believed I could be if I worked hard enough at what I was doing. My tutor nurtured these childlike dreams and he once told me, 'Nearly every child I teach will never be good enough to entertain the Third Reich, yet you have a talent which, if managed correctly, will see you rise above them all. Now do you understand me?' I nodded and asked how I could improve to these levels. To which he answered, 'You need more time with me to be able to teach you in greater detail; an hour will never suffice my dear girl.'

So, it was arranged for me to have an extended two hours with him and it was during this time that he became much more physical in his approach to the tuition. I would be seated on the chair and he would look at me and tell me my posture was incorrect, and he would physically position my arms, legs and body, like some toy doll. As I began to play, he would put his hands on my shoulders from behind telling me I was too tense, and it was affecting my playing. It began with his just placing his hands on my shoulders, but moved to him gently massaging them. I thought this was how he taught and did not think there were any other intentions there. After I finished playing the one piece, he took the violin from my hands and asked me to relax and raise my arms in the air. I did as I was instructed and again, he began massaging my shoulders but then worked down to my chest in circular motions. I had very little there but his hands remained there for some minutes. I remember thinking that what he was doing was wrong, yet I was fearful of saying anything.

That's where the abuse really began; he was testing the waters so to speak. He knew I was not the sort of child that would yell out or shout; that's why he chose me. Yes, I felt disappointed by what he was doing as I looked up to him and I felt he had let me down by not being the person I thought he was. He began filling my head with all sorts of stories about failure in the German Reich and what it meant for a female. He would tell me, 'I can give you a future much greater than any school; education is not the key to success, the key is who you know in life.' He worked on me psychologically, breaking down my barriers to the point where I had no defences against him and where I could never tell on him. He would say, 'If any of this gets out, what we are doing here, we will both become social outcasts. You and your family could end up in one of the camps.' Then he would say, 'But, it will never come to that, as we shall never speak of what happens here to anyone, shall we?'

So, it went from him putting his hands on me, to me removing my top where he could touch my bare skin. Soon it got to the stage where I would be completely naked with him. It was then he asked, 'Have you ever seen or touched a man?' I told him, 'No, I had not.' And so he sat me down beside him on his sofa unzipped his trousers and just got it out. I must have looked shocked as my heart began to race with nervousness and fear. He said, 'Don't be afraid, it won't hurt you; touch it, hold it in your hand.' I looked away from him and then he took my hand and placed it on his thing (as I called it). To me, as a child, it was disgusting. I didn't like the look of it nor the smell. It was a smell which reminded me of raw sausage meat; it was horrible. He encouraged me to masturbate him and the only one of us who gained the slightest pleasure from it was him, certainly not me. When it was over, I jumped up and grabbed my clothes and just wanted to leave his house. I didn't want this to continue to where I knew it was going to end, with him hurting me.

When I got home my parents would say, 'You are very quiet, Engela. Did you not enjoy your lesson today?' I just wanted to stop having the lessons and tried to think of a way of getting out of them. It was my sister Irmgard, who was five years older than me, whom I finally confided in. I begged her not to tell mother and father or we'd all be in serious trouble.

Irmgard just told me, 'I will sort this out; don't worry anymore. I know a lady teacher who will teach you, okay?' I could see how angry Irmgard was; her face was red and I could see tears in her eyes. Yes, she was very angry, and I was worried about what she was going to do. The only other problem was, how do I explain to mother and father the reason why I would not be going to that man's house again? I couldn't tell them what had really happened, but Irmgard told them that this man was no longer well enough to teach.

In fact, Irmgard and three of her friends had gone round to his home and threatened to tell his wife and the authorities what he had been doing with me and the others. Of course, they were blackmailing him, as he had not done anything to them, but the authorities wouldn't see it that way, would they?

After the war it all came out, I heard that the father of a boy this man had abused gave this man a terrible beating, almost killed him. He moved away but I was told he was later arrested for his activities as a member of the Nazi Party. I never learned what he had done but it must have been serious enough for him to have been arrested.

Did what he had done to me damage me in any way? No, it didn't damage me, and I grew up as a perfectly normal girl and I had boyfriends when I was older and led a normal life. I hadn't realized, not until the war had ended, just how rife this kind of thing was under the Nazis. So many youngsters had suffered sexual abuse at the hands of people like that man, people who felt they had protection from the state to the point where they could coerce or threaten you into doing them sexual favours. Yes, these creatures hid behind the swastika, and the power which it bestowed upon them was widespread. There was financial, moral and sexual corruption. The fact many preyed upon young girls such as me meant nothing to them; they possessed no empathy whatsoever. I count myself lucky. I could easily have been raped by that man. What chance would I have stood, alone against him, had he chosen to do so?

Rebecca Noetz was just 13 years old when she was molested by a male friend of her father. Rebecca wrote several letters to me in 1999 while I was still researching aspects of the female Hitler Youth in the Third Reich. Hers was perhaps one of the saddest stories I had heard to date, at the time. It was a difficult account to have to commit to paper, yet Rebecca was determined that her story should someday be heard. She recalled:

What happened to me took place now so long ago. It was in the autumn of 1942, yet I can remember it as clearly as if it happened yesterday. My father was a businessman and had all kinds of things going on during the war, so he was always coming and going. My father was a good man, he looked after us all well and we never went without anything even during the hardest of those years. I remember this business partner my father had with him for two years, a man in his mid-forties whose name was Anton Griebe. My father went off on one of his business trips, I don't have any idea on where he went or what he was up to, but this Griebe man was placed in charge of making sure me my mother and brother were well looked after while father was away. This Griebe often looked after us in our own home, while my mother went out to work a shift in one of the nearby factories. She would return home around 11 pm of an evening by which time we were in bed, though I would always hear her coming in through the front door.

Griebe was just a babysitter of sorts although I didn't consider myself an infant who needed to be told when to go to bed. I found this Griebe just an annoyance and I didn't like the man at all; it was what you might say a mutual dislike. It was one evening that autumn in 1942 that Griebe told us it was bedtime, around 8 pm. My younger brother went quietly yet I protested, saying it was too early, I wasn't a baby, and I wasn't going to bed until 9 pm. Griebe just said to me, 'Okay, 9 pm it is then,' and I thought that was the end of it. I sat in the chair by the fire just watching the flames consume the last of the logs. I had a nightgown on, and a thick blanket wrapped around me. Griebe sat at the table as he always did, either writing letters or reading something. When I looked across at him, I caught him staring at me more than once, but he would look away and carry on with whatever he was doing. He left the room and came back with two large cases and I saw him putting paper currency into the pocket of his jacket. The money was in thick wadges and I can remember thinking, 'That's a lot of money. What is he doing with it?' It was shortly after 9 pm that Griebe announced that it was my bedtime now, that I should be a good girl and go upstairs quietly to my room so as not to wake my brother. I got up and wrapping the blanket around me again, I made my way up the stairs to my room. I climbed into bed and lay on my side.

A few minutes later the door to my room slowly opened. For a moment I thought mother had returned from her work early, until I saw Griebe's silhouette in the doorway. The door closed and all was in darkness, I clutched my blanket as I could hear him walking toward my bed. There were some shuffling noises and then he actually climbed into my bed with me. He had removed his trousers and was wearing nothing other than a vest. He grabbed me, placed his hand forcefully over my mouth and hissed into my ear, 'You keep quiet and if you do as you are told all will be fine and I will say nothing to your mother about your terrible behaviour this evening.' Without saying another word, he took his hand away from my mouth and began fumbling with something. As he did this, I told him, 'But I have done nothing wrong to you. What are you doing? Please get out and leave me alone.' He said nothing and when he had stopped fumbling with whatever it was, he tried to roll on top of me. I kicked and fought him off, and I shouted at him to get away from me and get out of my house, that my mother would be told about this and my brother would be listening in the next room and also tell our mother. In the darkness I again heard him fumbling around. I froze with fear, wondering what was going to happen next. I lay there too terrified to move or cry out. I was crying but I lay crying into my pillow so as to minimize any noise.

He left my room in such haste he did not close the door behind him and I watched as he disappeared down the stairs. Then I heard the front door slam yet I stayed frozen to the spot, too scared to move until my mother returned home. When mother finally came home around 11.15 pm, I ran down the stairs screaming. My mother thought I had had a nightmare or something. I was trying to tell her what had happened, but I was so hysterical I couldn't get the words out. When I was finally able to tell her what had happened, I just remember how hysterical she then became. She went and woke my brother who had slept through it all, got him dressed, then rushed us over to our grandparent's house which was a twenty-minute walk away in the cold and dark, along a deserted country road. When we arrived at our grandparents, my brother was sent up to bed in the spare room, while mother explained to my grandmother what had happened.

It was my grandmother who examined me, asking what he had done and where he had touched me, and if he had put anything inside me down below – that is how she put it to me. I remember my grandmother weeping as she examined me, then turning to my mother and telling her, 'Thank God she is alright, he hasn't done anything to her.' The next morning the police were told, and I was examined by our local doctor who again reassured my mother I had not been penetrated.

When my father received the news, he came straight back home but he couldn't look at me. It was as if he blamed me for what had happened. Griebe had left with documents and a large sum of money, most of which was my father's. Notices for his arrest were issued but he was never found; it was as if he went completely off the radar. It was believed he had fled Germany somehow, but no one ever found out where he went, and he never paid for what he did to me. Up until that point I had felt safe and well protected within our society, yet after that I saw it for all of its flaws.

The relationship between me and my father deteriorated afterwards, and things did not improve until after the war, in 1947, when he finally apologized and begged me for my forgiveness. Even then despite healing the rift with my father I had problems with alcohol. I drank to numb the pain of what had happened to me. I married but soon after it fell apart; I met another nice man and married again, only for that to fall apart after five years. I would drink, swear and get into fights with people, I lost my sense of self-worth and felt that maybe I was to blame for what had happened. The last straw came when I got into a fight with a prostitute outside a Hamburg bar. I was arrested and charged with causing an affray and assault.

My father managed to get me out of that mess with little more than a fine, but after that I understood that it was down to me to change my life, to stop being a victim and try and make something of myself. It was not easy back in those times; there was no support for victims of child sexual abuse back then, the attitude being, 'Just shut up and get on with it, pull yourself together.' That's what they told you. From speaking with other victims later on, I learned some were thrown into mental homes due to their behaviour, triggered by rape or other abuse in childhood. Things like drunkenness were acceptable if you were a man but a woman who drank and got drunk could be labelled as suffering from Communism and thrown into an institution where they'd lobotomize you and things. Life was hard for women back then and it is still hard for many women today. I never had any children though I married a third time and it lasted and was normal in every respect other than it was a marriage without children. of course.

When I look back and think about the Hitler years, I recall there was this apathetic and chauvinistic attitude to females in general in the Third Reich. Was it this attitude which in turn emboldened the sexual predators who roamed in that society? Where young girls were concerned, they would say, 'Well, a female is at her best for breeding between the ages of 15 and 20 years of age. If a girl is menstruating, then she is perfectly able to fulfil her tasks as a woman.' It was that vile old saying: 'If a girl is old enough to bleed then she is old enough to butcher.'

I also gathered the recollections of Walter Reickart and his twin brother Ernst, who were 10 years old and living in Hamburg, in the west of Germany when they, too, had to endure sexual abuse during the reign of terror of the Hitler Youth. Walter's recollections of this time are particularly vivid:

It was not the boys of the Hitler Youth me and my brother became fearful of, but the local Hitler Youth Gauleiter and his hangers-on as we called them. One of these hangers-on was this skinny creature who always used to wear a suit which was clearly too big for him; he wore a golden Nazi Party badge on his lapel, and it was obvious to many of us that he had an unhealthy interest in the young of the Hitler Youth, the boys mostly. His colleagues, if they were aware of this, did nothing and turned a blind eye to it all. This man had sexually abused a number of boys, but this did not come out until many, many years after the end of the war. There was so much shame and stigma with this sort of thing and the attitude in Germany back then was, whatever happens behind his or her closed door is of no concern to anyone else, even the police. The abuse this man put me and my brother through was not as serious as some we heard about later, but it was bad enough.

The community of Nazism took you away from the relative safety of your home and into their clutches, where there were those who stood to prosper from their exploitation of you. With me and my brother it was sexual exploitation, paedophilia as it is known today. Yes, this man took us away from the others and forced one of us to wait while the other would be abused out of sight of everyone else. We were threatened that if we spoke out about it to anyone, we would all be sent to a concentration camp; he would say that to us. Most of the abuse consisted of us having to masturbate this man, that's how it started, but it quickly progressed to oral rape. It made me physically sick every single time, but fear is a very powerful weapon which these people use to ensnare their child victims; this is how they work, they will tell you terrible things will happen if you talk, you will die, your brother will die, your whole family will die.

The most serious point in all this happened after several weeks of this routine of abuse. This man actually attempted to rape me fully, but he couldn't do it. He attempted it from behind and also with me facing him, I felt him nudging against me and it felt soft and I think that is the only reason he did not go through with raping me, purely because he had become impotent or something. I don't know and at the time I didn't care.

It only ended weeks prior to the Allied forces arriving in Hamburg when all the Nazis suddenly disappeared, and no one knew where they had gone; they just fled. Reports of these abuses were made but our parents like many others were embarrassed about these revelations when they began to come to light. Victims of these dirty old men often had to suffer in silence for what they went through. The Hitler years took most of our young childhood and they have left a deep scar on both me and my brother; the abuse was everywhere in that so-called national community. It was horrible that is all I can say.

Thankfully, both Walter and his brother overcame the mental trauma caused by their abuse; they both settled down and married and had children of their own. I asked Walter what advice he might give today as a survivor of abuse, and he replied:

> Never let any government categorize and then take your children away so they are out of your sight and out of your control. You should know your children better than anyone else; if they try to confide in you, for God's sake listen to them. Our parents were not keen to listen to what was happening, as they were more concerned with what our neighbours, the local policeman, the shopkeeper and all the other locals would think, rather than sorting out the scum who abused us instead. That's how it was; it was a different time and thankfully it didn't last very long for us.

One of the most undeniable cases of paedophilia where the German military were concerned has to be that of the notorious Oskar Dirlewanger, born 26 Dezember 1895, in Würzburg, Bavaria. Dirlewanger was without any doubt one of the most evil, sadistic and sexually depraved individuals in the Third Reich. His appetite for alcohol, rape, sadism and violence shocked even the most hardline Nazis.

Dirlewanger had fought in the First World War and was wounded six times. He received the Iron Cross Second and First Class and finished the war with the rank of Leutnant (lieutenant). It is often believed that Dirlewanger's behaviour in later life was spawned amid the death and destruction of the First World War. There are no reliable records of Dirlewanger's childhood with which to ascertain his behaviour as a young boy and a youth, but it is highly probable that the traits of psychopathy were there from an early age, as is the case with many individuals such as Dirlewanger. It is possible that as a child he tortured and killed animals for no purpose other than his own pleasure. He may also have had sexual issues and maybe even suffered sexual abuse himself. A police report on Dirlewanger after the First World War described him as 'A mentally unstable, violently fanatical alcoholic, capable of erupting into a violent rage usually after ingesting various drugs which he was known to abuse'. Despite this less-than-glowing appraisal of his personality, Dirlewanger studied at the Goethe University in Frankfurt and obtained a doctorate in political science in 1922.

The following year he joined the Nazi Party with a particular involvement with its paramilitary arm – the SA or *Sturmabteilung* (Stormtroopers or 'Brownshirts'). Dirlewanger revelled in the violence that ensued in street battles with rival political parties in Germany at this time. He also harboured a virulent hatred toward Jews and Communists. When Hitler came to power in 1933 Dirlewanger was rewarded for his commitment to the party but was also a thorn in its side, thanks to his convictions for the illegal possession of weapons and embezzlement. In 1934 Dirlewanger's sexual appetite for both young girls and boys began to surface and he was found guilty of the rape of a14-year-old girl member of the BDM. Following this conviction, which included the illegal use of a government vehicle and the damage caused to it whilst under the influence of alcohol and drugs, he lost his job along with his doctorate and all military honours, following which he was expelled from the Nazi Party.

Following his release from prison he was arrested again for a sexual offence and was sent to the Weizheim concentration camp where many who were labelled sexually deviant were sent at that time, in Germany. It was through the efforts of his long-time comrade, Gottlob Berger, also a close friend and associate of the Chief of the Schutzstaffel (SS), Heinrich Himmler, that Dirlewanger was released from custody and reinstated in the general reserve of the SS. His doctorate was also later restored by the University of Frankfurt.

With the outbreak of the war, Dirlewanger volunteered to join the Waffen-SS ('Weapon-SS)', the fighting arm of what was the Hitler bodyguard and was given the rank of *Obersturmführer* (Senior Storm Leader). Eventually Dirlewanger would be honoured with a fighting unit bearing his own surname – the Dirlewanger Brigade. This was at first merely a battalion but was later expanded to a regiment, which went on to achieve brigade status. Initially comprised of a small group of former poachers and soldiers from a more conventional military background, the poachers proved to be both excellent trackers and shots, which were considered useful prerequisites for anti-partisan operations. As the war dragged on Dirlewanger's brigade was swelled by ever-increasing numbers of convicted criminals (both civilian and military), concentration camp inmates, men from lunatic asylums, homosexuals, interned Romany people (gypsies), and, toward the close of the war, even political prisoners of the Nazi regime. It was an unflattering military accolade even by Dirlewanger's standards.

One of the first duties with which Dirlewanger's unit was tasked was security, first within the general government of occupied Poland, where Dirlewanger served as the commandant of a labour camp at Stary Dzikow, with the unit known as the SS-Totenkopfverbände or SS-TV (the SS Death's Head unit). The SS-TV was the organization responsible for the administrative and operational duties of the Nazi concentration and extermination camps. With Oskar Dirlewanger effectively running the show at Stary Dzikow, complaints about the sexual abuse of the inmates reached the ears of the authorities. A judge in the SS judiciary, Georg Konrad Morgen, conducted an investigation into the allegations of rape and other sexual abuses carried out not only by Dirlewanger himself, but also the men under his command. What Judge Morgen's investigation revealed sickened him. Dirlewanger was accused of wanton acts of murder, sodomy and rape. The rape and sodomy in particular were in direct contravention of the Nazi racial hygiene laws. The majority of Dirlewanger's rape and sodomy victims were either young girls or young boys. However, a special regime of cruelty and perversion was reserved for his older victims. It was revealed that Dirlewanger particularly enjoyed having Jewish female inmates stripped naked before being whipped. There were also stories where Dirlewanger burned the genitals of women he abused with a petrol lighter. Yet, whipping was one of his greatest delights and once the whipping had finished one of Dirlewanger's men would inject strychnine into the veins of the unfortunate victims. He would then watch the spectacle in perverted delight as the victim convulsed to death before him. There were also reports that Dirlewanger had the flesh of his Jewish victims boiled with horse meat to make soap.

A former UK-based Waffen-SS source, who wished to remain anonymous, related this memory of Dirlewanger:

> The obscene antics of Dirlewanger and those men under his command were tolerated simply because Heinrich Himmler, who was *Reichsführer* of the SS, needed that sort of a man to do the really dirty work that others could not do, if you understand what I'm saying. If Dirlewanger was ordered to go into an area and kill every living soul without mercy, with his bare hands, then he would follow that order to the book, exactly as he was told. His organizational skills were excellent, considering he drank very heavily. In Dirlewanger's eyes it was merely a war against sub-humanity which had no right to life at all, not in any form. He considered

his victims sub-human, he was fighting a war against sub-humans, and I would say Himmler didn't care that Dirlewanger was a very naughty boy. He did as he was told, he killed without question as a good soldier should, in the line of duty. It may seem odd but we SS soldiers of units such as the Waffen-SS Liebstandarte viewed Dirlewanger's brigade as a scum brigade. They weren't like us, they were thieves, rapists, child molesters, lunatics, murderers and drunks. They were not intelligent in the same ethos as we were, and I would say if they were sent into a situation and were all wiped out no one would have been bothered; it would have saved the lives of better-quality SS soldiers. In that respect. Dirlewanger's brigade was assigned simply to carry out the worst possible tasks that might affect the sanity of a normal soldier; yes, they were the pig-swill boys alright.

I heard many stories about the activities of the Dirlewanger Brigade, in and around Lublin, and they came from a reliable and truthful source. I heard stories about how Dirlewanger and his men raped children, and I was genuinely shocked by what I heard. I heard that he and his men went into Lublin where they kicked in the doors to houses, extorted money, stole valuables and generally terrorized the population there. I was told that by the time they had finished their uniforms would be stained with blood and shit and things. Dirlewanger thrived on cruelty and sexual depravity, many were aware of this, but he was good at the task of being totally ruthless, and that is what counted at the end of it all. For Dirlewanger's brigade, the opportunity to kill, torture and rape was a love at first sight kind of thing, or should I say blood at first sight.

Dirlewanger's sexual lust for children knew no bounds. He was in most respects what one might describe as a trophy rapist who preferred children to adult females or males. He cared not whether his victim was a young girl or young boy; if the mood took him, he would take that child somewhere and rape or sodomize the child, and afterward, in many cases, he would shoot the child himself. Dirlewanger repeatedly sacked the ghetto at Lublin and it was here that many of his child victims fell into his depraved hands. Dirlewanger's entire career was characterized by child rape, murder, perversion, sadism and alcoholism. Yet, despite his violence and sadism, his activities went unchecked throughout the war and on 15 August 1944 he was promoted to the rank of *Oberführer* (Senior Leader), and in October of that same year he was awarded Germany's highest military decoration, the coveted Ritterkreuz (the Knight's Cross) of the Iron Cross.

In June 1945 time had run out for a man whom many describe as one of the most evil and depraved figures not only within the Nazi Third Reich, but throughout history itself. Dirlewanger was arrested near the town of Altshausen in Upper Swabia where he had been hiding out in a remote hunting lodge. When arrested Dirlewanger was wearing rather ill-fitting civilian clothes yet was recognized by a former Jewish concentration camp inmate. Following his arrest, he was taken to a detention centre where he was questioned, and some sources say beaten senseless by his captors. His death was reported to have occurred between 5 and 7 June 1945, at Althausen, yet details of his death are shrouded in mystery. French sources insist that he died of a heart attack and was buried in an unmarked grave. Polish authorities claim that he died of maltreatment in the form of beatings, while others contest that he escaped, to later join the French Foreign Legion.

To close this particular chapter and the sickening details of Oskar Dirlewanger, it must be pointed out that there has never been any proven evidence to suggest that Dirlewanger actually indulged in necrophilia. These rumours appeared to surface following the publication of two books which I have neither seen nor read. It is pretty evident that, if he had indulged in the disgusting practice of necrophilia, and in the line of his duties there would have been countless hundreds of opportunities for him to have done so, then, in turn, at least a handful of witnesses somewhere along the line would have come forward after the end of the war. Yet no reports of any such activities were forthcoming not as far as Dirlewanger was concerned. Even today, when searching for information about this man on the world wide web, the word 'necrophiliac' frequently appears alongside his name, despite there being no evidence in any of the narratives to connect him to this practice. One can only assume that such assumptions are the result of literary fabrication solely to support the promotion of the two books referred to above.

Otto Buchner's father, Peter, had been a member of the SS Totenkopf Division which was active in the East in the war. Otto revealed that his father had liaised with the infamous Dirlewanger Brigade during the course of operations in Eastern Europe and what he witnessed there had shocked even him. Otto explained that his father rarely spoke about his war, but once when a little drunk he began to talk about Dirlewanger, to whom he had taken an instant dislike. On this occasion Otto's father recounted:

> Dirlewanger, yes, he was definitely one of those mental cases, a man not at all sound of mind, quite insane in many respects. He was a man you could quite easily imagine standing at the edge of a mass burial pit, full of fresh corpses, masturbating over them. He enjoyed killing; to most of us soldiers killing was a job, a task we were expected to carry out in the course of our duty, to engage other soldiers in battle. We didn't revel in it like he did; he enjoyed the act of killing and almost all of those under his command were the same, they were a division of psychopaths who enjoyed raping men and women, girls and boys and even the elderly were not spared their sexual perversion, and when they had their fun, they then went on a rampage of murder and bingeing on alcohol. They were a law unto themselves and often given the worst tasks, because Dirlewanger was crazy enough to do anything he was ordered to do, without any hesitation or question – he would just go and do it. Hitler liked him for that reason. In Hitler's view Dirlewanger could do the jobs that even the most battle-hardened soldiers could not bring themselves to do. It spared the other SS units the job of doing the dirty work. Hitler had received in-depth reports of the rape and sexual torture carried out by Dirlewanger and members of his unit, yet he sat back and let Dirlewanger do what he wanted, probably for the above stated reasons, I don't know. I heard some terrible stories about Dirlewanger's men. A shocked comrade told me they once raped a woman before wrapping her in barbed wire and roasting her alive over a fire, like a hog on a spit.

Otto tried on several occasions to squeeze more information from his father, but said, 'He just clammed up on me; he wouldn't talk about it again and he never did, up until his death. I know the unit my father served in was responsible for many war crimes in the East, but I know that he wasn't involved in any such murders of civilians, which is one good thing I can say.'

As for Oskar Dirlewanger, he was a living embodiment of evil and depravity and all the proof that anyone could need that monsters do exist, and that most of them reside not within the realms of fantasy but within the human race itself.

Chapter 7

Sex and School

Sex education, in even its most basic format, was virtually non-existent within the Nazi education system. The sex education that many teenage girls and boys received under the Nazis evolved largely from two main principles, racial and natural biology. With the focus of attention on these two themes the true concept of sex was conveniently avoided. Young males often became sexually aware before the girls, discovering that the appendage between their legs possessed joys greater than just urinating. What male cannot recall that moment in his early youth when he was almost compromised by his mother's sudden and unexpected appearance at his bedroom door as he neared the point of no return, forced hastily to pull up his pyjama bottoms in a well-rehearsed drill to spare himself the humiliation of being caught in the act. Yet his mother still questioned him: 'What are you doing?' As if she didn't know.

The discovery by girls of their own sexuality is much the same. Sexual therapist, Dr Ilse Neumann, explains:

> It is perfectly natural to discover your sexuality; it is all a part of our evolution as human beings and there should be nothing embarrassing about masturbation as it is entirely natural and harmless. We all discover it, usually around our pre-teens by touching ourselves and discovering that it actually feels good and that we can gain either comfort or relief from it. Undoubtedly, masturbation is often the first experience of sex that most young people will ever experience.

The Nazis were keen to encourage the perception of sexual intercourse purely as a means of producing children, thus promoting Hitler's dream of a thousand-year Reich. When presenting the subject of sex to teenage girls, any aspect of sexual intercourse that may have been considered pleasurable was deleted from the conversation. The act was described as the application of nature, devoid of any of the usual widely accepted human emotional elements. All young Germans in the Reich were taught that only the lesser races indulged in sex for pleasure, and that lust and gratification belonged purely in the realm of the Jew. There were no diagrams to explain the process of human reproduction and the mechanics of conception in Nazi human biology textbooks – they were considered pornographic. Where young women were concerned, the sex act was merely an extension of the domestic functions expected of the German female in her role of housewife.

Masculinity being one of the defining factors of Third Reich society, in many instances it was left to the males to educate their women sexually, although many of the young girls of the BDM learned about the virtues of sex from their own private conversations with one another, or from an elder sister, or through accidentally catching their brothers in the act at home. On the other hand, boys, especially older boys in the Hitler Youth, enjoyed incessant discussion of the pleasures of sex. As the alpha males of their society, they were entitled to do so and their thoughts and opinions were never once construed as being in the 'realm of the Jew'. This is a reflection of the male attitude, in general, during the Third Reich, and it reeked of hypocrisy. Consider how the likes of Joseph Goebbels, Reinhard Heydrich and Martin Bormann conducted themselves in their own insatiable pursuits of the flesh, often for women considerably younger than themselves.

Kirsten Eckermann recalled the Nazi version of sex education:

> It was not sex education as we know and understand it today. It was all very confusing and contradictory, and we were aware of this as teenagers. The state-approved biology book only went as far as stating reproductive cycles through natural means as in nature itself. It was all examined through plants and seeds and things like that. It was just lucky for us girls that we had the girls' Hitler Youth and its weekly meetings, and the yearly camps held throughout the summertime. It was through these things that we as girls discussed such things as sex between ourselves. You couldn't talk about it with any of the troop leaders around, but we certainly did when they weren't there. There were always those older girls who knew all about the birds and the bees and were open to discussing with others. That's how many of us learned all about it, and there was no messing around, it was straight to the point, 'You get your knickers off, he gets a hard on and it goes in your hole like this,' and they would go into all the details [she laughs]. We couldn't rely on our so-called educators to tell us anything.

Parents weren't much better either. Mothers very rarely sat their daughters down and discussed what menstruation was all about, let alone sexual intercourse and pregnancy. Yet, the men always knew all about it and they were purposely educated that way. There were some boys who knew more about menstruation and the biological functions of the female body than we did ourselves, at first anyway. This is why so many young girls became pregnant by accident. Boys would always say, 'Oh, well, if I pull out of you, you won't get pregnant,' or 'If we have sex during menstruation, you can't fall pregnant.' It was all rubbish of course, as they'd tell you anything if they thought they could get your knickers off and get you into bed. The men of Third Reich society were obsessed with sex and women and some of the old men were among the worst.

Hildegard Kustin concurs with Kirsten on the issue of sex education:

I never learned a thing from any of the books we had in school, or the lessons for that matter. Everything I discovered about sex was from the other kids. Though I caught my brother and his girlfriend on two occasions when they were doing it on the living room settee. On the first occasion they didn't even hear me walk in as they were too engrossed in what they were doing. I watched in amazement for a few seconds as he was really giving it to her [she laughs]. He had her legs right up in the air and it looked so funny to me. I couldn't help but laugh and my brother went mad, shouting at me, 'Get out of here, get out now or I will throw you out.' I just went back upstairs into my room where I spent most of my time. I was later threatened, 'Don't you dare say anything to mother and father about it.' I taunted him back by saying, 'Dear brother, it's not like I haven't seen your willy before is it. Why are you making such a fuss?' So, in all honesty we learned in other ways about what sex was and the different variations that couples could have sex.

Martin Wengel a former member of the Hannover Hitler Youth recalled:

In the Hitler Youth for boys we had our own very simple way of understanding sex and what it was. For example, if a young man was asked by the older boys, 'How do you fuck a girl?' and he was unable to answer, he would be taunted and labelled as being a homosexual. My father explained a little about sex to me as they really didn't teach you anything in school. I told my father one day a boy in our Hitler Youth group was beaten up as he didn't know how to have sex with a girl. So, yes, my father tried to explain certain things to me, as embarrassing as it must have been for him at the time. It wasn't his job to do that; the schools should have done that as our educators, but they were too damn hypocritical, too afraid that this precious generation might become consumed with the same filth and lust as its leaders. What a crazy society we had become at that time. To be honest with you, as a 13-year-old boy I had no interest in sex or girls, I still preferred my cars and guns and things; I was too young to be concerned with adult problems, but the Hitler Youth forced you to be aware of it all, it was your obligation as a male, that was it.

Teachers in the Nazi era who were tasked with educating the Hitler generation were in many respects placed in a precarious situation. Even the most hard-line of Nazi teachers were fearful of being accused of the moral corruption of Germany's youth, so in some ways it is understandable that many did not relish the prospect of having to lecture on the subject of human reproduction, in its most basic form. Sex education in the Nazi era stood out in stark contrast to that of the former Weimar Republic, which was considered a cesspit of immorality by Hitler and his Nazi cohorts. In many respects it was a deliberate dumbing down of the education system, which would have far-reaching consequences for many, beyond the war.

Anna Dann, a young Berliner and former member of the Hitler Youth for girls, recalls:

Girls were taught very little on the subject of sex which I think was very unfair. If you had older sisters, it would usually have fallen upon their shoulders to tell you about these things, usually in late-night bedtime conversations. I never had that luxury as I had only a brother. So, for me, my way of finding out and understanding the rudiments of how sex was initiated, what it was and how it all worked, was down to my 'sisters' as I called them, in the BDM, the girls' Hitler Youth. In our small groups, particularly when away from home on the camps, we talked with the older girls and sex naturally came up in our conversations. Once it was all explained that the male puts his penis inside your vagina, then he starts thrusting in and out and reaches what is known as orgasm and the sticky stuff that comes out of his penis is the carrier of sperm, which makes you pregnant, it was all pretty much clear to me. Of course, the younger ones, me included, would pull faces, expressing our repugnance at the idea and say, 'Oh, no, my god, I'm never doing that.' The older girls filling us in on the sordid details would laugh at us and say, 'You won't be saying that when you are older; you are just babies at the moment, but that's how it works.' As a 14-year-old the whole biology of sex and childbirth was intimidating to a degree; it involved doing the unthinkable and then going through the gestation period and then the pain of giving birth itself. I personally was in no hurry whatsoever to discover the virtues of sex, but I did know teenage girls and boys who certainly were and admitted they enjoyed it. Sexual knowledge is vital for all young people as it is a process of life, yet our educators did not appear to be that keen to tell us certain things; it was like they were too embarrassed.

Martin Wengel concurs with Anna:

As a young male back then in the Hitler Youth I didn't care much for the differences in sexual education as taught to boys and girls. Only much later when I became a father myself was I concerned that my children be aware of what it was all about when the time was right to tell them. In fact, my wife had the task of talking to my daughter, while I gave my son a lecture on the birds and the bees. In the Hitler Youth I recall standing having a piss in the hedge once and this older boy walked up, takes out his dick stands there proudly as he too takes a piss and announces, 'To keep a girl happy you need a turkey neck like the one I have here in my hand, not a little worm like that thing of yours.' He came out with it in a very matter-of-fact way. I laughed nervously and walked off. Even at school at the open urinal where we would line up to piss at breaktimes there was competition between the boys who would say, 'Mine is bigger and longer, mine is better than yours,' as if this was somehow considered an aid to fertility. The one was mocked for his short stubby penis, but he replied cockily, 'Mine is a howitzer, short but powerful.' The competition and obsession with sex and size began right there in the toilets at school and in the showers after our physical education classes.

Theresa Moelle was scathing of how sex and human reproduction was taught in Hitler's schools:

It was a soulless formula. We didn't learn anything about sex in school to be honest; they often appeared embarrassed to educate us as to the mechanics of human reproduction, especially in the way it occurred. Being raised on a farm, I soon learned what sex was all about. There were a few occasions I happened to be walking and I would hear strange noises coming from the barn; we had two such barns just a stone's throw from the main house. I soon learned in my teens that these strange noises were nothing other than the music of love, two people making sweet music. I recall being fascinated by it and quietly sneaking up to see if I could see anything [she laughs]; it was too dark inside to see anything but judging by the noises, they were really enjoying themselves. Most of those who used the hay barns were the farm labourers who didn't have anywhere private to take their girlfriends. The next day at school we girls would get together on our lunchbreaks and talk about things like this just as modern teenage girls do today – we were really no different in that respect. In a sense we educated ourselves; we didn't need school to tell us how babies were made as we learned ourselves.

As we grew older, and especially in the girls' Hitler Youth of course, we grew curious of what fucking was all about. We understood, apart from it being a biological obligation for German women to have many babies, that it felt good and generally most women loved fucking once they'd tried it a few times. There were of course some girls who remained ignorant to sex for whatever reason and if they were taught nothing in school or discreetly by their parents, they never stood a chance and you knew they'd end up pregnant very quickly, often before they'd even married; it was sad really.

Chapter 8

Virility and Velvet
(The Martial Law Manual for Making Love)

It is only in recent years that the three Hitler Youth organizations – the Hitlerjugend for males, Jungmädelbund (Young Maidens League) and its senior equivalent, the Bund Deutscher Mädel (League of German Maidens) – have become sexualized in the perceptions of many modern-day Third Reich enthusiasts. I say enthusiasts because, from experience, I have found that an enthusiast has a different outlook when compared with an historian. Consequently, there can be a gulf of difference in opinion between Third Reich historians (me included) and the average enthusiast.

This chapter examines the views and experiences of former female and male members of the three Hitler Youth organizations, in regard to the subject of sex, and whether or not the Hitler Youth as a whole was inadvertently sexualized, either by the Nazi state itself or the casual observations of foreign outsiders.

The Deutscher Jungmädelbund and the Bund Deutscher Mädel

The Deutscher Jungmädelbund (for girls aged 10 to 13) and the Bund Deutscher Mädel (for girls aged 14 to 18) were never intended to be anything other than a means for the successful indoctrination of Nazi Germany's female youth. They were intended to ensure, through various physical disciplines, education and a strict, racially oriented ethos, the fitness and long-term health of the girls themselves, so they could go on to raise healthy Aryan German offspring. The closest British equivalent to the Jungmädelbund and Bund Deutscher Mädel would have to be the Brownies and the Girl Guides. The only disparities between the two groups, apart from the obvious political and geographical differences, was the fact that membership of the Brownies or Girl Guides was never compulsory, nor did the girls have to endure violently racial teachings combined with a demanding regime of physical exercise. It is perhaps down to both the foreign and Nazi press agencies, along with the Nazi propaganda machine itself, that the medium of photography portrayed sexualized images of the girls of the Hitler Youth. Internet websites certainly display more images of Hitler Youth girls engaged in sporting activities, than posed images of the girls in full uniform. In the original Nazi view images of the girls in their white sports vests and black shorts were designed to convey to the world the physical prowess of young German women; they were certainly not intended to emphasize any sexual element that may have been conjured in the minds of viewers. This point having been made, amateur American photographer Jess Steiner recalled a visit to Berlin in the summer of 1936, and his encounter with a group of Jungmädelbund girls at their Saturday afternoon sports activity, which took place every weekend:

> What I saw was a camaraderie not unlike that of our cheerleader girls back home during a football game, or high school girls participating in a PT class. Yet, this appeared somewhat different; there was no individual competition, the girls worked as a team in most of the activities. I was also surprised at the young ages of these girls which ranged from 10 to early teens. I saw one group of girls form two lines and hold hands with the girls opposite them in the lines. Then one girl would take a run-up and jump up into the centre of the two lines where she would be bounced along to the end of the line before the girl would jump off, landing gracefully on her feet and standing to attention like a soldier might on parade. Then there was another group of girls who formed themselves into a human pyramid three to four girls high. The tallest, strongest girls formed the base of the pyramid while the smaller less physically powerful girls climbed up them to form the top of the pyramid. The stronger girls would help pull them up while holding onto one of the other's hands. I had never seen that before outside specialized gymnastics classes yet for these German girls it was all incorporated into their education formula. You could see that even the smaller girls of the group were quite physically well defined, by the muscles in their legs and their dexterity during the exercise routines they had to perform. All the time there was a leader watching them, encouraging them and shouting out instructions.
>
> When they had finished, I approached the girl who was in charge of them and in my rather poor German, I told her I was an American photographer and then I asked if I could take some photographs of her

girls. She stood there with her hands on her hips and with a proud smile she said, 'Yes, of course you can. Which ones do you want to photograph?' Subconsciously, I found myself choosing the pretty girls though I was making no conscious attempt at photographing them in any sexual context. My idea was to capture a pleasing photographic aesthetic. I photographed one girl who told me her name was Lottie and that she was a 12-year-old from Berlin. She leaned against a wall and smiled for the camera as I took a series of photographs of her at different angles. I then asked if I could take some photographs of an older girl who was standing on the sidelines watching the others. The girl could speak clear English and told me she was 18 years old, was a gymnast and in the last year of her youth service. She explained she was here to help teach the younger girls the physical arts of gymnastics. I simply asked her to perform some of the routines she was teaching and as she did them, I took photographs of her. It was only upon my return to the states a week later, when I began developing the roll of film I had shot that day that an image of the German girl emerged as perhaps the most striking of the series, despite the fact she was doing nothing other than performing a handstand without any support.

When I showed my photographs to some of my colleagues it was this handstand photo that they all whooped over. I recall the one guy saying, 'Jesus Christ she's hot! Did you get her telephone number?' Another remarked, 'Wowie! I think I'm in love!' With hindsight, when I looked at the photograph, I guess it was sexy in one sense. The girl was wearing nothing other than a white sports vest and a pair of tight-fitting gym shorts. She was tall, with blond hair, and in every respect she was the personification of the perfect female, in the view of Adolf Hitler and his Nazis. The only thing which detracted from that otherwise wonderful image was the swastika badge she wore on her sports vest. That was certainly sinister, looking back on it, all these years on.

With the above statement in mind, it was no surprise that whenever the Nazis held their huge sporting events, and national party rallies, prior to the outbreak of war in 1939, the girls were always the focus of the photographer's attention; the young men were often ignored, particularly by members of the various US press agencies.

Ilse Baumann, a 13-year-old member of a South Berlin BDM troop at the time, recalled the attention given to her and some of her friends during a party rally in 1938:

They [the foreign press] were everywhere. We couldn't go anywhere without having a camera pointing at us and some funny-looking guy wearing a raincoat shouting and gesturing for us to smile while he took photographs. I remember one came up to me; he was a balding, middle-aged gentleman with a mouth that appeared too big for his face. He gestured for me to stop and look at the camera as I could not understand what he was saying. I did not know any English. I gathered he wanted to take a photo, so I stood still, posed and then smiled while he blinded me with the flash. I think he found it amusing but when he smiled it revealed rows of large yellow teeth, I began laughing at him and I thought to myself, 'You look like a chimpanzee.'

I told a friend about it later and she said, 'Ilse, they drink a lot of coffee and smoke a lot of cigars in the USA, this is why their teeth are yellow and their physicality is poor.' Yes, the photographers, particularly the foreign ones, were very amusing to us. We didn't take the photographs seriously as we knew we would never even see any of them, so what was the point? Were any of the photographs sexy or sexual? Well, that depends on how you perceived them, I guess. Photographs of us in our sports kit may have turned on many young men across the Atlantic [she laughs]; I really couldn't say. I can imagine many of them would have liked to put their 'iron in the fire' with us, as we used to say.

Katrina Niekerk, another former member of the BDM, recalled:

We knew how to be sexy just like the Hollywood movie stars. We were sometimes cheeky with the foreign pressmen at the big parades and sports events. I remember once I was joking around with three of my friends after we had finished a running event. We walked past this photographer who we could tell was not from Germany. As we walked past him, I pulled up my vest showing him my belly. He caught me doing it with his camera. We all laughed and one of my friends said, 'Katrina, I hope for your sake that photo does not make the *Deutscher Beobachter* (*German Observer*) as your mother will kill you.'

If the floors of the press agency darkrooms of the world were made somewhat sticky in places (and not from the leaking jam of lunchtime donuts), then what might the press have made of it had they heard of the antics of Hildegard Schwarz, an 18-year-old BDM girl from Leipzig? Hildegard wrote the following revelation in her diary, in July 1940, shortly prior to embarking on her compulsory *Landjahr* service (a year on the land). Her diary entry would have been unprintable in its day. Yet today it provides another perspective on the sexual attitudes of some of the more mature girls of the BDM:

> The German Reich is charged with sexuality, it is everywhere. The physical might and sexual prowess of both German males and females is conveyed through almost every statue in the Reich capital and every piece of propaganda, all conveniently packaged as art. My boyfriend and I have recently been to the capital [Berlin] where we shared a hotel room and not for the first time. It should have been blatantly obvious to dear papa that we as two healthy young people would not have opted for separate rooms and single beds, and we weren't sharing a huge bed just to sit and read each other poetry or romantic stories, or to feed each other strawberries of a morning, whilst listening to the birdsong outside the window. We were here purely for the purpose of having as much sex as we possibly could. We booked in as Mrs and Mrs Bauer and of course it was a barefaced lie, as marriage couldn't have been further from our minds. I had had my first sexual experience a year and a half previous. I have to admit that I enjoyed fucking as much as I like drinking alcohol. Alcohol in small measures complements greatly the sexual act by nullifying all inhibition. My boyfriend understood to perfection the geography of the female genitalia; he gave me lightning bolts from my urethra which permeated the whole of my body. There are two distinct sexual poles of north and south. The southerly most region is often viewed with the disdain of an English Victorian-era slum. Yet there is no greater delight than that of having a man thrust his tongue into your arse providing you have washed thoroughly beforehand. The northerly most region is like some well-trodden path to some socialist soup kitchen, hardly adventurous, dull, boring, and doesn't everyone just instinctively go there? The act of sex itself is an artform that has to be mastered, despite the state's reluctance to admit this. One has to learn through practice as with anything else. I learned very quickly the delights of oral sex in particular. My boyfriend of the time would never have admitted it, but it was one way for me to always ensure complete control over him. I knew my technique was a good one. I would hold him with my index finger and thumb then work my way from his balls using just the tip of my tongue, working up to the tip of his penis. It was at the tip of his penis where most of my stimulative efforts were focused. I would work my fingers back and forth along his shaft while flicking my tongue over that super-sensitive spot at the tip. The idea is to do it softly, never hard, barely making contact at times. I actually liked giving oral sex, but I did not do it with every boyfriend I had, only the ones I had genuine feelings for, or had fallen in love with, because giving oral sex to me was something very intimate and personal. I could not have

done it with a stranger or someone I had only just met. Yes, as I have said, I loved fucking and getting drunk, but I was only young and what I did had to be done in total privacy too. I wasn't a slut – that's the English word for a girl or woman who sleeps with anyone, isn't it?

For a young girl of her particular era Hildegard's memoir may surprise some. Yet it was only some thirty or so years later that young couples of a very different era would be doing the same, jetting off to exotic locations, dining on freshly caught octopus, enjoying hot nights beneath cool sheets, with mini-bars and complimentary Sybian machines for an enhanced sense of decadence.

Gabrielle Haefker concurs with Hildegard Schwarz, at least on the issue of the Reich being charged with sexuality. She recalled the Nazi Party rally held at Nuremberg in 1936:

People were having sex all over the place, even the girls and boys of the Hitler Youth. In fact, the youth outdid the adults. As there was no segregation at this event boys and girls were able to mix freely, unchaperoned, and a lot of girls found themselves pregnant upon their return home. It caused the government some embarrassment as they were blamed for it, particularly by the parents of the girls. But young people like to have sex, that is completely normal, and why shouldn't they? But at Nuremberg in 1936 many forgot or couldn't be bothered with using birth control. The abortion rate rose sharply as many of the girls who fell pregnant were not at an age where they could just marry; no these were young girls of 15 to 17 mostly. They have said that after Nuremberg 1936 some 900 girls came back pregnant. I know for a fact that figure was conservative and based upon those girls who had received treatment, allowing it to be recorded by the authorities. There were several hundred more who had their pregnancies terminated privately or in neighbouring countries; these for various reasons were not recorded. There were a few that actually had their babies and handed them over for adoption afterwards. The state assisted the families of those girls who went through with their pregnancies. Efforts were made to try and inhibit wanton sexual behaviour within the Hitler Youth, in future. The Hitler Youth Streifendienst (Hitler Youth police), or SRD as they were known, were instructed to keep a closer eye on all members of the Hitler Youth thereafter. The Hitler Youth were also given lectures on their moral conduct at their weekly gatherings and at school. It didn't work though, as boys and girls were still having sex whenever they could. Even Nazism could not erase the basic human nature of its youth, despite efforts made to the contrary.

Theresa Moelle recalled that, at age 15, in 1943, she and her brothers and sisters were messing around at a pond in one of their livestock fields:

> The normally still water was foaming with a curious slick of clear gelatinous covering. The water had overnight become a thick soup of amphibian seminal fluids. We were mesmerized as we sat at the side of the pond poking sticks into it. In the middle of the pond there was this mass of writhing toads, embracing one another; in effect they were in the throes of mating. We were paddling our feet in the water when this old woman came hobbling past us with her dog. She stopped and told us, 'Don't dip your feet into that water while the toads are in there mating, you will become pregnant with deformed babies.' We looked at one another puzzled, and being the oldest I told her, 'That is rubbish.' The woman shrugged her shoulders, hissed at us then walked on. The old lady's remark was just old German folklore, what her mother had obviously told her. I knew enough about reproductivity and sex to know when someone was trying to pull the wool over my eyes. At the time I was aware of what sex and sexuality was all about.
>
> In the BDM, when we got together, we sometimes discussed sex as all girls do. Did the BDM make us feel like sex sirens? Well, when you are out on a field in PT kit with a huge crowd looking at you, all those people will be looking at you and thinking all kinds of things. The men will more often than not be focusing on your looks, things like your legs, arse and tits. The women will be looking at the boys in their PT kit and thinking along similar lines, zeroing in on their physique, muscularity and of course their bulging groins.

Alessa Goberg's view on the BDM and sex was predictably light-hearted. Here was an atypical German woman who despite old age possessed no regrets, embarrassment or inhibitions whatsoever, on the sexual aspects of her youth in Nazi Germany. Alessa recalled:

> Were we girls of the BDM somehow the sexy side of National Socialism? That depends upon how sexy you yourself felt as an individual. I think a great many outsiders thought we were sexy. It may sound unkind, but the BDM had its fair share of what we used to call trolls. These were what I can only describe as the less attractive girls in the physical and aesthetical sense. It was much like any community of females or males, there would be the good-looking ones and then there would be the not-so-good-looking ones, who were what we would call rather large in stature, manly, if you like, and as a result slightly less confident in themselves. Of course, you

were aware in yourself when you looked in the mirror as to whether you were pleasing to the eye or not, as most people can tell when they come of age and begin to take notice of themselves. For example, from the age of 14 years old I would stand before the mirror in my room and examine myself intensely. I wouldn't stand there drooling or anything, but I could see that I was of a good physical form, and I knew boys found me attractive despite the fact I was what many today would call flat chested; yes, I had small breasts. My best features were my good looks, so I was told, my long legs, slender frame and the fact that my backside wasn't too big [she laughs].

As a result, I was confident and confident people exude the quality which men find naturally attractive in a female, I think. Anyone can look at themselves and think, 'Yes, I am pretty,' or 'Maybe I'm not as pretty as others.' This is basic human nature and both girls and boys possess the same attitude to themselves today. Our society back then was one which promoted naturism and nudity as being healthy attributes in people of all ages. This may have been construed as being sexy or sexual. Not everyone embraced naturism where you walked around the countryside naked or swam in the rivers and lakes without a bathing suit on, but my family brought me up not to be ashamed of being naked or other people seeing me naked. It was all perfectly normal to those of us who lived out in the countryside of Germany. So, as I grew into my teens and my body developed, I was not shy or embarrassed about anyone seeing me naked. I knew very well that I looked good.

In the BDM we girls participated in many outdoor activities, especially on the yearly summer camps where we would be naked some of the time. These activities included swimming and dancing. These activities were not an attempt at sexualizing us, they were just normal, though I know outside observers such as foreigners, both men and women visiting our country might have thought otherwise. Some may have thought we were fair game for them, but we were not. Of course, I had boyfriends and our families and society were strict on what was considered permissible behaviour for young girls. But what they didn't know didn't hurt them, was the rule, and to be honest many of us were much the same as teenage girls today, no different really. We weren't robots, we had feelings, emotional and sexual feelings as we grew up; that is all perfectly natural. Anyone who tries to convince you that we were these upright, hard, totally clean-living Nazi stereotypes, totally committed to the state, is lying to you. Even those in power were getting up to all sorts of things. We heard all sorts of rumours about them. I was a healthy, fit young girl and I enjoyed having boyfriends and I enjoyed having sex with some of them. I was around 18 when I had my first proper sexual experience. I'd had many 'dress rehearsals' if you like, where I gave boyfriends 'hand relief' as they call it today. If I felt comfortable, I would let them do the same for me. I sometimes let them dry hump me [simulated lovemaking, usually fully clothed] which was okay, I guess. After a while masturbating each other becomes boring though and the boys get frustrated with it. I was curious to experience sexual intercourse with the boyfriend I regarded as my first love. There was no planning or anything; it just happened naturally. My family were farmers, and it was almost a tradition among girls from farming families that they lose their virginity in the hay. You couldn't do it in the house for fear of being compromised by either your parents or younger siblings; that would have been far too embarrassing, so doing it outside in one of the hay barns was the next best thing. Couples still do this today and there is nothing at all wrong with it in my view, provided no one can see you doing it. So, we went into the hay barn where we had less chance of being disturbed.

The act of making love was more or less instinctive. We undressed one another and I remember being amazed at how incredibly hard his penis was. As I grasped it in my fingers, I felt the scrotal tissues tighten like a canvas, we kissed then I lay down on my back and I lay there watching him put on the birth control which I had of course insisted on; I then let him lie between my legs. I took hold of him and guided him inside me keeping my fingers firmly around his penis so as I could control the degree of penetration. I knew it would hurt if he tried to thrust too quickly, too soon, so I insisted on controlling the pace which he was not bothered about at all, I think he was far too excited and lost in the moment to think of becoming the all-conquering domineering male that the Hitler Youth expected of him. It was several minutes before he had fully entered me, and I felt comfortable about letting go of him. The sensations were quite incredible compared to masturbation, oh yes it was much nicer. The most difficult thing of all was keeping the noise down in the throes of passion; that is never easy. You get to a point where you don't care about anything other than the goal of reaching orgasm. He was a considerate lover and gave me my first proper orgasm shortly before he had his pleasure. Afterwards we just lay in each other's arms for a while. We felt relieved, relaxed and happy and I was happy having given myself to him. After that first time we couldn't get enough and with each time the sex became better as we explored other methods of intercourse.

I learned much with that one boyfriend, including the joys of oral sex. There is not a man on this planet that can say he doesn't enjoy fellatio and it is the same for any woman. Some women see the act of performing fellatio as being domineering, but I just enjoyed seeing the pleasure I was giving; it wasn't about control or anything. For a male there is nothing sexier than watching a pretty girl as she goes up and down on his cock with her mouth. Most males blow their load very quickly when you give them fellatio, but I didn't see that as a problem, as I could always have seconds. I definitely wasn't selfish, but I knew many girls who were, by the things they would talk about. Some women hated the taste of semen too, but I didn't mind it; I would just spit it out of my mouth. 'Double ending' was another thing I enjoyed very much. In most countries it is called '69'. It was good as it enabled you both to give simultaneous oral pleasure. I enjoyed having anal stimulation too and there was nothing dirty about it if you made sure you were clean. 69 allowed for the male to easily stimulate the woman's anus with his tongue. I often returned the compliment by doing it for them too, but it meant the male having to kneel down and not every male wanted to do this as they felt it was too submissive. Once they had it done to them once, they usually very quickly changed their minds though [she laughs]. The idea was to stimulate their anus with the tip of your tongue while wanking their penis. This often culminated in a very intense orgasm which was pretty messy and it reminded me of when I was milking cows [she laughs].-

Yes, the girls' Hitler Youth professed this air of innocence, obedience to the Nazi state and living a moral existence as a good Nazi should, but that was all rubbish. While yes, we were honed to become accomplished keepers of the home and could cook, clean and care for a husband and our babies, we did what any normal healthy girls would do. Some did not have proper sex until they were 19 or 20 years old. Compared with today you would say we were late starters. The only difference today is that we didn't advertise the fact then that we were having sex. This may appear contradictory with me telling you this now, for the purpose of a book, which people will read, but if I don't tell you how it really was then no one will ever know or understand, will they?

So, Hitler Youth girls were not about sex or portraying a sexual image to the outside world. We were raised and educated to serve a particular purpose within our society at the time, what our then leader Adolf Hitler expected of us, and we thought nothing else about it. The fact we sometimes wore very little in sporting and exercising activities is irrelevant. You can't compete in a sporting tournament or exercising routine wearing restrictive clothing, can you? What we wore back then was much the same as what many school children wore for PT classes at the time, no different really. The only difference being the vests we wore had swastikas on them. Whether a girl wore plimsolls, dancing shoes or carried out PT in bare feet was another issue some construed as being sexual. If a girl chose to wear nothing on her feet, it wasn't because she felt it looked sexier, it was down to her own personal preference. The same can be said for the boys. Of course, there were males who had serious foot fetishes and for them a pair of expertly manicured feet attached to a pair of slender legs must have been quite a turn-on. The same can be said for women though; there were women who liked a man with nice feet – it worked both ways. That said, some girls and boys had feet like gorillas [she laughs].

Feet were quite a study for the Nazi authorities during physical inspections: they had to be clean with the toenails cut squarely and no nail varnish was allowed. Anti-fungal foot powders were often used to ensure the feet of both girls and boys remained free from infections such as athlete's foot. Yes, there were creepy characters in our society who looked at you and drooled, more than likely fantasizing about fucking you, yes; we knew they were out there, but we could handle them in most cases. I know there were some creepy men who abused their positions of power within the regime, to molest both boys and girls; some of them were dealt with at the war's end by local people.

There was an abuser of young boys and girls who lived near our little community. Nobody dared say or do anything while the Nazis were still in charge; he was untouchable and felt he could do what he wanted. Shortly before the surrender he was found floating face down in a lake, he had shot himself in the head, it was believed. But I think the locals sorted him out and killed him. It's ironic in a sense, as despite all of that flawless preparation toward motherhood, I married yet never had any children. I took over my parents' farming business in 1955 along with my husband and there never was a right time for having babies. My husband passed away four years ago, and I can say I had a good marriage with neither of us having any regrets about not having children. Between us from our siblings we have five nieces and three nephews, and they were enough for us.

Having interviewed Alessa previously, whilst working on the manuscript for another book, *Hitler's Housewives: German Women on the Home Front*, I was already well acquainted with her no-nonsense nature and frank approach to the subject of discussing sex and sexuality in the Third Reich. I was neither shocked nor surprised by the things she told me, despite the intensely personal nature of her narrative, yet I was concerned that some readers may find the above just too fantastic for the Third Reich. When I put this particular issue to her, Alessa responded:

Is it really that difficult to believe that I can sit here and talk in an adult fashion about sex and how we once were, so long ago, under Hitler? Is it really that difficult to believe? It is much like the thousands of German female rape victims after the so-called liberation of our country. No one believed them either back then, but by God, they do now.

The issue of unwanted sexual advances experienced by girls in the Jungmädelbund and Bund Deutscher Mädel is a far-ranging one. Many former members have talked openly in some of my previous books about unwanted sexual remarks, advances and actual physical assaults, including rape. The perpetrators of these acts varied from Hitler Youth boys, district Nazi Party members and officials, old men in their communities and, rather surprisingly, foreign visitors to the Reich.

Erica Gordon lived in Mannerheim, Germany throughout the war and was a former member of the Mannerheim BDM. She has provided a typical example of unwanted sexual attention. Yet this unwanted attention was not from one of the males but a female in her BDM group. Erica told me during our interview about the BDM, that on a forest camping trip in the summer of 1942 something happened to her. She explained:

> It was so hot all the girls in our tents slept naked. This was quite normal for us girls to do if it was very hot at night. Up until that point, I had no problems with it at all. One of the girls was the younger sister of the BDM leader in charge of us, I knew this girl well and never had any previous problems with her, despite the fact that she always seemed to want to get close to me. I never suspected anything as I had no reason to. I felt unwell one afternoon, so I was excused further activities by our BDM leader. The leader instructed her sister to go back to the tent to keep an eye on me whilst I rested. The other girls continued with their activities.
>
> All I wanted to do was lie down and rest my head as I had this bad headache. As I lay down this girl lay down next to me, and she just put her arm across me. I thought nothing of this, assuming it was just a comforting action which I had no problems with. I fell asleep only to wake up with this girl's fingers between my legs, I jumped up and I said to her, 'Get off me! What do you think you are doing?' I was still feeling ill, but I decided to rejoin the other girls, rather than stay a minute longer in that tent. The other girl quickly caught up with me and stopped me by grabbing me by my wrists. She firstly apologized saying, 'I'm so sorry Erica, I didn't mean anything.'
>
> When I told her what she had done was wrong and she could be in very big trouble, her attitude changed. She snarled at me, 'Don't you dare say anything about it; remember who is in charge of this group. No one would believe you over me or listen to you, it was just a bad dream that's all.'
>
> In that respect she had bought my silence. I was not mistaken about what had happened: she was moving her fingers around between my legs. It didn't matter that it was carried out by another girl, it was still unwanted attention and should not have happened. I had no sexual or romantic

feelings for this girl at all and I was not aware that I had maybe given her the wrong signals or anything either.

Katrina Niekerk recalled a girl in her BDM troop whom she and her friends suspected of being attracted to other girls:

She was just one of those girls who didn't fit in. She was quite a bit larger than the rest of us and was always slower in the PT routines. The other girls gave her the nickname 'Bovinia'. Bovinia was basically a nickname which referred to bovine or cows. This girl rarely talked about boys like the rest of us did and she showed no interest in them at all. Whenever we talked about sex with boys amongst ourselves, she would say we were being infantile and stupid, and she would get up and walk off. I myself was never unpleasant to her but I did think her very odd indeed.

What the Nazi authorities would have termed inappropriate behaviour between girls of the BDM, and females in Nazi Germany in general, occurred more frequently than was previously thought. The right to love freely, whether with a member of the opposite or same sex, is a luxury taken very much for granted in today's so called 'modern society'. In Nazi Germany sapphism and homosexuality were both considered serious offences. Yet, despite the severe penalties imposed upon anyone accused of sexual deviance, including girls and older females of the Reich, romances and full-blown relationships flourished. The irony here is that many of these clandestine romances would outlive the Third Reich itself and for some would last a lifetime. I have covered this particular subject in some of my previous works, and, not wishing to revisit old ground, I will recount the following example which previously has never been published in any form.

Dana Busch and Elise Bettmann were both from Vienna, Austria, but had never previously met or known one another until they joined the girls' Hitler Youth. Following the German annexation of Austria in March 1938 and the Hitler Youth laws becoming compulsory for all Austrian children, both joined the BDM organization. Neither girl was exactly enthralled about having to join what their parents viewed as a violent, political and alien organization, spawned by a country which had forced itself upon the Austrian people. Dana Busch recalled:

I met Elise through our local district BDM or Hitler Youth for girls. Every district had its own Hitler Youth area grouping. The Germans made it compulsory for all young people to join so you had to get on with it. My parents were not happy about it as they used to say, 'We are Austrians, we are not Germans.' They were not happy about Hitler taking over our country and merging it with Germany, yet they understood there were many Austrians who felt it was the right course of action. So you see there was tremendous support for the Germans and many Austrians looked upon them as liberators, as opposed to these political invaders of our country. No shots were fired, it was a bloodless invasion and the Austrian people became part of the German Reich. Our indoctrination into the politics of the National Socialists began in school almost immediately following the Anschluss. Then there was the call to join the Hitler Youth which I absolutely dreaded. I was not keen on school and to me the girls' Hitler Youth would be yet another form of school. In our BDM group there were girls I knew as friends and some I had never met before. One of the girls I had never met before was Elise, and we just clicked as many girls often did. We were both 13 years old, both disliked school and soon discovered we both shared a dislike of the Nazi system. When I say we clicked almost instantly, I don't mean in a romantic sense. We clicked in the way that we shared the same views and opinions which we knew we could never openly voice, so long as Hitler was in control. We both disliked the BDM and what it was teaching us, particularly the sports activities we used to have to do. Neither of us was keen on sports yet every Saturday afternoon we had to attend this bloody sports afternoon which we both absolutely hated. We just weren't interested in it despite the fact they gave you these awards and certificates for good performance. Rather surprisingly I obtained a few certificates which were officially approved by the Hitler Youth, and they had these oakleaf motifs attached to them. We couldn't not participate, as the whole thing was compulsory. They kept telling us that we must be raised as supremely fit, and not be like the spoiled indulgent masses of countries such as America. This was so that the children we would go on to produce, eventually, would not emerge as weak and sickly.

Both our parents hoped that we would marry and have children as any normal parents would wish of their children, but our parents didn't want us marrying Germans. Oh no, both my parents and Elise's parents hated the thought of that. At the time we had never really thought of what marriage might be like; our only role models were our parents, both of whom had good stable marriages and, despite Hitler being in control, they raised us as best they could under their principles, albeit secretly of course. Me and Elise spent a lot of time together both in and out of school and in the BDM. I wouldn't say we were tomboyish, but we did get up to a lot of things the boys did. We would go out climbing trees, scrumping apples and try and catch fish from the river and things. When we were both around the age of 15, we began to discuss fashion, hairstyles and makeup and things, and wished we had these things which western girls took for granted. We were not permitted makeup, western fashion and our hairstyle had to be the Nordic style. The Nordic hairstyle was something both Austrian and German females shared, so that was not a problem, but we could never experiment as we would like to have done with things like makeup.

It was around this time we began to look at each other in a different way. Our hormones were changing, for one thing. We both went to local dances, where our parents thought we might meet some suitable Austrian boys, and we used to go but would often decline to dance with any of the boys there. It was quite permissible for a girl to marry as young as 16 or 17 back then, provided both sets of parents were in agreement and were happy with it. In this sense families would have been aware their daughters were probably having some form of sex but trusted them to be sensible up until their wedding day.

Elise and I finished our sports afternoon the one Saturday and afterwards went back to Elise's house to change. We always changed back at Elise's house before going for a walk into town. There was no one else at home as her parents had gone out visiting which they always did on a Saturday. Elise complained that her left leg muscle was aching, so I told her to sit down and place her foot in my lap and I gently massaged her sore muscle. As I massaged the back of her leg, I thought to myself what beautiful legs she had. I could feel that her calf muscle was very tense but after a few minutes she said it began to feel better and complimented me greatly on my 'gift'. I just smiled and said I was happy that it had worked. Then she asked me if I would massage her back for her. She took off her vest and as she did, I marvelled at her firm torso. This was the first time we had been virtually naked with each other, completely alone, and it felt exciting in a way I couldn't explain.

Like me she was not a big girl, at around nine stone. She lay down on her bed so I could massage her back. I told her that to do this properly I would have to sit astride her lower back, if this was okay, and she told me that would be fine. I began to move my fingers gently up her back in swirling motions paying particular attention to her shoulder muscles. She told me how nice it felt and that she didn't want me to stop, that it felt so wonderful. As I ran my fingers up and down her bare back, I felt pangs of excitement, excitement that I had never experienced before. It felt strangely erotic, and I remember thinking it was a good job I still had my PT shorts on, as she would almost certainly have become aware of my rapidly moistening state.

After some twenty minutes or so I explained that my hands were beginning to tire so I had to stop. I got up and as I did so Elise turned over then reached out and took my hands in hers and began rubbing my fingers while pulling me toward her. The next thing she was pulling off my vest and we both began kissing; it was intensely erotic as our breasts brushed together as we kissed. I removed my shorts and we both got into her bed and continued kissing. It felt like we had both been waiting for this moment ever since we had met, yet it was totally unplanned – it just happened, so naturally. Nobody had ever touched me sexually before, yet as two females we knew our bodies and what we could do to give each other pleasure. It was wonderful and then it happened every time we could get time alone to ourselves. It was me who told Elise after some weeks had passed that I loved her, and she told me she loved me too.

We were lucky. Before the war ended in 1945, we had to leave Vienna as the Russians were coming. Our families left with other groups of Austrians heading west, so we were able to stay with one another. After the war and some difficult times, we started working and were able to share a small cottage together. We were very happy, despite our family's objections to our lifestyle. The fact that we had fallen in love and had embarked upon a relationship was nothing to do with the Hitler Youth whatsoever. While the Hitler Youth had brought us together and planted the seed, it was by no means a sexual organization. However, I think it is often wrongly perceived that way, by many people today. Me and Elise were in a very small minority of girls who became partners. Many would never dare speak about their lives as it was not the done thing. Today things are different; it is easier for same sex couples, and they have more rights and freedoms in certain societies.

Why am I so open about it all? The answer is simple: we helped these changes to evolve, we are not embarrassed about it and we are not ashamed to be honest, and say what we feel, or to talk about it. What is there to be ashamed about? Why is it so difficult to believe? Sex and its associated emotions are perfectly natural, and we all do it one way or another. Both myself and Elise were never going to make our families proud for what we did, but we were proud of ourselves. Today lesbian couples can enjoy the freedoms many couldn't previously, and we helped bring about that change. While we became secret lovers in what was a totalitarian society, our teachers were telling us in school:

> Your first love must always be for the community that is Germany. We cannot afford to become distracted by becoming doe-eyed romantics

with false perceptions of love; your first love should be your duty to your Führer. Whatever your Führer requests of you should be the single most important facet of your young lives. Your Führer requires children of you and this does not necessarily imply that love be an essential element toward this goal.

I sat there listening to this emotionless tirade and I couldn't help but laugh to myself and think, 'If only you knew!'

All good research requires an understanding of both sides of the story, so I was eager to gain some male perspectives on the Hitler Youth, not only to attempt to balance the subject matter, but also to ascertain opinions from the male point of view. Many German males who had once been members of the Hitler Youth as boys are now well into their old age, yet they are surprisingly willing to give their opinions and share their reminiscences, provided you use a diplomatic approach to certain issues.

The Hitlerjugend

Martin Schröder and his younger sister, Melissa, joined the Hitler Youth as soon as it became compulsory for all children. I was keen to speak with him to discover his views as a young male in the boys' Hitler Youth movement, and what he felt were the attitudes toward sex and sexuality at that time, and if he had any reminiscences that he might be willing to share with me for this work. I had never spoken to Martin previously, as I had done with his sister, Melissa. I had asked if he would like to add anything to the project I was working on at the time, but he declined. Later, perhaps emboldened by seeing his sister's contribution appear in print, he contacted me through Melissa, agreeing to tell me not only his thoughts, but to share some stories he had never told anyone before, other than his closest friends:

It's all so long ago now that it hardly seems real. Was it all a bad dream, I used to ask myself.

I remember the furore when Hitler came to power; there was a real sense of hope, pride and belonging, so when it became law that you had to join the Hitler Youth, me and my sister Melissa enrolled. If you didn't enrol you were the odd ones out and you stood out to a point where people questioned you about why you hadn't joined. You risked being bullied by the other kids at school and things too. Refusing to join could also be detrimental to your long-term educational prospects. When I joined my local boys' Hitler Youth organization, from that very moment we were treated as soldiers; yes, it was what you would call today a very macho institution, all about strength, virility and aggression. Weaklings were quickly weeded out of the gang and if you failed to fit in it could be very hard for you indeed.

The Hitler Youth nurtured the natural aggression prevalent in the psyche of young males. They told us we were the masters of our nation, the Jews were our deadliest enemies, that we were the fighters and the warriors and that our women were the ones responsible for looking after our interests in the home. They made it clear to us that females did not possess the same physical attributes of males, that we were stronger in both body and mind, that only males could rule the Reich. We were told the women were there for our comfort, to feed us, keep us strong and provide a stable home and to have and look after our children. As males we would not be concerned with any duties in the home, other than to further the gene pool, as they put it.

At home we never showed our mother disrespect, we would never have dared; our father was the alpha male and as the man of the house, he was the boss. As a young lad in the Hitler Youth the sexual side of girls was never a thought inside my mind. We were around the girls on many occasions, especially at the Nazi Party rallies where we paraded together. It was only when I was around 14 or 15 years old that I, like many of the other boys, began to take a serious interest in girls. There were girls we fancied and sometimes we had to fight over them [he laughs] if more than one boy desired the same girl. Fighting was nothing out of the normal for us, as in the Hitler Youth we had to carry out mock battles where real fist fighting ensued, in order to subdue and beat the other side. The winning side stole the other's flag – that was the reward. Afterwards some boys would be left with bleeding noses, cut lips and blackened eyes. Some were even knocked unconscious from the blows they received. No one dared shed any tears as it was considered weak to cry in the Hitler Youth. So, fighting over a girl was just another fight for us, it was nothing. If another boy liked the same girl you were after, you would beat him up and he would try to do the same to you, sometimes.

I only ever fought over three girls but that was enough for me. With the third one I came off worst and he gave me a right hiding, as he was bigger than I was. Afterwards I got up, brushed myself down and he walked off with the girl. He had won, it was as simple as that, no messing around; it was a courtship of violence which mirrored the whole of the German Reich itself. Were my sexual attitudes toward girls warped by the teachings of the regime? Maybe, as a young man, for a while I may have been influenced and of the opinion that our females were there just for us, merely as servants, both sexually and domestically. This was not unique to the Nazi regime and it was something which women experienced in other societies of the world back then. When we boys got together on our Hitler Youth camps, particularly in our teens, the subject of sex arose frequently in our conversation. Some of it was purely boasting, some of it amusing, whilst some was totally serious.

One of the lads, a 16-year-old, told me that having sex with a virgin is painful, as they are naturally frigid and 'tight' as he put it. He said if you are not careful your foreskin can split, and people will think you are a Jew. He laughed as he said this, yet he was being serious. Hearing this made me apprehensive of the mere thought of having sex with a girl. It was something that stuck in my mind right up to the point where I met my first serious girlfriend, the daughter of a Heidelberg greengrocer. Her name was Heidi, and she was the same age as me, 15. I always felt slightly intimidated by her as she was blonde, blue-eyed and very pretty. I didn't think she was the kind of girl who might be interested in me. I didn't consider myself handsome, or good looking enough, for the likes of her. We got talking and discovered that we shared similar interests in music and literature. We hit it off, as they say these days, and she became my girlfriend. I began to go out with her into the town on many occasions over the course of our two-year romance. Her father made it perfectly clear to me that he wanted no naughty business with his daughter. He told me that if I were to get his daughter pregnant, he would do something terrible to me. I acknowledged his request and shook his hand, knowing full well that he was serious about removing my testicles with his bare hands.

We used to go to the local cinema, often meeting up with friends on the way, so time alone was infrequent and rare. When in the cinema all you did was maybe hold hands or put your arm around the girl; you couldn't do much more with all the other people around you. As me and Heidi became more relaxed with each other we would take walks in the countryside. We used to catch the tram out of the city and walk into the woods and along the river. It was very nice.

It was beside the river one summer's day that Heidi said to me, 'Are you afraid of my father?' I told her, 'No, of course I'm not. Why?' She then asked, 'Then for heaven's sake Martin, why don't you ever kiss me or touch me?' The truth was I had little experience of kissing but I could not admit that to her, though I think she knew anyway [he laughs]. Being the one to make that first move was not so easy. I was afraid she would be offended if I made efforts to touch her. For the first time in my youth, as a strong, aggressive prospective German male, I was alone with this lovely young girl and I was dithering like a child.

Heidi owned the initiative as I stood there like a rabbit in the headlights. She put her arms around me, so we were face to face. Then it happened. Within seconds her mouth was firmly attached to mine. She then pulled away and said to me, 'Martin, you are kissing me like you would kiss your grandmother, not how you should kiss your girlfriend. Let me show you the right way to do it.' So, I stand there, and she tells me, 'Close your eyes and open your mouth.' I followed her instructions and it was totally different this time. It felt very nice indeed; this was proper kissing. There was one slight problem though. How she was kissing me stirred the pit of my stomach and as much as I tried not to think about it, I could feel myself becoming excited. My legs began to tremble, I admit I thought I was going to faint. She pulled back and with a concerned expression upon her face asked, 'Martin, Martin, are you alright, are you okay?' To make matters worse the rather embarrassing bulge in my shorts seemed to be getting bigger and bigger, which no attempt to conceal proved successful. I couldn't pull away from her, so pretty soon she was going to notice it, which of course she did. She casually looked down and putting her hands over her mouth she began to giggle at me, and she said, 'Oh, my god, Martin, look at you.' I could feel myself turning red through the humiliation of it all, yet before I could say another word, she smiled, grabbed my hand and dragged me off under the shade of some trees. She wasted no time in pushing me down and then pulling my shorts and underwear down around my ankles. She then lay down by my side and told me, 'I will sort this out; it will be nice, I promise you.' So, there she was, on her side in front of me, kissing me while giving me what was my first wank, as they call it [he laughs]. For once I wasn't flying solo as we used to say [he laughs]. All the time I was quite nervous but the feeling of her soft hand around me and her beautiful mouth against mine really was very overpowering. I'm afraid as much as I didn't want to make a mess on her dress, I had no control at all, and it was like a fire hose being switched on for a few seconds. The feeling was difficult to describe. I had heard other boys in our Hitler Youth group saying it felt as if birds were flying out of your arsehole, or butterflies were flying from your dick.

It was the first time a girl had ever done this to me, and I definitely wanted more of it after that first time. Afterwards Heidi quickly ran down to the stream to make sure that she had removed all trace of the sticky mess with some water. When she had washed it off, she came back as I was pulling up my underwear and buttoning up my shorts. The whole experience had been wonderful, and it made me feel somewhat more mature, like a man. I had just had sex, it wasn't full sex, but it was a milestone of my youth, I was no longer in the 'wanking club' and I was no longer an innocent boy anymore [he laughs)]

Today such a thing would be laughable and quite the norm, but back then that was quite something to brag about though I would never have dared to do that, out of respect for Heidi and for fear of invoking the wrath of her father. I'm pretty sure he would have given me a hiding had he found out. It is a known fact that all boys begin to masturbate when they come of age, it is perfectly natural, but to have a girl do it for you, that was much nicer [he laughs].

After that we would go to the fields and woodlands often throughout the summertime when it was warm. Heidi taught me the virtues of how to pleasure her using my fingers. It took a bit of practice to get it right, but she enjoyed this immensely. I remember the first time we made love; we were both 16 by then. I remember it very well as most people remember their first time, don't, they? We had to do our Saturday sports with the Hitler Youth first, this was always in the afternoon on a Saturday. We both loathed it as neither of us was particularly athletic, but we had no choice, so once we were released from our Hitler Youth duties, off we went and caught the tram out of Heidelberg as usual and headed off into the fields. We didn't waste much time in getting down to things; my confidence had grown, and I knew what I had to do. Strangely there were no nerves, we were both relaxed and I took charge of this beautiful blonde girl, taking off her shorts and vest before hastily removing my own. She assisted in the fiddly task of securing a contraceptive on me then I was soon on her like a rabbit, and it was a marvellous feeling. All the time we were looking into each other's eyes – yes, it was very erotic. We did it a few times after but soon my time with Heidi was up. I had to report for military training as all boys had to do, back then. She ended our little romance and I suspected she had begun to fall for another boy in our town. It hurt at the time, as my male pride was dented but I was not going to cry over her as I felt that things had run their course. I had learned much from her and the fact that we are not as macho as we like to think we are.

In the Hitler Youth I kept these views to myself; it wasn't considered manly to praise womanhood or look upon them as equals back then. I was always respectful of the girls I went out with; I never pushed them to do anything they were not sure about, and I was happy for them to take the lead when it came to the sexual act. I did not return home to Heidelberg until mid-1946. I saw Heidi a few times and we would say hello but that was it. Soon after I met the beautiful woman who would become my wife, so I was sowing no more wild oats after that.

While discussing the subject of male sex and sexuality in the Hitler Youth, Martin also recalled how boys suspected of being homosexual were treated:

> The other boys used to say, 'There is something about him, or there is something wrong about those two.' This is quite common in young men though and I didn't really take much notice of it back then. There certainly were homosexuals in the Hitler Youth. If discovered, they would be beaten up and thrown out. A friend from Berlin suspected that one of the leaders of his group was a homosexual – he and another lad were always going off together. This leader was such a fine example, with a string of sporting awards and certificates to his credit, that if the Hitler Youth authorities had known he was a gay, were they prepared to turn a blind eye to it? I think that is generally how it was right up to the leadership itself. It was a case of do it, but don't get caught doing it.

Peter Rickmann recalled, as a 15-year-old member of the Hannover Hitler Youth:

> We had *'Blond Arsches'* [blond arse – slang for a homosexual] in the Hitler Youth, as we did everywhere else in our society. There were two kinds of homosexuals; the ones that fitted in and those that didn't or couldn't. Many people in Third Reich society despised homosexuals. They were looked upon as sexual deviants, ungodly if you like; they were on the same level as Jews in the view of many Nazi citizens. I remember my father talking about homosexuals when I was about 13 years old. I had never heard the term being used much before and naturally I was curious as to what it all meant. So I asked my father, and in response to my curiosity my father replied, 'A homosexual is a male who desires the flesh of other males, rather than females. What they do is quite unacceptable. It is filthy and unclean and is not permissible in any civilized society, especially ours.'
>
> I understood the basics of his interpretation, but my sister, Erica, who was 17, told me in a much more explicit manner what her idea of a homosexual was. She said, 'A homosexual is a boy or man who will bend you over and fuck you up your arse when you are sleeping. He is a man who likes kissing and fucking other men.' [She then went on to say]: 'There are boys who like fucking other boys up their arse and boys who like being fucked by other boys.'

Arnulf Scriba, another former member of the Hitler Youth, recalled:

We boys did so much together besides our Hitler Youth activities. When we washed, we stripped off all our clothes and could see one another naked. In the summer, we often wore only our boots and shorts, on camps especially. There were always one or two boys who were suspected of liking other boys, but it could not be proved so they were not treated any differently to the rest of us. As far as we were concerned, they were Germans, and they were good comrades and as long as they kept their hands to themselves there would be no problems. If there had been anything going on, then they kept it well away from the Hitler Youth, which was advisable.

The Streifendienst or SRD, which was our own internal Hitler Youth police force, kept a keen eye on us all. Sex was not discouraged but it was made very clear that homosexuality could never be tolerated and that males could only ever have sex with, and cohabitate with, females; that was it, no other way. Yet I heard stories from other boys I knew who told me that homosexuals had been discovered and kicked out of their Hitler Youth unit. What became of them after that I cannot say; at the time I wasn't really interested. As a young lad you stuck to the rules and did as you were told and had to think what they told you to think.

I recall outsiders within our group, boys who for one reason or another just didn't fit in. One was a fat boy and the one day he was squatting down and some of the other boys pointed at his arse, saying, 'Look at that.' It was weird. This boy had what looked like scabs which went down to the crack of his arse – anal eczema. And the others shouted and laughed. The Hitler Youth was no environment for what would be termed a poor specimen.

Kurt Ulling has fond memories of his teenage years in the Hitler Youth:

It was great, I enjoyed it all very much, apart from the political lessons which I found boring. I was a normal red-blooded male and I liked girls. We didn't have mixed Hitler Youth camps: boys and girls had separate camps. There were of course times where we mixed, and we would get talking to girls and arrange to meet them. The sexual interest was mutual, we were curious about sex and keen to try it, so we did. I remember a girl I met from Brandenburg; she was coming up for her eighteenth birthday while I was 16. She was certainly not shy and taught me a lot in the short time I had with her. Our parents would not have been happy with either of us had they found out. Parents preferred their boys and girls to be at least engaged to be married before having sex, so that it didn't come across as being promiscuous. Our girls were certainly not promiscuous; in my younger days I had only had full sex with three or four of them before I settled down and married my wife. Couples back then were expected to marry younger and start having children while they were at their physical peak. Lecturers in the Hitler Youth would say to us a girl is in her biological prime from 18 to 24 and the same for a male, and after that it is all downhill. But that is what we were taught as young people in the Hitler Youth.

To bring this particular chapter to a close I felt Dana Busch's final statement was very apt. Summing up things she said:

> The Nazi elite were getting up to far worse than anything we could have been accused of doing. They were screwing all over the place. Some of them liked young boys, others young girls, but it was okay for them to do it as they were in charge. It was all so fucking hypocritical, as if they themselves were writing the *The Martial Law Manual for Making Love*.

Chapter 9

Orgasm and the Nazis

It can be said that the industrial revolution, now known as the First Industrial Revolution, was the transition to new manufacturing processes in Europe and the United States in the period from 1760 to 1840. However, it was only from the early 1900s that electrical appliances became more commonplace in the average home. Whilst male masturbation devices came somewhat later, the electrically powered vibrator for females was said to have been the fifth home electronic device ever invented for commercial use, preceding the electric vacuum cleaner by some nine years, the electric iron by ten, and the electric frying pan by more than a decade. It gave all women of the developed world the choice to climax in the privacy of their own homes. If the statistics above are indeed one hundred per cent correct, as is stated through official documentation on the subject, then they certainly represent the priorities of consumers at the time. However, there were more clinical applications than recreational uses for electric vibrators, particularly in western societies of the nineteenth and early twentieth centuries.

It was generally accepted that through these times certain mild behavioural problems, particularly in young males, could be resolved through the simple act of masturbation – any pent-up stress or aggression could easily be relieved through this natural process of self-stimulation. Yet, there were some physicians who argued that not all females who masturbated themselves achieved orgasm, which made them 'stroppy' and 'disobedient'. As preposterous as this sounds to us today, it was the clinical theory of the time and a proposed remedy for what was termed 'hysteria', particularly in young females who were yet to bare children. It was an absurd clinical response to nothing more complex than the greatly misunderstood physiological changes and conditions that applied to male and female puberty.

In Nazi Germany the administrative bodies of both the Nazi girls' and women's leagues wanted sexually athletic females who could produce large families rapidly. Rather unsurprisingly, some figures within the clinical branches of the SS, where all manner of diabolical racial, physical and sexual theories were emerging, were of the belief that females who could reach orgasm at will stood a far better chance of conception than females who couldn't. This warped theory could only ever serve as a rubber stamp for unscrupulous individuals in the Nazi medical profession to abuse girls and women, under the sanction of the SS and the Nazi state.

Anyone who perhaps is still thinking at this stage that this work is somehow not serious, or that it is an attempt at titillation, should be appalled by the following material. It does not make for pleasant reading and whilst it did not surprise me in the least, it did leave me feeling slightly nauseous.

As a 17-year-old girl Ruth Götze reported to the Ravensbrück camp located in the Fürstenburg area of Havel, in July 1943. Her role in the camp was as a junior overseer of the female inmates. She related these two particularly disturbing events which she witnessed at the camp, and which she believes have never been documented before:

> Most of my duties revolved around the escorting of small parties of female labourers at the camp. I reported to other areas of the camp, including the medical section. It was while performing duties at the medical section that I twice witnessed some form of sexually orientated experiments being carried out on two of the Jewish female inmates there, both of whom subsequently died. I remember seeing this comatose female inmate, her wrists restrained by large leather straps to one of the examination tables. Her legs were held up and apart in a contraption which looked like part of a gynaecological chair. At first sight I thought the woman was in labour or they were trying to induce labour or something, I didn't know. I was curious and as I looked closer, I could see that there was some kind of plug inserted in her vagina, the plug having several electrical wires attached to it. Before I could see what they were going to do, I was asked to leave, as I was only meant to be handing over an envelope of papers for one of the camp doctors.
>
> A couple of days later in the same medical room I saw another inmate, clearly pregnant and fully conscious. She was restrained in the same manner with her legs held up and apart in these leg braces with electrical wiring coming from her vagina. One of the doctors had a small panel with three black coloured dials on it. He was moving them in clockwise and counter-clockwise directions and as he did so the woman's body convulsed violently. Every time the dials were turned, she would arch up her back

from the table. I could see the straps which bound her wrists, the skin beneath was turning white every time she convulsed. It looked as if the straps would break open from the force. Every time the dials were turned, she convulsed and moaned out. I was unsure as to whether her moans were of pleasure or pain, but I should imagine they were more out of pain than anything else.

What they were doing this for I never found out; all sorts of things like this went on and we were not always privy to the information gained from it all, so I don't know. As a woman myself I did feel sympathy for the victim of this experiment, I thought to myself, 'What if that was me, how would I feel?' The only thing I discovered is that two dead bodies came out of that medical room in the days after what I saw. The doctors had killed them by whatever it was they were doing to them.

The above 'experiments', if you can refer to them as such, were not perpetrated exclusively by Nazi doctors in the camp system of the Third Reich. Similar experiments, which were nothing more than vile sexual abuse, were carried out on unfortunate human beings who had been labelled as criminally insane, or mentally deranged, in many of the institutions that were termed 'lunatic asylums' in the western world. The above-mentioned Nazi experiments which Ruth Götze inadvertently witnessed may well have been a sadistic and perverted twist on the clinical theory developed by Plato, the Greek philosopher, for the cure of what he called 'hysteria' in females. In my opinion, female hysteria has never existed; it was an invented affliction and the means of treating it reflected the derogatory attitude possessed by males toward womanhood in general.

As with parts of the western world in the nineteenth and early half of the twentieth centuries, there were physicians in Nazi Germany who, in the pursuit of Aryanism, agreed with Plato's theory, that 'hysteria' in young women was caused by the affliction of a 'childless womb' In Greek times it was believed that a childless womb could move throughout the body, damaging organs and causing a variety of health issues. A number of ancient remedies for female hysteria included marriage, heterosexual intercourse, becoming pregnant, the application of scented oils to the female genitals and external vaginal stimulation. It was believed that these treatments would anchor the uterus back in its proper location in the pelvis. Of course, these so-called theories were quite ridiculous and

Prostitutes peddle their trade in a street in Weimar Germany. (*Source unknown*)

A representation of the hedonistic gay scene of the Weimar clubs. (*Weimar History Archive*)

Young women enjoyed a high degree of sexual freedom in the pre-Nazi era of the 1920s. (*Source unknown*)

Tula Kubiczek on the left, her sister Anna in the centre, and a friend. (*Courtesy B. Werner*)

Johannes Kriebst poses for a photograph in happier times. (*J. Kriebst collection*)

Katharina Briedenich on the right, recalled how sex became manualized under the Nazis. (*Courtesy K. Briedenich*)

Ursula Vogel at age 14 in her BDM uniform. (*Courtesy H. Vogel*)

Ursula Vogel relaxing in the Vogels' garden in Heidelberg, in the summer of 1947. (*Courtesy H. Vogel*)

Arnold Hilbe in Hitler Youth uniform. (*Courtesy A. Hilbe*)

Balthasar Kramer experienced sexual abuse in the Church. (*Courtesy Kramer family*)

An 18-year-old Engela Losch plays ball in a lake with a friend. (*Courtesy A. W. Muller*)

Hildegard Kustin. (*Courtesy H. Waller*)

Alessa Goberg questions: 'Were we the sexy side of National Socialism?' (*A. Goberg*)

Dressing up appealed to both sexes, often as a prelude to sex itself. (*Source unknown*)

Olga Kirschener in the BDM. (*Courtesy O. Kirschener*)

Chief of the SS Heinrich Himmler was obsessed with astrology, the occult and satanism. (*Deutscher History Archive*)

A Jewish synagogue which has been turned into a brothel for German soldiers. (*Wikimedia Commons*)

German soldiers enjoy the hospitality inside a French brothel in the Second World War (*Wikimedia Commons*)

German soldiers at the entrance to one of their military brothels. (*Wikimedia Commons*)

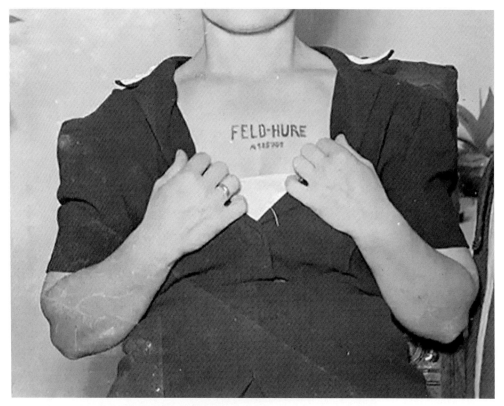

A woman bearing the tattoo *Feldhure* which translates to 'Field whore'. (*Wikimedia Commons*)

Chief of the Luftwaffe, the ever-ebullient Mr Toad of the Third Reich giving a speech. Göring battled not only drug addiction but impotence and obesity. (*Source unknown*)

Propaganda Minister Goebbels possessed the sexual appetite of a rabbit and was a notorious serial adulterer. (*Source unknown*)

Für Goebbels ist der Krieg nicht schlimm,
Er sucht den Star für einen Film.
Indem die andern sich verbluten,
Beschäftigt er sich mit den Nutten.

Allied propaganda openly ridiculed the legendary appetite for women and sex displayed by Goebbels. (*WW2 History Archive*)

Reinhard Heydrich. A hard-on for death and cruelty. (*Wikipedia Commons*)

Heydrich's death mask. Even in death he appeared to smirk. (*Wikimedia Commons*)

Heydrich pictured with his wife, Lena, and one of their young sons. (*Wikimedia Commons*)

Hitler's deputy, Martin Bormann, the man who had sex with his boots on. (*Wikimedia Commons*)

Bormann with Hitler. Bormann never strayed far from his master's side. (*Wikimedia Commons*)

A typical *Lebensborn* facility in Nazi Germany, in the Second World War. (*WW2 History Archive*)

Oskar Dirlewanger, one of the most sexually depraved men of the Third Reich. (*Wikimedia Commons*)

Jörg as a boy plays at a swimming pool in a private complex in Argentina.
(*Withheld by request*)

A family snapshot taken by Jörg's father in Germany before leaving for South America.
(*Withheld by request*)

Martha Hutter. (*M. Hutter*)

Klara Busch, the mother of Ingrid Pittman. Klara became good friends with Margarete Braun, the youngest sister of Eva Braun. (*Courtesy I. Pittmann*)

A fine example of Allied anti-Hitler propaganda originating from the Allied Special Operations Executive (SOE). (*Source Propaganda in Warfare*)

Margarete Braun with her husband, Hermann Fegelein, who would later be executed for desertion by order from Hitler. (*Wikimedia Commons*)

Eva Braun. Often described as the bird in a gilded cage. (*Braun family archive*)

Even artistic photography can be construed as exuding sex appeal. (*Courtesy C. Wootton*)

Sexual fetishism existed in Nazi Germany as it does in the twenty-first century. (*Withheld by request*)

Arnold Hibzicht's photo of Erica. (*A. Hibzicht*)

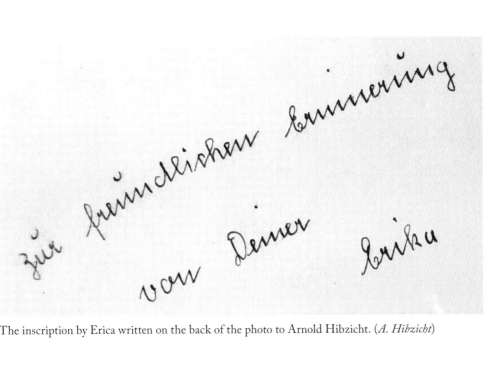

The inscription by Erica written on the back of the photo to Arnold Hibzicht. (*A. Hibzicht*)

Luise Butschelle with Heinz.
(*Courtesy L. Frisch*)

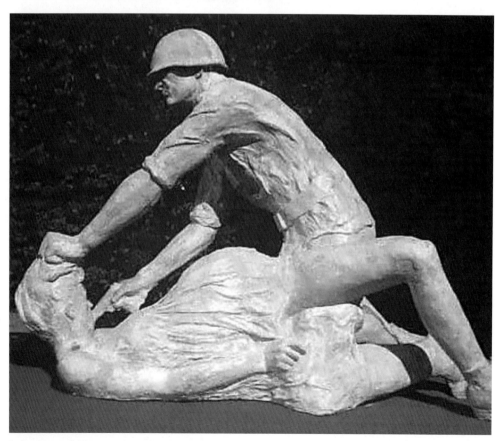

Jerzy Szumczyk's controversial sculpture *Komm Frau* ('Come here woman'), depicting a Russian soldier raping a pregnant German woman. (*Hyperallergic.com*)

humiliating to any of the women forced to undergo such procedures, despite the fact that external vaginal stimulation was not regarded as a sexual act, unlike that of penetration of the vagina. Either way, there is evidence to suggest that some clinicians in the Nazi SS supported these ancient abuses as a cure for behavioural problems in young German women. At the time it seemed there was a general consensus of opinion among men, and not just those in Nazi Germany, that if a girl had begun to menstruate then she was ready for sexual intercourse and motherhood. As abhorrent a theory as this undoubtedly is, it is still perfectly acceptable in many cultures around the world today, and it looks doubtful as to whether they will ever change.

The following account was related to me by Theresa Moelle:

My problem was as a child and young teenager due to my early childhood and the abuse I had suffered in the religious order I had been placed within from birth, I had so much aggression within me. This was not considered natural at all for a girl. I often argued and fought a lot with my adoptive parents, and I know I put them through hell at times, but they never gave up on me. My adoptive mother once took me to see a doctor to find out what was wrong with me. The so-called doctor took me into his care and decided I was suffering from what they called hysteria. This of course was rubbish and when he suggested I was held down while they forcibly attempted to make me orgasm by manipulating me, my adoptive mother took my hand and dragged me out of there and never took me to a doctor again. In their view I was becoming a young woman, my body was preparing for motherhood and as a result my body was 'craving *kinder*' [children] as they put it. As I was still too young to marry and have children, I should be stimulated to relieve the building tensions of my own biology and then I would be fine.

It was quack medicine and a ticket for unscrupulous dirty old men to abuse young girls. Yes, stroppy teenaged girls could be carted off to the doctor who would look at them, then gleefully announce, 'She needs to be with child, her body is ready for reproduction and motherhood. Yes, of course, we can help her through this.' Then they would suggest genital stimulation, the girl would be taken into a room out of the mother's sight, where the process would be carried out. There were more than just a few of these doctors with the Nazi mentality on biology, who were of the opinion that without having regular orgasms either through their own or other means, that teenage girls became hysterical, almost as bitches do in heat. It was their belief that the act of reproduction naturally calmed them down, making them more rational human beings.

Does it sound that unbelievable to you or others? There were many things thought to have been fiction or propaganda that are now common knowledge. The practice of forced genital stimulation among young females in particular was far more widespread than many today are aware; if you read up on it you will see. Thankfully, I never saw that doctor again and my parents thought his assumptions were diabolical. They just put up with my terrible behaviour until I came to my senses and settled down, which of course I did very soon after the war as I met and married my husband, Raif. I married young but for me it worked, and I had a very happy marriage and wonderful children and great grandchildren.

Chapter 10

Dressing Up

Within the context of their own intimacy, couples of all ages, all around the world, have taken part in the act of dressing up, or role play, with the introduction of various fetishes into their sex lives. This of course is down to individual tastes and preferences. There are individual fetishes for all forms of sexual activity. Apart from the aesthetics of a pretty face, there are those who have an affinity for selective physiological traits in their partner, such as lips, eyes, breasts, legs, bottom or feet. Of course, within the context of normal relationships with couples, regardless of their sexual preferences, there is nothing at all wrong with this. In Nazi Germany role play may have entered the sex lives of German couples or the girlfriends of German soldiers inadvertently. There are countless stories of the French girlfriends of German soldiers in France dressing up in their boyfriend's military uniforms as a prelude to the sexual act, but what of Germany itself?

Olga Kirschener recalled the antics of her elder brother whenever he came home on leave during the first two years of the war:

> My brother was with a Flak unit; he was in charge of the sighting of enemy aircraft, quite an important task as he used to enjoy telling us lesser mortals in the family. He was issued with a very smart uniform, and he was never short of girlfriends; he was always sneaking them into the house whenever mother and father were away. In fact, the only stick in the mud regarding his activities was me, of course. He would have to bribe me either to stay downstairs whenever he had a girlfriend round or to go out to my friends for an hour or two. He would offer me cigarettes and I would say, 'Don't be so silly, I don't smoke.' Then it would be sweets and I would retort, 'But I'm not a baby you know.' In the end he would become annoyed and slightly frustrated at the prospect of me ruining his little plans. He would throw several banknotes at me and shout, 'Oh for god's sake Olga! You are costing me a fucking fortune!' I would just say, 'Well, what am I expected to do for two hours?' 'Just go and buy something or go and see a film, I don't care, just get out!' was his reply [she laughs]. So, yes, I would go out

for a couple of hours and in many senses, I was a good sister, I didn't tell mother or father even though I knew they'd go raving mad if they knew their home was being used as my brother's cat house.

Did I know what was going on? Well yes, of course I did, I was young, but I wasn't totally stupid you know [she laughs]. I knew he was having sex with her while I was out of the house. I remember one day in November my brother had been on leave for a week and he wanted me out of the house as usual for a couple of hours on a chilly, dark and wet Monday evening. I agreed, with the usual act of bribery having been accomplished, and I left the house at 6 pm, telling him I would return at 8 pm after visiting my friend's house nearby. As it happened, my friend's father came home rather the worse for wear; a row soon broke out in the kitchen between my friend's mother and father, and I was forced to leave earlier than expected. I walked the block twice in the cold, dark and drizzle, and thought to myself, 'To hell with this, I am going back home.' I walked down the alleyway at the back of the houses, which were all in a terraced row, and I crept through the back door of our house. I went and sat down in our living room and picked up a book and started reading. I could hear all sorts of funny noises coming from upstairs and I sat there and laughed to myself.

As with most youngsters I soon became bored and wanted to go into my bedroom and lie down and read my book. I walked up the stairs and as I arrived on the landing I was greeted by a half-naked girl with smudged lipstick and a cigarette hanging out of her mouth. I scared her and she shrieked in fright. I recall her saying, 'Who the fuck are you? What are you doing here?' Before I could reply my brother rushed out of his bedroom wearing only underpants, demanding to know what I was doing here as it was not time yet. I replied sarcastically, 'Well, I'm going into my room, you do what you like.' What I noticed, before he grabbed her hand and dragged her back into his bedroom, was that she had my brother's uniform jacket and side hat on, and nothing else, at all. I think my presence must have proved a passion killer as it remained very quiet in my brother's room until I heard the door open, footsteps going downstairs and the front door open and shut.

My brother burst into my room, grabbed me and shook me, shouting at me, 'What did you do that for? Now she has fucking gone.' I shouted for him to get off me and our argument was suddenly brought to an abrupt halt as the front door opened and mother and father walked in.

Luckily, they did not hear us arguing, or they would have wanted to know what was going on; my father would have certainly beat it out of me if he thought it necessary. As it happened, they heard nothing and suspected nothing. Later on, my brother came into my room and told me he was so sorry for shouting at me and shaking me, as he didn't mean it. In fact, he said to me, 'Thank god you came home when you did, as mother and father would have caught us.' I told him it was okay and not to worry about it, then I asked him, 'Why was that girl wearing your uniform?' He laughed, then rolled his eyes and told me, 'Olga, you will find those answers for yourself someday.'

Selina Mayer, an 18-year-old from Spandau, Berlin, joined the Deutsches Rotes Kreus (German Red Cross) and remembered the sexual allure of her uniform:

> My first proper boyfriend, who was two years older than me, used to love my uniform. I was aware of the age-old attraction that some men felt toward a female in uniform, particularly nurses, and how yes, they might appeal sexually to them. Sex was something that did not really give me that much pleasure at first, I have to admit that. It was my first proper boyfriend who suggested I put on my DRK uniform one evening, not all of it, just the blouse part. I wasn't too sure about it at first; things like that back then could be construed as being kinky and I didn't like that idea at all, but he persuaded me and so in the end I gave in. It is stupid I know, but wearing just the blouse and the little hat we had to wear, suddenly turned our sex life into a hurricane of lust. The fact that I became so much more desirable to him, wearing part of what was just my work uniform, gave me a tremendous sense of power over him. I could get him to do anything I wanted while wearing this uniform during sex; that was not a bad thing, in my mind. He would tell me to do this and do that, but I always had control over him, something I would not have had during normal lovemaking. It was as if by wearing my DRK blouse I suddenly became this superior being. I enjoyed it and yet at the same time I found it quite amusing.

Jens Ehrler, who had joined the Wehrmacht in mid-1940, recalled an old flame of his in the days of his youth, when he was just 19 years of age:

> All the women loved a uniform, for some it was a great turn on. The girlfriend I had at the time was more an on-off relationship. We had been friends since infant school, so we could pick up with one another without any complexity or having to go through lengthy courtships or anything. If we wanted sex, we would go with one another primarily for sex; it was as simple as that, no messing around. She would insist I take off all my clothing but once naked I should put my jacket back on. I found wearing the jacket in this manner a little itchy and uncomfortable, yet it turned

her into a nymphomaniac; there was nothing she wouldn't do to me while wearing the jacket and we would have sex two or three times in one go. In many ways it was much like the German girls we would see wearing various uniforms – they did look, what you would say, very sexy, and the girls thought much the same about us no doubt.

My only problem with this was the horror of getting semen on my uniform jacket or damaging it, I could get into a lot of trouble in that way from my superiors.

I had another girl interested in me later on, and as part of our sexual routine she would often put on my army jacket. She looked better than me wearing it and I would often say to her, 'Put these shoes on too,' and she would put these high heel shoes on which she had stashed away in what she called her secret cupboard. She would get down on all fours on the bed and tell me to take her from behind … as that is how she liked it best. It was all very erotic and exciting for a young man, and I would pull the jacket off her so as I could see all of her body. It was lovely and the sex was some of the best I have ever had. We all did some crazy things as we were young and there was a war on, we might not live long and had to make the best of that time we had left; that was our thinking. I knew another girl who told me her boyfriend enjoyed wearing her bra and knickers as a part of their sexual foreplay. I remember her saying, 'We used to do it the normal way, but this way gives us the best fucking ever.' I told her I was not interested in wearing women's clothes, no matter how good the sex might be. I was never kinky, but I was definitely adventurous and never afraid to try new ways of having sex or the girl wearing uniforms and things.

Gunther Reissner recalled his time in the Hitler Youth and his first girlfriend, Hilde, a member of the girls' Hitler Youth, the BDM, who lived in the same town:

I had seen Hilde on a number of occasions although she had not grown up in our town; her family moved in when I was 13 years old and she was 14. We never even really spoke that much but if we met, we would politely acknowledge each other as we all did at that time; we were the new community, the future of Germany and as such we got on with both boys and girls. We used to have sports activities with our respective Hitler Youth organizations of a Saturday afternoon, and this was always known as sports afternoon. Although we did our activities separately from the girls, afterwards we often walked home in groups with the girls, as some of the boys walked with their sisters back home. I noticed Hilde was walking alone as she had no brothers or sisters so I decided I would walk with her.

After that we became good friends but did not become close until just before my sixteenth birthday.

In that short space of time, I began to look at Hilde differently: yes, the sight of her in her white sports vest and black shorts was enough to put all kinds of feelings in me. As we began meeting to go for walks and things, inevitably we became more attracted and intimate with each other and started off sharing kisses, proper kisses as she called them. I learned everything about sex from Hilde, as she certainly knew more about it than I did. She knew she was an attractive girl and when we had time alone, she would always wear those black shorts and vest and nothing else. To be honest, it was all very innocent at first and she was more than happy to just pleasure me by hand without expecting me to return the favour. Yes, it was immensely pleasurable for me and as we built up trust we went further until we were having sex as much as we could. Our only problem was getting birth control, rubbers as you call them in England. You could not just walk into a shop and buy them like that in our small community, as someone would always tell your mother, 'Your boy came in earlier to buy contraceptives.' Then you'd have your parents moaning and scolding you for being a dirty young rascal and things.

Me and Hilde often got our contraceptives from Wehrmacht rations. Most of the soldiers didn't use them and if you had the balls to go and ask them, they would often throw you a packet; it was worth the embarrassment and your parents would never get to find out. Hilde liked me wearing my uniform too and she once tried the shirt on, but I preferred her in her own attire. Did her uniform make her any sexier than she was, is the question. In some ways, yes, as you could admire her body more as the vest was quite tight fitting so you could see how big her chest was and her shape, if she had a flat stomach and things. Her shorts revealed her well-defined hips and her long legs which I also liked very much. So, yes, in a sense her sports kit did make her look sexy because you could see her body better than in the other uniform she sometimes wore, or her normal dresses.

Dressing up as a precursor to having sex was great if you could find the privacy to do it; that was the issue. It was not always easy for teenagers in Germany at that time to find somewhere comfortable away from prying eyes where they could enjoy sex. In the summer we often went out into the woods, but you couldn't do that in the middle of winter or if you lived in one of the cities. But yes, as I grew older and me and Hilde grew apart and then went off on separate paths through life, I appreciated how certain clothes could affect one's sexual behaviour and enrich the experience itself. After all, who doesn't dress up these days and do far more than we ever did? It's nothing, now is it?

Kirsten Eckermann recalls the antics of an 'influential local family' with party affiliations, who lived in her borough:

> Every New Year's Eve up until 1944 they would host these private parties. This was nothing out of the normal as everyone still tried to celebrate New Year, even with the war going on. I heard from a reliable source that the parties these people were indulging in were not all as they seemed. They would dress up usually in Roman- or ancient Greek-style attire, partake in all manner of merriment, fuelled by alcohol, and when the kids were put to bed the whole thing became one huge Dionysian orgy. Of course, this became public knowledge once due to a drunken party guest stumbling out of the house; he staggered across the lawn at the rear of the house and was found staggering around the village wearing nothing other than a loincloth and a fake crown of thorns. It was said that he was smothered in love bites and lipstick.
>
> The authorities picked him up yet instead of being arrested he was taken back to the house and put to bed. People with influence, or Nazi Party membership, could get away with these things, while anyone else would be put in jail for the night and heavily fined. They were not the only ones who used a fancy dress party as a means of engaging in sex orgies. Whispers were widespread across the Reich of the capers of Joseph Goebbels who, it was said, at least privately enjoyed dressing up, even in female clothing, for sex. How true this is … who knows for sure? But there can be no smoke without fire, as they say.
>
> There is nothing in the rule book which states that it is wrong for couples or groups of people to dress up in the attire of some ancient psychopath, such as Caligula or Genghis Khan, but dressing up like that purely to heighten the sexual responses just seems weird to me. I've never done it as such things have never interested me, and I am pretty sure had my husband came home to find me dressed up as some Greek or Roman nymph waiting on the couch for him, he would probably have laughed his socks off or thought I'd gone mad [she laughs].

Chapter 11

The Pleasure and the Pain

When one becomes familiar with the modus operandi of the Nazi state, one should not be too shocked or even surprised by the fact that the pursuit of pain and suffering often continued into the domestic arena of the home, as if it were a seemingly normal component of romance, love and marriage.

Helena Voight, a young Austrian girl from Vienna, was much like many young girls of her generation. Obliged to marry when she reached the aged of 18, she married a young Austrian-German named Bernhard Falck, whose family had strong Germanic roots and were among those who supported the German takeover of Austria. With the Germans in control of the country the populace was expected to express where their loyalties lay. Helena had been married for three years when the Germans invaded. Her husband was a farm labourer who had been happy working in that occupation until he was convinced by other young men that the work he was doing was the kind of work that slaves, negroes, Jews and Slavs should be doing, not a German. The ordinary life that Helena had enjoyed up until the German invasion was short lived. Bernhard Falck felt obliged, more through peer pressure than anything else, to join the German military who had convinced him that greater rewards lay with loyalty to the Third Reich than any romantic patriotism for defeated nations. Helena recorded in her personal writings:

> It is like the happy, contented man Bernhard once was has disappeared. He left home and was away for six weeks, returning in this hideous uniform bearing a skull and crossbones. I never questioned at the time what he was doing or where he was going, but I knew the uniform he was wearing was that of the General SS or Allgemeine SS as they called it. These units were tasked with the running of the camps. I wasn't happy with this at all, but if one complained you were told to shut up and not to question. All he would talk about was the training and the camaraderie of his unit and how nice it felt to finally 'have a job with a purpose,' as he eloquently put it. I would

sit and let him ramble on and pretend to be happy for him. I loved him but sensed the dynamic of our relationship was changing in some inexplicable way that I was unable to coherently interpret.

It was only months later when he would return home to spend a little time with me that I realized he was no longer the same person, not the contented young man that I had married. His behaviour became increasingly bizarre, especially where sex was concerned. We had always enjoyed what I felt was a normal sex life' it was nothing special but we both enjoyed it. When I say things became bizarre, I mean in the sense that our lovemaking had evolved to the point where if I was not completely submissive to him, if he was not inflicting pain upon me, he could not gain any pleasure from it. He would restrain me painfully during lovemaking, at first using his own force and then by means of tying me down. At first it was with two ties with which my wrists would be bound to the frame of the bed. If I protested, he would physically force me to do it; there was no choice. Then he would insist I do the same to him. I received no pleasure from this at all. I would be told to kneel down, and I would be spanked while being penetrated, which again was painful and humiliating, as the blows were not light but often full force which left reddened welts across the skin.

This only stopped when he told me, 'The next time I return home I will bring a whip with me – that should be good.' When he left I went to my parents, who were furious with me and berated me in their own words for 'deserting a good husband'. I asked my mother to speak with her in private, and then I showed her the wounds that had been inflicted upon my body by 'my dear husband'. When my mother saw them, she burst into tears. She then had the unenviable task of telling my father the truth, which was embarrassing and humiliating again.

When father was told, he was very angry and shouted, 'I will kill him if he dares to come round here.' I was sent away to my grandmother's house, as my parents were worried that the authorities might intervene in matters. I basically had to hide away there until the end of the war. Even at the war's end I did not return to Vienna, as the Russians were there and I was advised to remain where I was, that things were better under the British than the Russians. In my eagerness to gain legal separation from Falck, I even reported him to the Allied authorities who had already arrested and questioned him but had released him without charge. They had no evidence that he had committed any crime. I divorced him and never saw or heard anything from him again.

The explanation for the sudden changes in his sexual preferences I can only assume were due to his work. He was in the camp system ... in that system cruelty, pain and suffering were everywhere. The brief times he was home it felt as if he wanted to bring that same cruelty and suffering back home with him.

Helena's story is by no means unique, yet the infliction of pain during lovemaking was not entirely a male sexual fetish, as Max Woessel confirmed in an interview during the writing of a previous work. Max Woessel was 18 years of age and had hoped to join the Luftwaffe in February 1943. Due to poor academia, Max had failed aircrew selection on three occasions, which he admitted caused him much anger and frustration. It was then he was offered training with the Flak arm of the Luftwaffe, which he accepted. In his own words he was 'only a lowly munitions handler' but the smart uniform gave him a great sense of personal pride. It also proved an instant aphrodisiac for the girls in his local town on off-duty periods. Max recalled:

> The girls loved the uniforms we in the military wore. It didn't matter that my job in action stations was to pass the ammunition to the gunners. I was in the Luftwaffe and they didn't think much beyond that [he laughs]. I had plenty of money in my pocket when I went out and it was easy to get the best girls. I recall the one girl, whose name I will not mention here, was the one and only young girl I have ever tried to avoid. That may sound silly but believe me there were good reasons for doing so. She was 22 years of age, tall and very good-looking, a brunette who liked to show off her long legs, which were of course very nice. I had been warned off this girl by some of the other boys who had nicknamed her 'The Lioness'. Looking at her I couldn't understand the logic behind either the warning or the nickname.
>
> As I drank my beer, I became less interested in all the warnings and gossip and more in this girl herself. I was intrigued by her, and I kept looking at her which, of course, she noticed, and began to reciprocate my interest in her. We struck up a conversation and she explained she was married, yet her husband was away and would probably remain so for the duration of hostilities. It was an obvious cue that she was available and when she asked me to walk her back home, of course I obliged, in slight disbelief of my luck. Yes, I wanted to fuck her, and I wasn't concerned about her nickname either. She had dangled a carrot before my eyes, and no, I couldn't resist finding out what she was like sexually. We left the bar where my other pals were blind drunk by this time, and most were asleep with their heads resting on their arms. Only one of them managed wearily to look up and attempted to call me back, but off we went.

I was excited at the prospect of maybe having sex with this girl, yes, I was just like any other red-blooded male: I liked having sex and the better looking the girl the better the sex in my opinion, totally natural. As soon as we had walked through the front door of her house, she leapt upon me and began pulling off my clothing. I thought to myself, 'This is great!' We kissed and groped each other as we slithered up the stairs toward the bedroom. Once on the bed I helped remove her remaining clothing and she pushed me down and began kissing my inner thighs. I lay back as she worked her way slowly up my thighs with her tongue. It was all very erotic until she took hold of my dick with her hand and began pushing down really hard on it. That hurt and I yelped out and said, 'That hurts! What are you doing?' She replied bluntly, 'What do you think I am trying to do? I want your knob out,' to which I replied, 'I am not circumcised you can't do that.' The oral sex she began to give me was rough and painful. I cautioned her several times but she took no notice at all. In fact, she slapped me hard and told me to shut up and obey her. She seemed to be getting off on the fact that she was inflicting pain on me.

Deciding that she was now ready, she mounted me and began thrusting so violently it hurt; she dug her nails into me as she ran her fingers down my chest. I tried to take her hands and pull them away but she grabbed my wrists and held me down, and as hard as I tried, I could not get her off me. She bit my neck so hard that it hurt, I could feel her teeth actually digging into me. As we kissed, I could taste a mixture of stale tobacco, alcohol and blood. Her thrusting was so violent it really hurt and although she was brought to orgasm several times. I remained unfulfilled due to the pain she had inflicted throughout. She rolled off and again headed down below and I thought, 'Oh no, not again,' yet this time she was very sweet and careful and within a few minutes I had blown my load into her throat. She gulped it all down, something that surprised me as many of the girls who had given me the pleasure of oral sex in the past had almost vomited and spat it out.

After I had finished, she sat up, lit herself a cigarette and smiled at me. I asked to use her bathroom and after showing me the way I shut the door behind me and looked into the mirror hanging over the washbasin. My neck was an unbroken mass of red and purple blotches, it looked terrible, my chest was covered in scratches some of which were oozing a small amount of blood where the skin had been broken by her nails. I flushed the toilet, returned to the bedroom where we shared a drink together and I made my excuses to leave. She begged me to stay for the night, but I was determined that what I had experienced was quite enough for that one night.

To all intents and purposes Max had found himself ensnared in an emotional entanglement that was every bit as sharp as barbed wire. Yet here was a young man who went back for more, who could not resist the proverbial playing with fire, the caressing of flames which at some point were going to burn him badly. Max continues:

> That first bout of lovemaking with the girl, whilst not exactly pleasurable in the normal context, had me mesmerized. I felt that with time I could somehow harness her, reign her in, make her the girl next door and everything would be rosy. That was my young immature perception of love and romance, through the mentality of a teenager. I was effectively playing with fire as (a) she was older than me and (b) she was married, and nothing could ever become of this dalliance of ours. My colleagues tried to warn me I was heading for an emotional implosion but being young I could not be persuaded to see sense.
>
> In reality, all that me and that young woman were sharing was a penchant for casual sex. We met again some two weeks later in the same bar. As we drank beer, she bragged that there were few girls who could say that they had lost their virginity in the back of a Kübelwagen like she had done, or had been walked around naked on a Persian rug while wearing a dog collar and chain. She went into lucid detail on how her husband enjoyed doing this to her. He would demand that she beg like a dog before kneeling on all fours where he would then penetrate her anally as he did not wish for her to fall pregnant. She must have noticed the slightly horrified expression on my face as she went on to explain, 'Yes, my husband talks to me as we fuck; he says, "You are my bitch and I am the hound."' She also explained how strangling her almost to the point where she would pass out was one of the greatest thrills and whipping and kicking were good too, if done properly. As the last dregs of beer were sipped from our glasses it was clear she had no intention of staying here any longer; she was obviously aroused enough from our conversation and was eager for us to go back to her house for sex.
>
> When we arrived at her house the routine was much a repeat of the last time: she tore at my clothes and at the same time we began climbing the stairs toward the bedroom. This time she leapt upon the bed with all the athleticism of a cat … and assumed a kneeling position with her head resting on her arms, demanding that I lick her arse. I told her I wasn't so sure I wanted to do that, which I wasn't as the prospect of having my mouth around even a beautiful woman's arse just repulsed me slightly, yet at the same time I wanted to try it. Then she barked, 'For fuck's sake, I bathed before I came out. I am perfectly clean, now get on with it.' So, I did as she asked as she continued to give instructions on what I had to

do. It was actually not that bad; there was no unpleasant taste or smell as much as I can remember, the only smell being that of the musky scent of her vagina. It was not long before she was writhing around and droplets of warm sticky vaginal fluid began to moisten the bedsheet. I felt her whole body stiffen as if about to go into some form of shock, then shudder violently as she let out a series of loud gasps before collapsing onto her side. As she lay there panting, she smiled and then said, 'Now it's time to play the rusty trombone.' 'What on earth do you mean the rusty trombone?' I inquired? She then got up and while standing behind me she motioned for me to bend over. I felt her dropping down to her knees and wondered what the hell she was going to do now. I then felt her tongue probing about my arse, and it sent shivers of delight through me in a way I had never expected, then she grabbed my dick and began to wank me – this is why it is called playing the rusty trombone, as the act resembles just that, someone playing a trombone.

The orgasm I experienced in that one method of sex was the best I had ever had; it was very intense indeed and afterwards I felt completely shot and tired. The fact we had both drunk a lot of alcohol beforehand didn't help and the rampant sex we had just enjoyed had been very intense, despite there being no intercourse. We fell asleep naked on the bed, and I awoke in the morning to her performing fellatio on me. I almost pissed in her mouth as I told her I was bursting to go to the bathroom. She let me go and when I returned, she continued performing fellatio until I was ready. The sex was rough again, only this time I wrestled with her for advantage. I held her down and she grunted through gritted teeth 'Fuck me' several times. I was aware that I was thrusting into her very hard and that it might be hurting her, but I didn't care; she was enjoying it and so was I. It seemed the more we fought with each other the more intense the feelings were sexually; yes, it was wonderful. In the end I was doing to her exactly what her husband had probably done with her many times. I had her legs over my shoulders bent as far back as I could get them and I thrust into her very hard, I felt her fingernails digging into the cheeks of my arse. Her face was reddened and moistened with sweat by the time I ejaculated in her. She lay there gasping for breath. I rolled off her and we just lay there for a few minutes, fighting to get our breath back. We had a bath and I helped her change the sheets on the bed before we had coffee and some breakfast.

I left around midday and before I left, we arranged to meet up the following week. On this occasion which was the last time I would ever meet with her I called at her house as it was a Wednesday evening, and I was due to go on duty at midnight, so I was forbidden to drink any alcohol. It was on this occasion that she demanded I have anal sex with her. I had misgivings about this as I felt it was dirty and that only a homosexual did this. In fact, I told her that and she snarled, 'That is rubbish! Lots of married couples do it!' I agreed, more out of curiosity than anything else, to do this with her. The foreplay seemed more hurried this time, yet her biting and scratching were still the same, like being thrown into a sack with an angry cat. We would fight and I would grab her by the wrists to stop her digging her nails into my skin which she found very amusing. I threw her down on the bed and was about to enter her when she insisted I stop. At that point she got up and went into the bathroom and came back with some soap in her hands. She grabbed my dick and smothered it with the soap. I was looking at her puzzled when she beat me to the point by telling me, 'This is for lubrication!' She then turned around assuming the kneeling position and resting her head on her hands. She then mumbled, 'Give it to me; fuck me in my arse.' I admit I was not that keen on doing this at all, I had always thought sticking anything up anyone's arse was dirty. I had visions of withdrawing from her covered in faecal matter and blood. Yet, I was too aroused and so I lined up like an archer about to loose an arrow and slowly pushed. How do I describe it? It was incredibly tight, and I thought for a moment that I would not be able to do it to her this way. Once the glans had passed through that incredibly tight muscular ring that forms the sphincter, it was not too bad. The stimulation gained was greater than vaginal penetration, yet it felt somewhat different. She enjoyed it greatly and that was that. When I withdrew from her, I recall how it seemed that her anus remained open, gaping if you like. It's peculiar but I remember thinking how it reminded me of a whale's blowhole. I washed myself thoroughly afterwards then I had to leave to go on duty.

I had hoped to see her again, but I heard some news, some days later that the woman's husband had returned home with a battle injury, so that was that. She told me it would not be possible to meet up with me anymore, that it had just been a bit of fun and that her husband needed her now more than ever. I was disappointed as the sex I had enjoyed with this woman, The Lioness, had been some of the most intense and adventurous of my youth. I have to admit I do look back on her with a degree of fondness.

Max admitted to still having erotic almost semi-nightmares about this girl even when he married some years later. Max was not forthcoming as to the content of these dreams, but happily dismissed them while shaking his head and smiling. She had already served him the half-cooked corpse of what the reality may have been on hot coals with her heavily sweetened menstrual blood. Did 'The Lioness' reappear through the dark veil of time itself, presenting herself as a frightening spectre with fangs and urticating vaginal hairs? Did she stand over his prostate form, a cutthroat razor in her left hand as he lay convulsing in a pool of his own testicular blood? Or did she appear as some kind of Frankenstein's bride with Tesla rays blasting from her vaginal orifice? Either way she remains locked safely away within the psychological black box of the minds of all who encountered her in the physical sense.

Diana Roehoff recalls a conversation with her best friend, who revealed that her boyfriend had begun to insist on tying her up during sex. The friend explained that the tying up was not a problem, yet on the last occasion her boyfriend had tied her up and began tickling the soles of her feet with a feather. She screamed for him to stop as if you are ticklish, it is not the least bit funny or pleasurable. I asked Diana what happened afterwards, and she told me:

> Well, after he untied her, she hit him over the head with a rolling pin and threw him out of her house and threw his things out after him. She never wanted anything to do with him again and always referred to him as 'The Pervert'. I told her that maybe she had overreacted as I didn't think tickling was that bad, but maybe he should not have tied her up. She didn't agree in the slightest and even considered some form of vengeance ... She told me, 'Well, I could always lure him back, take him to bed and maybe massage warm oil mixed with powdered glass into his foreskin. Now that would teach him, wouldn't it?' It struck me as being a bit of a weird suggestion, but I laughed it off. Whether she was serious or just joking, I couldn't tell.

Sadomasochism is far from a recent sexual practice and there is ample historical evidence to suggest that it has been practised for centuries and was relatively common, particularly throughout the medieval period. It resides on what many consider to be the darker aspects of the sexual fetish spectrum. Numerous factual and fictitious works have been written on the subject, two of the most notable being *The 120 Days of Sodom*, written in 1785 by Comte Donatien Alphonse François de Sade, better known as the Marquis de Sade, and *Venus in Furs*, written in 1869 by Leopold von Sacher-Masoch, a semi-autobiographical account which caused outrage in Sacher-Masoch's home city of Lemburg and which has been subject to frequent bans ever since.

It is believed that the surnames of these two authors is where the term sadomasochism originated. Whatever its origins, the word sadomasochism relates to the sexual practice of erotic release from the infliction of pain, either by one's own hand or by a sexual partner. Degrees of severity in the types of pain inflicted vary considerably from case to case. Generally, a degree of control is retained by the masochist during the act and he or she will often cease what they are doing prior to any serious injury being inflicted. Sadomasochism has been practised by couples regardless of their sexual orientation and has taken place in the highest echelons of society all over the world. Some of the more bizarre cases documented include the insertion of needles into the perineum (the space between the testicles and anus, also known as the 'gooch') and the rubbing of genitals with sandpaper.

Anilingus (the sexual stimulation of the anus by the tongue or mouth), as mentioned in the above narrative relating to The Lioness, is another practice of sexual stimulation that dates back centuries. In its historical context anilingus was used as a form of punishment, usually for prisoners. The use of anilingus in the Thirty Years' War in Germany (1618–48) was described by Von Grimmelshausen in *Simplicius Simplicissimus*, written in 1668. In this work it is referred to as 'arse licking', and the term survives today to describe a person who is overly respectful or helpful to someone in authority, or obsequious. In some prison systems anilingus is one of the ways in which a male prisoner can be made to pay his dues to another.

However, anilingus has only recently become commonly acceptable as a sexual practice, largely as a result of the internet and the parallel emergence of online hardcore pornography, and its ease of availability to the masses. Today, anilingus, the practice of a sexual partner stimulating the anus of the other by means of his or her lips, tongue or teeth has been labelled in slang terms as 'rimming', 'rim job', 'eating arse', or 'tossing the salad'. The anus possesses a relatively high proportion of nerve endings and is today considered an erogenous zone, depending of course on your own personal view.

In fact, the term anilingus first entered the English language in 1899 through F. J. Rebman's translation of Edition 10 of *Psychopathia Sexualis*, the literary work by sexologist Richard von Krafft-Ebing, first published in 1886. Anilingus can be performed in a variety of positions, utilizing different techniques to stimulate the anus, including kissing or licking; it may also involve the tongue moving around the edge of the anus or up and down the insides of the cheeks of the buttocks and in and out the anus itself.

What is fully understood today, which may not have been decades ago, are the potential health risks associated with the practice of anilingus. The primary risk with this sexual practice, even if the person receiving it has washed thoroughly, is the risk of oral contact with faecal matter. Diseases which can be transmitted from oral contact with human faeces are shigellosis (bacillary dysentery), hepatitis A, B and C, poliomyelitis, human papillomavirus (HPV) and herpes simplex virus (HSV). There is also the risk of parasitic infection such as intestinal parasites, including chlamydia, gastroenteritis, conjunctivitis, gonorrhoea, lymphogranuloma venereum and other sexual diseases. As with any oral sexual activity clinicians also believe there is a strong link between oral sex and some types of throat cancer. Surprisingly it is believed that the human immunodeficiency *virus* (HIV), which causes Acquired Immune Deficiency Syndrome (AIDS), is not easily transmitted through anilingus.

Anal sex is another controversial sexual practice, the origins of which go back centuries. In some ancient cultures anal penetration, or sodomy, was carried out as a punishment, and not just as a means of a woman avoiding unwanted pregnancy. In warfare of both the ancient and modern world there have been recorded cases of vanquished enemy males and females being subjected to the pain and humiliation of anal rape, including cases as recent as the Vietnam War. Anal sex was always traditionally an act associated purely with homosexuality, yet today there are many heterosexual couples who practise what was once an illegal activity, punishable in many countries by imprisonment.

In the Third Reich homosexuals were condemned to death if discovered, yet some married German couples admitted having at least tried this method of sex at some point in their marriages, particularly early on when the use of condoms became boring, yet pregnancy still had to be avoided. One of the prerequisites for indulging in anal intercourse is ensuring the bowel is empty prior to penetration if one is to avoid expected effluent such as 'bum gravy'; the other is a suitable means of lubrication, for obvious reasons. In ancient times, long before Vaseline and KY Jelly made lubrication easier, many different items (often those which were easily and readily accessible) were used as lubricants. These included olive oil, various animal fats and soap. Elements within the Third Reich hierarchy were also partial to this method of sex, despite its association with homosexuality, something the Nazis viewed as totally abhorrent. Again, this contradictory attitude was reinforced by the belief that having anal sex with a woman was somehow okay.

Today, this subject provokes a variety of reactions; there are those for anal sex and those against it. Obvious concerns, apart from the risk of internal injury, are the fact that certain diseases can be contracted from anal intercourse. AIDS is one such example. It was conveniently labelled as the 'Gay Plague' back in the 1980s when the first cases began to appear around the world. A few high-profile deaths caused by this disease prompted an urgent television advertising campaign which warned people, 'Don't die of ignorance!' While AIDS is no longer the death sentence it was when it first emerged, it has not yet been eradicated. Today a plethora of drugs and medications effectively manage the symptoms of the disease and its effects upon the body.

Those who practise anal intercourse also run the risk of contracting Anal Intraepithelial Neoplasia (AIN) which is caused by the Human Papilloma Virus (HPV). This is basically a form of cancer that develops in the anus, primarily as a result of anal penetration. Most people will contract HPV at some point, but their immune systems rid their bodies of the HPV infection before it can cause any problems. However, a small number of these HPV infections will lead to cancer developing in the body.

It is not the intent of this work to lecture the reader on what he or she should or should not do. It's your life and I am merely pointing out some of the facts associated with a sexual practice which goes back centuries, spans many cultures, and which was not, by any means, something unique to the Third Reich or the members of its sexually active society. Personally, I cannot see how anyone could gain pleasure from such a practice, but then the 'don't knock it until you've tried it' brigade might advise to the contrary. It's a free world and each to his or her own preferred consensual activities in the privacy of their own bedrooms.

Sexual and/or genital torture has also been recorded as sadomasochistic behaviour, yet from research it would appear it was rarely pursued in the everyday home of the Third Reich. Many people with whom I have talked over the years, particularly on sexual subjects, have largely had no experience of this dark area of human sexual perversion.

Yet it was prevalent in the concentration camps, usually as a form of punishment meted out to the unfortunate inmates. Among the entire catalogue of abuses suffered by those interned in the concentration camps, sexual torture rates amongst the most abhorrent. Jewish inmates were usually the primary victims selected for this type of punishment, which included sexual abuse using sticks, knives, or heated objects, purely for sadistic rather than sexual gratification. In many of the concentration camps male inmates were subject to beatings where their testicles were struck with sticks or clubs, poked with knives or bayonets and even burned with cigarette lighters or other hot objects, and sodomized with sticks. Female inmates often had sticks or other implements inserted into their bodies, and it seems that one of the favourite methods of torture, applied by the most sadistic and depraved of female concentration camp guards such as Irma Greese, was burning the nipples of female inmates with cigarette lighters. Most of the victims who were subjected to these disgusting practices, and who survived the war, were so traumatized by their experiences they would never talk about them.

Two such victims, one female and one male, did come forward in an attempt to reveal what they went through at the hands of sexually sadistic camp guards at the Ravensbrück and Buchenwald concentration camps, yet in the end they just could not talk about it. It is these poor souls I feel for most. After the passing of all these years they are still suffering the physical and psychological effects of the damage inflicted on them during their incarceration, in what can only be described as hellholes of the worst possible kind.

Chapter 12

The Antichrist's Astrologer

It is not the aim of this work suddenly to plunge those readers who have remained with me, up to this point, into a confusing miasma of uncorroborated narrative, which at some later stage may be construed as some form of convenient literary padding. Many myths surround the subject of the Nazis and the occult – this is quite clear – but what is not entirely clear is the subject of sex in the Nazis' own occult rituals. Were there consensual or non-consensual ritual abuses and if so, how widespread was this? I have found that formulating a lengthy analysis of this sub-generic issue regarding the Nazis and the practice of sorcery was difficult. A considerable amount has been written on the Nazis and the occult but virtually nothing on any sexual practices which may (or may not) have been involved. Without doubt there were those in the Nazi leadership who were fascinated with astrology, satanism and the occult in general. As most occult practices endorse at least some form of ritual sexual activity, can one be sure that the Third Reich was any different?

Heinrich Luipold Himmler, born 7 October 1900 in Munich, Bavaria, had a long association with Nazism and rose rapidly through the ranks of National Socialism to become one of the most powerful personalities in the party, second only to the Führer himself. Himmler's rise to prominence was indeed aided by Adolf Hitler who regarded Himmler amongst his closest advocates. Most of us are aware who Heinrich Himmler was and the duties he carried out in this role as the Reichsführer of the SS. A virulent antisemitic and racist, Himmler was also one of the main protagonists of the Holocaust.

Himmler became fascinated by astrology, clairvoyance and satanism, and was convinced that the three separate entities could be utilized toward a singular goal of predicting certain future events. In turn, this could be militarily beneficial to the Nazis and their propaganda machine. Karl Ernst Krafft, a Swiss astrologer and clairvoyant, is reputed to have predicted that a man born on Hitler's birth date, 20 April 1889, would rise to power as Germany's leader, and there would be assassination attempts which would ultimately fail. Generally, astrologers and clairvoyants were persecuted under the Nazis but Krafft soon found himself in the embrace of the Third Reich's elite.

It is true that Krafft made some very accurate predictions regarding certain events which would later occur in the Second World War, so much so even the British intelligence services became spooked that the Nazi war effort was somehow under the guidance of some mystical power. The British attempted to employ their own astrology experts in a bid to counter this unseen force possessed by the Nazis. An astrologer employed by the British, Louis De Wohl, was soon quietly sidelined due to a lack of faith in his actual ability to garner any knowledge of Krafft's work. A rather ominous warning among Krafft's predictions was his alert to the Nazis that, for them to emerge victorious in the war, they must effectively win the war by the year 1943.

Of course, 1943 was a year which would become pivotal in the later defeat and destruction of Nazi Germany. Despite all the technical innovations being made in weaponry, such as the V-1 and V-2 rocketry, the new jet-powered fighter and bomber aircraft, which had begun to enter service late in the war, the Nazis still believed that, if harnessed, some higher power could be called upon to bring destruction to the Allies and victory for Hitler and Nazi Germany. These were romantic notions with no plausible foundation whatsoever. There was no spiritual power which could suddenly be summoned to destroy the Allied forces bearing down upon Germany. What the Nazis required at this time was considerably more manpower than they had, together with greater numbers of tanks and aircraft. Nazi Germany would be defeated through the Allied war production facilities, not some otherworldly power which certain prominent Nazis were convinced existed. As a result, certain occult rituals and ceremonies were performed throughout Germany, from the big cities to the sleepy rural villages, in some vain hope of summoning the destruction of Germany's enemies.

One might ask at this point: what possible links with sex can be found within the context of this subject? The answer is quite simple: sex, satanism and the occult are more or less entwined and wherever related rituals are performed, traditionally some form of sexual activity also takes place. Ancient Greece used beautiful young girls as oracles to predict future events, and it seems that young women were used in occult rituals enacted by the Nazis, in particular the SS who viewed themselves as the vanguard of Aryan Germanic culture. This area of Third Reich history is very shady and little factual information exists regarding Nazi occult or satanic practices, including rites involving sexual intercourse or other sexual activities.

A man capable of shining some light on this dark area of the Third Reich was an American-German known to me only as Jörg. Jörg's father had served in the ranks of the SS and had held a brief appointment on Adolf Hitler's personal guard. During the course of a video conversation with Jörg he showed me his father's awards, SS identity book, and an extensive family album showing Jörg with his father in what he called their Southern American community. I wanted to see if there was any truth in the rumours of even the most obscure satanic or other occult rituals having been performed in Nazi Germany, which involved sexual activity of any kind. I was told that if anyone knew about this, Jörg did. Before our video conversation took place, I was warned there could be no photography or recording equipment present; only a pen and paper would be permitted, and this should remain in view at all times throughout the conversation. In all my years of research I have never encountered a more bizarre situation, yet all research has to begin somewhere, and this was as good a place as any, for a book of this kind.

On the subject of Nazi occult or satanic rituals Jörg explained:

> Himmler was not always directly involved as there were many independent rituals that took place around the German countryside in the war. Himmler gave his blessing for these rituals to take place and said those involved in conducting these rituals should not be interfered with by anybody. Himmler had a very deep fascination with astrology, and clairvoyance and satanism in some respects, and shared the view that if greater unseen powers could be harnessed then they might be used as a weapon against the Allies. It was as simple as that. It mattered not to Himmler the spiritual allegiances of these powers which participants in the rituals were intent on invoking, whether they were good or evil; this didn't matter to Himmler.
>
> Now to the point which we are talking about here. You are asking me, basically, did sexual activity take place at any of these rituals as is commonly found, particularly with satanic rituals? My father told me he

had witnessed many rituals where the SS elite attempted to appeal to the unseen forces. My father was nothing more than a torchbearer forming a circle of light around an altar upon which a young female lay, in what he thought at the time was a drug-induced state. She wore a white gown and was obviously naked beneath this gown. From what I remember my father telling me, the girl was baptized with chicken's blood on her forehead, in the form of an inverted crucifix. A ceremonial blade was placed in a cup containing what looked like wine. The point of the weapon, which was decorated with the SS insignia, was dipped in this cup and then held over the girl's mouth so the liquid could drip off it onto her lips. There was what he termed 'a consummation of the passage of spirits' chant, before some male wearing a mask constructed of twigs, leaves, grasses and two of what he thought were goat's horns, entered the ceremony.

At that point my father and the other torchbearers present were asked to turn their backs and focus on the forces present in the fields, rivers, lakes and trees of our land and focus on the destruction of the Allies, and for the death of British Prime Minister Winston Churchill to occur. My father told me it was obvious that whoever was wearing the mask had sex with the girl, as part of the ceremony. Who he was and who she was he didn't know as he was never told, and he was sworn to secrecy as part of his SS oath of allegiance.

Himmler certainly was a participant in rituals held at Wewelsburg Castle which was considered the spiritual and cultural epicentre of the SS and its ideology. In my father's words Himmler saw himself as the self-appointed high priest of the spiritual embodiment of the SS, its supreme spiritual being in physical incarnation if you like. In this context it is possible that Himmler himself indulged in ritual sexual activity. It was known that Himmler was having an affair with his secretary as were most of the males in the various offices of the Third Reich.

How do I know? That is easy; my father told me that everyone knew what was going on regarding sexual affairs, yet within the SS it remained largely a secret. So long as these affairs did not become too much in the way of public knowledge, Hitler wasn't too worried. My father was not present at every SS ritual, of which there were many. Participants were chosen very carefully; normally only high-ranking officers of the highest level were permitted to take part in or witness the rituals. Sex often forms part of ritualistic ceremonies as it has done over the centuries. Performing sex acts during rituals often serves to promote virility, fertility and power. Those females chosen to be on the receiving end, far from being the proverbial virgins snatched from their beds in the middle of the night, were often volunteers who felt they were fulfilling an honour to the state. It probably never occurred to them that they were just there to be sexually exploited.

It is likely that there were many young girls, particularly from the Hitler Youth, who gave their services willingly to these SS rituals. Why am I telling you this? That is quite simple. I am not bound by such allegiances or silence, my father died years ago and as far as I am concerned there is little harm in revealing what I was told, to you today. It doesn't really matter anymore, does it? My father was not prone to making up stories; if he caught us telling lies as children, he would thrash our hides for us. He hated liars more than anything, so I am very comfortable telling you all that I know, even though on this subject it is not very much.

This was by no means the first time I had heard of young females being used sexually in bizarre rituals, particularly in quiet rural villages of Nazi Germany. Most of those who were involved in these rituals were quietly viewed as crackpots by many of the locals, as Kirsten Eckermann explains:

There was this strong undercurrent, like we were pawns in some alternative religious philosophy at the time. As in many countries Germany had its traditional celebrations particularly in the rural regions where the seasons were celebrated, harvest time in particular. There would be ceremonies at night under torchlight to thank the spirits of the land for the bounty received; as the night went on people would be drinking and the next thing the drinking would lead to them fucking each other and so on. This was not frowned upon and was accepted as a ritualistic activity.

It's quite easy to see where the line was crossed into devil worship and other crazy things. People still had a great fear of witchcraft, black magic, demons and werewolves back then. I sometimes heard whispers of things that went on, but as I had not seen them with my own eyes, I could not prove that some of these things had actually happened or whether it was just people assuming things, so I cast them aside. Now I am not so sure; young women were used in many ways under the Nazis. It's not difficult for me to believe that some were abused in the process of performing rituals which it was hoped would bring about the total destruction of Hitler's enemies. In my opinion it was just another way for weird males in the community to pass their time, and in the process pursue their sexual predation of either boys or girls.

Theresa Moelle, a former member of the girls' Hitler Youth who lived in the rural outskirts of Berlin, recalled:

I wouldn't say that Germany at that time had an unnatural obsession with the occult, devil worship and associated sexual ceremonies, but Himmler and his SS certainly did. The SS were dark and satanic and much of their symbolism was derived from the occult. I was always brought up to understand that occult stood for evil, that you didn't get involved with it or you would be selling your soul to the devil himself. As a young girl I never really thought much about it; as I grew older, I did and I began to understand it all.

There were times at the Moelle farm, when I was young, that I would look out of my window and see small torchlit processions heading out across the fields into the woods. I never quite understood what was going on. My adoptive father tried to put a stop to it once but he was told what was happening was government business and nothing to do with him, and to go back inside the house after being threatened with the words, 'You have seen nothing!' Yet, it was his land, for god's sake.

The next day we would sneak up into the woods to see what had been happening and find that the grass had been flattened over a wide area and the remains of a fire were evident. I recall the embers of the fire still being warm. One of the boys I knew told me that some astrological ceremony had taken place there, and some women were apparently naked and had sex with the males among the group. My adoptive parents forbade any of us to go into those woods afterwards, but the torchlight processions and rumours of girls having sex with men in ancient-style costumes continued for some time. The logic behind these things were totally beyond our understanding. What was really going on, who knows? I think it was probably another excuse to abuse or instil fear in people. That said, nothing should surprise anyone where the SS and the party leadership were concerned.

Doris Grunnemayer's father, Dieter, served in the Waffen-SS during the war. Doris recalls some of the things her father told her before his death from cancer in 1989:

I don't really know why he told me what he did; maybe close to death he felt that somehow, he was relinquishing some form of sin or something. He had told me things before but wanted to tell me more while he was still coherent, as he put it. It was shortly after he had been diagnosed with liver cancer, in the spring of 1988, one evening while my mother was not at home that he told me there were things I needed to know, and that he needed to tell someone about it. I knew my father had been in the SS and that it had been classified as a criminal organization, yet my father would not talk about his service that often. Maybe he felt that was the right time, I don't know.

He told me that during the war the SS were involved in all kinds of things, secret ceremonies where they attempted to conjure spirits and things and girls were brought to these ceremonies as oracles, as they had been in ancient Greece. My father said that the girls were often reduced to a state of hypnosis and that one of them made a chilling prediction that Germany would lose the war, Hitler would die, and the nation would be divided as a punishment. How could she have made such an accurate prediction? It frightened those present and the girl in question was taken away and what happened to her afterwards remained a mystery to my father. Everyone present was sworn under threat of death never to speak of it.

My father also told me that Himmler had planned a special SS museum of race and culture which would be built in Berlin, after the war had been won by Germany. It was a proposal Himmler had put to Hitler and Hitler was in verbal agreement; he felt it would be a good idea from a racial science point of view, something with which to educate future Germans. The building was to be a grand construction and some rough drawings were prepared but I don't think this building ever reached the planning phase. Either way the design of the building would most certainly have fallen into the lap of Albert Speer. Hitler loved Speer's architecture, so he would have been the man to design the proposed building.

Himmler proposed to create a gallery where there would be human taxidermy displays of Jews and what Himmler termed as 'the other lesser races' of the world. They would be mounted in the same way as trophy hunters mounted animals they had shot. The human taxidermy gallery would have contained a section devoted to deformity and mental illness, a kind of freak show of death if you like. These displays would also include anatomical specimens of internal organs. It would be a kind of SS-created human natural history exhibit. My father said that specimens of brains, and sexual organs had already been collected, preserved and placed in a special storage facility. My father was one of a team of SS personnel tasked with destroying it all in mid-1944.

He said there were jars and jars of male and female sexual organs all neatly labelled; some of the specimens showed signs of sexual disease and some had been cross-sectioned. There were also glass jars with human brains inside. There was not much at that stage as by 1944 it was clear even to the likes of Himmler that Germany was going to lose the war, so the whole lot – which amounted to some 500 individual specimens – were all destroyed by being burned in pits of gasoline. I was horrified by hearing this, but I wasn't surprised either. I knew my father had been involved in darker areas of the SS and as he neared his own death, he was possessed of a genuine fear that he would go to hell for his association and the things he had been involved with as a young soldier. He even had a local priest visit him and they talked privately, and the priest prayed for my father and offered him absolution.

Himmler was the driving force in all these things, yet there is still much to be revealed about what was really going on and I only wish I could tell you more about it all. I am pretty sure that had Germany won the war, Himmler would have delighted in having lampshades constructed from mongoloid hides and skulls in his private offices; that was the kind of man he was.

Heinrich Himmler, the *Reichsführer* of the SS, hid behind the persona of a devoted father and husband, which he may well have been, but he was also thoroughly evil. Many people who knew him sensed immediately that there was this malevolent side to the man's personality. Theresa Moelle recalls that after the war, whenever Himmler's name was mentioned on the radio, or later on the television, her father Walter would curse and say, 'Oh no! Not again, that antichrist's astrologer.'

Theodore Oest, an acquaintance of Bruno Gesche, was able to shed more light on the Himmler sexual debate. Theodore had remained friends with Gesche until Gesche's death in 1980. Bruno Gesche was a former member of the SS and one who proved a thorn in the side of the feared *Reichsführer* of the SS – Heinrich Himmler. Theodore recalled a conversation he had with Gesche in the winter of 1951 and naturally Gesche's old enemy, Himmler, became the primary topic. Oest explained to me that although it was obvious that much bad blood had existed between Gesche and Himmler, Gesche was by this time something of a recluse and not the kind of man to make up fairytales about his former associates. Gesche recalled during their conversation:

> Himmler, yes he was a ruthless bastard, quite prepared to sacrifice a lamb or two if it meant getting into the Führer's favour, which of course he was. Himmler once derided me for being a drunk. Yes, I may have been a drunk, but I was not a hypocrite like Himmler was. He professed to the nation and to the SS the virtues of being a model German citizen, totally oriented to the German community and way of life, yet Himmler was chasing women all over the place. Everywhere Himmler went he was having sex with women. He undoubtedly promised these women all sorts of things as he had his wicked way with them and it is likely they were flattered by his attention and the power he held, yet these women he had sex with

were merely his whores. His wife was well aware of his philandering ways yet permitted him to sleep with these women. I know that his daughter Gudrun became aware of her father's serial infidelity, going so far as to beg him to spend more time with her and her mother. Gudrun tried to reason with him and questioned her father's moral responsibilities to her and her mother. Himmler always referred to Gudrun as 'Puppi', his pet name for her.

But Himmler didn't care about his daughter's concerns, as he was as perverted as the rest of them. He was addicted to casual sex with women of all ages, just as he was addicted to the pursuit of ultimate power. He hosted these clandestine SS ceremonies where he and others attempted to petition the gods of the ancient world just as the Greeks had done. Sex was a part of all these secret SS ceremonies, and he was there, and he took part and I know this as I have been told by more than one former comrade about it. Himmler really thought of himself as this spiritual being and reaching the top of the SS was his destiny, to be the 'black prince', as I used to call him. He even once told a comrade that one day he would succeed the Führer and be Germany's ultimate and most revered leader of all. Do you know there were rumours that Himmler was responsible for the death of Reinhard Heydrich? Heydrich was the man who proved to be a one-time threat to Himmler's plans to succeed Hitler. When Heydrich was assassinated, it was Himmler who deliberately delayed the best treatment for Heydrich. If Heydrich died there was no other credible opposition to Himmler within the higher echelons of the SS.

I didn't like Himmler and he didn't like me, and we almost came to blows on one occasion. Himmler was a weasel; he would have been no match for me in a fist fight and I could have knocked him out like a boxer would his opponent. Lucky for me Hitler liked me and that kept me from receiving the severest reprimands that Himmler might have otherwise been free to hand out to me. Himmler tried having me assigned to the infamous band of drunks and sexual deviants that comprised the Dirlewanger Brigade of the Waffen-SS, operating in the east. This failed as I knew too much about the Führer's security for me to be possibly caught and interrogated by the Russians, so that fell through. My previous roles in the Führer's bodyguard had been exemplary and even Himmler couldn't take that away from me.

But no, Himmler was no clean-living family man; he fathered two children with his secretary Frau Hedwig Potthast, and there were likely others who were then threatened to keep quiet by members of the SS internal security. You didn't mess with these people, or you just simply disappeared. Hitler was aware of my spats with Himmler so it would have looked very suspicious indeed had I just vanished one night, so maybe that's why Himmler did not order me to be silenced as he did with other lesser individuals who became aware of his sexual antics.

I heard all kinds of things about Himmler, that he once even took part in bestiality. Was it true? Well, there is rarely smoke without fire, is there, and these things began to come out after the war, when Himmler was dead. I had to be very careful what I said about Himmler, as his daughter, Gudrun, was still devoted to her father's memory, and I have received death threats from unknown persons probably associated with her and the neo-Nazi political groups with which she is actively involved and affiliated. She runs a group that aids former SS personnel, but I am certainly not in her good books. She doesn't frighten me, but I have to be careful.

Bruno Gesche was right to have been fearful of Himmler's daughter, Gudrun Burwitz, who remained loyal to her father, defending his reputation at every opportunity, despite the truly overwhelming evidence as to his complicity in the Holocaust. Burwitz actively supported former Waffen-SS soldiers looking to hide from the scrutiny of the postwar authorities. She was a staunch National Socialist and was actively involved in many postwar Nazi political groups, up until her death. Bruno Gesche died in 1980 in Western Germany, while Gudrun Burwitz died in Munich, Bavaria, on 24 May 2018, aged 88. I made two attempts to speak with Burwitz during the course of my research, before her death, yet on both occasions she refused to speak to me.

Chapter 13

Sex on the Side

By mid-1944 young men all over Germany were noticeably absent. Young men of the Hitler Youth were being called up to replace those who had been severely injured or killed in the fighting on the Eastern Front. For those young men, fresh out of the Hitler Youth, who were serving on the Flak batteries in and around German cities, the situation sometimes spawned something of a sexual bonanza, as explained by Walter Gollob, a 17-year-old from Berlin who was called up for duty and served as a crewman on one of the many 8.8cm Flak guns situated around Berlin. Walter recalls:

> It was not a bad posting at all really, as many young men were being sent to the Russian Front as casualties there were horrendous. Yet I would say that our job was at times probably as dangerous as being on the Soviet Front. Sometimes bombs dropped by American aircraft would fall five miles wide of their targets; if one landed on you, it was the end, simple as that. So, we didn't really have it that easy, we were in action a lot of the time both day and night. I was with an 8.8cm Flak unit based in the suburbs of Spandau in Berlin. When action stations were called, my job was to hand the 8.8cm ammunition to the fuze setter who would set the explosive detonators. Between the air attacks we would often see young women whose husbands were away fighting, and they would often stop and make conversation with us. I knew many of the young men with me had already earned their bragging rights where women and sex were concerned. Most of them were already sexually experienced and it was pretty clear to them that I wasn't. I got teased about this from time to time but it was all in jest, as we say now.
>
> On one occasion a group of young women approached us and struck up conversation and one of them, who introduced herself as Maria, made a beeline for me. She asked me things like where I was from, did I have a sweetheart and things like that really. It helped to break up the monotony while waiting to go into action. Maria often came by and stopped to talk with me after that and after a while I became more relaxed about having a pretty young woman showing an interest in me. Maria was 20 years old,

quite tall with dark hair and brown eyes and I have to admit being a bit smitten with her and looking forward to seeing her each day when it was safe to go out walking. Eventually, some weeks passed by, and she asked me if I ever had any time off duty and what I did. So, I told her I often just visited my mother and father, mostly, nothing else. At that she asked if I would like to visit her next time I was off duty, so naturally I told her yes, I would. I asked her where she lived, and she turned and pointed to an apartment block near the park in Spandau, not that far away I remember thinking.

We did get the odd day here and there where we could go off duty to visit our families but on the next occasion I met up with Maria at the park and we enjoyed a stroll and just talked. Maria made it very clear that she loved her husband, but she missed the physical side of having her man with her. I understood what she was saying or rather what she was getting at and told her I that I understood what she was saying. At that she asked me if I would like to go back with her to her apartment and again, I said yes, I would, so off we went. As we entered the apartment block, we walked across a long concourse that led to rows of doors; hers was number 33 and soon we were inside, and I was closing the door behind us, extremely nervous yet excited at what was going to happen.

She wasted no time manoeuvring me toward her bedroom, beckoning me to follow her. As I stood watching her, she began taking off her clothes and I was aware of the growing bulge in my trousers which as hard as I tried, I could not conceal from her. I was amazed by her body; she was physically a very beautiful specimen. Her body had no doubt been honed to perfection as a result of her years with the Bund Deutscher Mädel and she had not had any children as yet. She stood and smiled at me for a moment then asked me, 'Have you ever done anything with a girl before?' I replied honestly that I hadn't, to which she replied, 'Well, the thing is to relax, not to worry and enjoy it.' She then helped me out of my trousers, shirt and underwear and pushed me down onto my back on her bed. She climbed upon me and sat astride and began kissing me, first on the mouth, then my neck, before working her way down my torso, using her lips, tongue and her mouth. I lay back and let her do all the work on this, my first time. I watched as she worked her way down my torso, kissing and licking gently with her tongue until she reached my groin. I felt her take hold of my penis and then slide it between her lips and into her mouth, where she began a gentle up and down rhythm. I watched mesmerized as her head bobbed up and down; she would stop momentarily and flick her tongue over what was soon becoming an exploding volcano. She must have anticipated my oncoming orgasm and stopped for a few minutes before sitting astride me again, taking my penis with her hand and guiding it into her already moistened hole. She began a steady rhythm with her hips which became quicker and quicker. She was the master and I the student. I remember thinking, before a sensation like seagulls flying out of my arse occurred and I experienced my first proper orgasm, without having had to wank. It was wonderful. Afterwards, we both lay on her bed and talked about all kinds of things, I avoided all conversation about the war as we were warned about the danger of spies even though I knew she was no spy.

After some thirty minutes we were both ready to go again, this time I mounted her between her legs face to face but again I didn't last that long, but she told me afterwards that I had given her two wonderful orgasms. When I left her apartment, I felt ten foot tall and as I walked to my parents' house, I thought to myself, 'Well, Walter boy, you are no longer a virgin.' Yes, I finally felt like a man, at last, and not a boy. I met up with Maria on several more occasions after that.

Eventually we had to abandon our association due to the advance of the Red Army and I never saw or heard anything from her again, and I had to forget her. I did think about trying to find her after the war, but it was not easy. I also knew what the Russians had done to any pretty German girls and women they encountered during the fall of Berlin, and I felt that what I might discover might be too upsetting. Of course, I still think of Maria today, otherwise I would not be relating this story to you, now, would I?

Looking back do I feel any guilt for having sex with a woman whose husband was away fighting? The answer is yes, I do now, but back then I didn't really think about it, as most young men didn't.

Ernst Neissau from Essen was a young man aged 21 and served with a searchlight detachment, based around the Ruhr, in early 1945. Having been wounded in Russia the previous year, he had been declared unfit for further duty with the army and had transferred to the Luftwaffe on ground operations. Ernst recalled:

Everyone in the Ruhr was thoroughly miserable at that time, as we had been subject to some of the most intense bombing raids of the war. I recall all these young boys of 15 and 16 arriving from the Hitler Youth; all had been mobilized under the emergency decree. It was madness. There were young women sent to us too, and I struck up a very close friendship with one of them. She was 18 years old and we just got on from the start, clicked with one another, as you might say today.

We went everywhere together when off duty and things began to develop between us: first it was just kissing then we were sneaking off anytime that we could, to make love. We even talked about marriage after the war was over. The problem was, I was already married and the father of a young son. At the time I just didn't care; I had gotten involved and I had really fallen for this girl, even though I had a lovely wife waiting for me back home, which was just a short distance away. It is one of those things I can't explain – I felt I could talk to this girl about anything, we ate, slept, worked and laughed together and yes, I found her most attractive, and I desired her.

The thing was we were both so stupid. I never used birth control with her once and we made love many times. Then she broke the news that she was pregnant, and the child was most definitely mine, as she had never had sex with anyone else. The officer in charge of us had to be told as it could not be kept secret from him for long. He was far from sympathetic and he sent her away back home to her parents and gave me a very lengthy verbal berating for my disgraceful conduct, as he put it. He intended to take things further and have me charged but the war ended before that could be done.

Yes, I returned home to my wife and son but couldn't get this other girl off my mind, as hard as I tried. I knew it was wrong but I made efforts to track her down in the months after the war had ended. When I finally found her a year and a half later, she told me the baby she had given birth to had been given up for adoption and she was sorry, but she could have nothing more to do with me, as her parents forbade her to have any contact with a married man, especially one who had got their daughter into such a mess.

I suppose it was my punishment for having what they called a bit on the side. I had to accept it and go home to my wife and son who knew nothing of this illicit affair. It is an irony really as we separated when my son was 13 years old, and then we divorced, despite both our parents being strictly against it.

Since then, I have remained single; life is less complicated when you live by yourself. You can do as you please and there is no one to hurt but yourself. Do I have regrets about the wartime affair? Yes, I do, but I can't change what has been done; it happened, as it did to many others too, no doubt.

Martha Hutter considered herself happily married despite her husband being away, on the frontline at sea, and the everyday privations brought about by the war. She had never imagined becoming involved with another man. Martha recalled:

I'd never considered myself foolish at all and never imagined that I would become embroiled in an affair with another married man. This was in

1944, I was 23 years of age and my husband had been away for the better part of three years; I had hardly ever seen him yet I was determined that the marriage vows which I had made to him would remain intact during our lengthy separation. My husband was in the Kriegsmarine [the German Navy] and the service at the time was very unpredictable. I never even knew if he would ever return home, but I was determined to wait for him. I had lots of male friends in the town where we lived, which was nothing out of the ordinary – I had as many male friends as I had female friends. I worked as a tram driver and came into contact with lots of people every day; life didn't stop despite the fact there was a war going on.

I became friendly with one of the regular passengers, who was always polite, cordial and cheerful and was a real lift compared to some of the moaning old people whom we often had to deal with. The thing was he was quite a bit older than me, yet things just developed, an attraction of sorts that neither of us was able to resist. He was a widower in his early fifties yet looked better than a lot of men much younger than him. I knew little about him really, but we became very chatty every time we met, and it just happened that he asked me to meet him one afternoon, quite innocent as I thought, and I never expected things to go any further than maybe a chat with a drink. Our town had not suffered greatly from the bombing as there was nothing there worth bombing, which I suppose was a good thing for us. There was a café in a quiet street that still served small amounts of alcoholic drinks; coffee was in short supply and so was tea, so it was mostly Schnapps that we would drink, and I think on this one occasion I had one too many. I agreed to go back with him to his home, I knew what was going to happen even before we got there, and I felt excited at the prospect of seeing whether or not I could resist if he tried to kiss me or anything.

When we arrived at his little house, I was shocked to discover that he had some real coffee. He explained that he saved it for very special occasions such as these. I then asked, 'Why, am I not the only girl you have brought back here then?' He replied, 'My dear Martha, I am far from the habit of bringing women here to my home. I have invited you here because I genuinely like you and I enjoy your company greatly.' I walked around his living room as he brewed the coffee which was served black in tiny little China cups. He brought the coffee in and asked me to sit down, and we talked about our lives, hopes and desires, not that anything was certain anymore as Germany was not doing so well in the war then. He asked about my husband, and it was at that point I became emotional. He consoled me and I don't know why but I ended up kissing him on the lips. For a second, he appeared shocked by the kiss but then leaned into me and began kissing me more, while cupping my breasts in his hands.

We stood up and clumsily removed our clothes and threw them aside. He pulled me down onto the floor; there was little in the way of any foreplay as he quickly lay between my thighs and proceeded to make love to me there on the floor of his lounge. He was a very considerate lover and knew what to do to please a girl. He took his time with me, ensuring I had my pleasure before allowing himself relief. After, I got dressed and rushed off without saying much, as I felt disgusted with myself for what I had done. Yet as I lay in bed that evening, I could think of nothing else but what I had done earlier that day. It had been very erotic, and I could not dismiss it from my thoughts, so much so that I felt myself becoming ever more aroused. I thought to myself later, 'Martha, you stupid woman, what are you playing at?' I made up my mind that it would never happen again, that I would never go back to this man's home, that being friends was fine but nothing more. The thing is lust is such a powerful emotion, and what one will do for those few seconds of utter pleasure that is the orgasm. One can pleasure oneself, yet it is not the same as physical sex with a handsome male partner. I found myself saying no, never again, yet I ended up going back to his house again around two months later.

Again, we had coffee while sitting down in his lounge and talking casually, yet there was this overbearing attraction – maybe it was his maturity and the mature way he made love to me that was so captivating. As we talked, I found myself becoming uncomfortably hot and unbuttoned the top of my blouse. I would begin to feel myself becoming moist and tingly. At that point I initiated a passionate kiss, which led all the way to his bedroom. He kissed me all over this time and did something to me no man had ever done before, not even my husband – it was something they referred to as oral sex, and it felt so good. I was completely under his spell as he turned me around and entered me from behind. He made love to me in this position for what must have been forty solid minutes, using his fingers on me at the same time. It thrilled me so much, in such quick succession, that I was soon begging him to stop as I was exhausted. I felt his body go tense and then he ejaculated in me, and then he withdrew, falling on the bed beside me. I lay and watched the fluid slowly ooze out from of the top of his penis which was still stiff. I asked if I could smoke, and he agreed, provided that I open the window to let the smoke out. After I had finished my cigarette, I had planned to get dressed and leave. I gave him a kiss, but we became so engrossed the next thing I knew was he was on top of me, between my legs and making love to me a second time.

When I finally left his house, it was getting late. Later, I again reflected and cursed myself for allowing myself to become embroiled in what, by all intents and purposes, was a full-blown affair. I was an adulteress and that went through my mind for the remainder of the evening; my sleep was fitful, tormented by the thoughts of what I had done, things I knew were wrong.

What finally shook me out of this madness was a letter from my husband telling me he would soon be home and that he loved me dearly and when he arrived, we would have a wonderful reunion. I told my lover by meeting him at the café that we could meet no more, and that it was over. He was very understanding, wished me well before kissing my hand and disappearing up the street. I found a new job away from tram driving so there could be no chance of an accidental encounter and that was it, that was my illicit wartime romance, my bit on the side as you'd say.

It's not something I am proud of, and I would advise any woman in similar circumstances today not to be as foolish as I was. I can give no explanation other than lust as the primary cause of my misdemeanour. Lust is as addictive as heroin and it takes considerable self-control not to give into it, especially when you know that you can give in and never be found out.

Adultery today is not considered the age-old sin that it once was in society. But what has not changed is that those who commit adultery, especially those who do so without any foundation for their misdemeanour, rarely reflect upon the emotional destruction that they will cause, all round. All too often the perpetrator seeks to blame the victim, in an attempt to absolve themselves.

A soldier who returned home from his war a few months after the end of hostilities in 1945 discovered details of his wife's infidelity through the neighbourly gossip of his community. What were his feelings about this?

I can vividly recall myself stewing upon the sheer scale of Sarah's infidelity. It would not have been so bad had her dalliance been with a total stranger, but no, it was someone I regarded as a friend. His name was Martin and yes, I trusted him. You expect your friends to keep their equipment in their pants, you don't ever expect them to stab you in the back like that. So, I sat and thought about it all and wished I could be a time traveller, going back to the very moment of her birth, grabbing her rat-like form as it emerged from her mother's body, before biting her fucking head off and then flushing what remained of her down the toilet.

Does that sound harsh to you? It didn't to me at the time, and never has divorce been such a blessing.

Chapter 14

Deutscher Militarbordelle

Many people will associate the name of Joy Division with that of the popular 1980s English rock band, fronted by the late Ian Curtis, and an equal number will be completely unaware of the sinister origins of the name. The 'Joy Division' was the slang term for the German military brothels that operated in many of the conquered territories, throughout the war. In this context the term 'joy' is wholly inappropriate – there was rarely any joy for those enslaved within its services.

There were two distinct types of military brothel in operation in the Third Reich. The first is what I term the 'fixed installations', which were the brainchild of none other than the *Reichsführer* of the SS, Heinrich Himmler. They operated within the confines of the concentration camp system and the women procured for these brothels were female inmates, usually from the all-female Ravensbrück camp, who were provided as a reward to the male concentration camp inmates, for hard work, etc. An example of this is the Auschwitz I Stammlager, a brick building which is visible in many photographs in the immediate background of the infamous sign which reads *'Arbeit Macht Frei'* (Work Sets You Free).

The second type of military brothel was established in the occupied zones for use by the Heer, the Luftwaffe and the Waffen-SS. These brothels were not mobile and did not move with the German military forces as they advanced, being positioned well behind the front, usually in local towns. Soldiers could then make use of these services on periods of rest (conditions permitting). Local women were often recruited for these brothels and the reward for their services often took the form of extra food and/or household goods. The women were rarely paid any cash and many were told their services were obligatory, and they should be happy to be serving the men of the mighty German Heer. A former German soldier recalled:

They served the purpose of giving us a chance to let off some steam, as they say. We often called them Wailing Stations, due to the cries of pleasure that could be heard emanating from them at times. There was nothing in it other than having sex and the women were grateful for certain luxuries other women could not get. Younger soldiers were not permitted to enter these brothels; you had to be what they termed a responsible age. This did not stop some of them trying, though. I remember more than one lad, around 17 years of age, being dragged out of one of these brothels by his ear, by an officer who then threatened a court martial if any repeat of the offence was discovered.

The saddest of these two military brothel institutions has to be those that operated in the concentration camps. The non-Jewish female inmates were often selected from camps such as Ravensbrück. Selected according to the merits of their age and beauty, they were then given a thorough medical inspection to ensure their health and hygiene were satisfactory. The next stage was termed 'Hooker School', for women who were unaware of how a prostitute should perform, and who needed to be educated on their roles. These unfortunate women, most of whom were young girls, were never willing volunteers; few had any choice and a refusal could lead to serious punishment or even death. Once the women had been given sufficient education about their new activities, they were shipped out to other camps as the reward for those male prisoners who made extra effort to work harder and keep their German captors happy. Male prisoners who took advantage of their reward were often paired with women of the same nationality. Many people are unaware that the health and physical condition of a great many of the male prisoners was so poor that even had they wanted to have sex, they were often unable to perform. The simple comfort of being held in the arms of a beautiful young woman often was reward enough for these wretched souls.

Martha Ozols was a 17-year-old Latvian national who fell foul of the German authorities following the German invasion of the country in July 1941. Martha's journey to the Kaiserwald concentration camp near Riga and ultimately into the German military brothel system began in the November of 1943, after she was ordered to report for compulsory work duty. Martha spoke bravely about what she'd called her 'descent into hell' during an interview with me in 2002. At the time I was still heavily involved in researching stories of the German occupation of

Europe, particularly those citizens who had suffered under the Nazis in the eastern territories. What she revealed was both shocking, and sad, and yet typical of many such stories I had heard over the previous years. Martha recalled:

> When they [the Germans] arrived, many Latvians joined them as soldiers; there was even a Latvian branch of the SS. There were many of us who had no interest in helping the Germans; we just wanted to be left alone to get on with our lives. There were calls from the Germans for Latvians to assist in the war effort by providing labour. They rounded up many Latvians for transport out to factories and workshops all over German-occupied Europe. When they came to us it was clear they did not want my parents, as my father was not considered physically fit enough. They demanded I go with them, but I told them I didn't want to. After arguing with them my parents told me, 'For god's sake, Martha, don't argue with them as they will shoot you; just go, go with them.' A large group of us, both men and women, were herded like cattle to the nearest railway yard to await transportation to various places, where we would be sent out to work. We were not exactly prisoners and we would be fed and watered in return for our labour, but in many respects, we had no choice: we were forced into it, yet they told the world that we the Latvian people were volunteering to help Germany win the war, that is what their propaganda told the world.
>
> I remember we were all standing in a clearing in front of a dense forest. I remember looking and thinking to myself that the forest is around 200 metres away, I can run, I can get away and hide and go back home. I looked around and there were four Germans visible to me – one to the right of where I was, around thirty feet away and the others were standing about talking. Most of the group were resigned to the fact they were going away for a long time. I seemed to be the only one looking around and slowly backing off to the rear of the group where I could make a run for the forest. I looked around one last time – the nearest German, an officer wearing one of those peaked caps, was looking in the opposite direction – then I bolted for the trees. I ran as hard as I could; the distance wasn't great, but it felt like the trees were miles away. One of the Germans noticed me, and I heard the shouts of, '*Halt! Halt!*' but I kept running. I recall hearing strange sounds and the snow on the ground being blown up into the air, then a crack, crack sound, which were bullets being fired at me. I was running so hard and had just made it into the cover of the trees when I was knocked almost unconscious by a low hanging branch. My head began to spin, and I fell over, I tried and tried to get to my feet and keep running but every time I seemed to fall backwards on myself. I was aware that I was

being pursued and knew I would have to get away fast if I was to escape but they caught up with me and grabbed me by the collar of my coat and began to drag me back to the group of people waiting for the transport. They threw me down and one of them kicked me in the backside and told me if I ever tried that again I would be shot and killed on the spot. Some of the other people in the group, including some I knew, called me names like 'stupid' and asked, 'What did you do that for, you stupid girl, are you trying to get us all killed?' My head was throbbing, yet I was lucky as I had only grazed my forehead in the collision with the tree. I cursed myself for messing up probably my only chance of getting away. I knew they'd be watching me now, but I was determined to get away.

When the train arrived, we climbed up and spread out into the wagons and sat down. We could hear the whistle blowing, then the jolt, and the gradual momentum of the train as it began to pull off and gather some speed. I sat in the corner of what was like a big horsebox with a line of slit windows; there were around thirty of us in there, but it was not too cramped, and we could all sit down at least. I tried to imagine how far we were away from home as the train clattered along the tracks. I would say around two or three hours had passed when the train began to slow and finally came to a halt. The doors were opened, and we were told we could come out for twenty minutes and there would be hot soup and bread for us to eat. I decided at that moment I would try to get away again if the chance arose. It looked like we were in the middle of nowhere, only a small platform and a hut, nothing more. Outside the hut hot soup and bread were being given out as we were told to line up to get our food.

Again, I glanced around and there were woods to the one side, but I'd have to run across the train tracks in full view of the Germans; I was worried they would shoot without hesitation. I was very hungry and longed for some hot soup and bread, but getting away from there outweighed my need to fill my grumbling belly. I took several deep breaths and bolted as fast as I could for the woods which were not that far, maybe only fifty metres away. I was fast and determined they would not get me this time. I knew from the position of the sun which direction I should head to try and get home. It hadn't occurred to me I was hardly dressed to spend a night in the cold, but I wanted to go back home and thought of nothing else. I picked my moment and just took off like a greyhound in pursuit of a hare. I flew across the tracks into the long grass the other side and again I heard a commotion behind, and shots being fired but I didn't stop and this time I made it into the woods and kept running until my lungs felt as if they'd burst. You get to that point where you just can't run anymore and you have to stop. I tried to judge how far away I had run and for how long. Would the Germans just give up and leave me or would they send soldiers to find me? At that time all was deathly quiet in the woods. I knew it would be dark soon and found the base of a large tree to shelter beneath for the night. I would start heading back for home at first light. As much as I tried to sleep that night, it was hopeless. I was cold and hungry and my thoughts were with my parents back home; I just wanted to go home.

As soon as dawn began to break, I continued my journey but knew I would probably have another night and possibly day of walking to get to familiar territory. I was tired and my concentration was not as it should have been. In the event I ran into a patrol of Latvian soldiers who had volunteered to join the Germans: they wore German uniforms yet spoke Latvian. This patrol was one of the many anti-partisan patrols being carried out all over German-occupied Europe. They aimed their rifles and demanded I stay still. I was searched and then questioned as to what I was doing out here. I told them I had been out walking and had got lost as I had fallen and hit my head. They examined my head and saw the graze and slight bump from the collision with the tree the day before, yet they didn't seem convinced by my story. Maybe they thought I was a member of the Latvian resistance. They took me with them and after a short distance put me in a truck and I was taken to the nearest authority where my identity was revealed along with the fact that I had escaped a labour duty the day before. They slapped my face calling me a 'fucking liar' and a 'race denier'. A race denier was considered a political offence and as it was reported this was my second escape attempt, they told me I would not be returning home, that I would be facing severe punishment for my crime. They held me in a cell for two days and in the two days I was fed only once.

I was sent to the Kaiserwald concentration camp where my battle to survive began, and my descent into the hellish perversion of the Nazis. In some ways I put my survival down to the fact I was not a Jew. Had I been a Jew I probably would have not survived until the liberation. The Germans running the camp began selecting young women the one morning. They picked me out and said, 'Look at her, she is very good, she will do.' There were seven of us picked out and we had no idea what for. It was not long before we were told if we wanted to have an easier time of it, we could provide services to the Latvian and German soldiers. We were told we would not be paid money but if we were good enough, we might receive some extra food and things that the other prisoners would never receive. I thought for a moment, 'Well, this doesn't sound too bad; maybe they are not all monsters after all.' It was a childish thought which I soon dispelled as we learned we would be offered as prostitutes to the German forces, and those Latvian members of the German military, in one of their brothels. The idea filled me with dread in an instant. I was 17 years old and I had never experienced sexual intercourse at that point in my life. I was scared of what was going to happen to me. I was the youngest of the seven of us and the other women who were in their twenties tried to offer some comfort to me, but they could do nothing else.

We were taken from the camp to this large house on the outskirts of Riga. I recognized the area well as I had been there with my parents in past years, so I knew where I was and that I was around forty or so miles away from where my parents were. It made me feel like crying for a moment, but I understood I had to be strong, I had to survive. The house we were taken to had many separate rooms like bedsit apartments. Each room had a bed, a table in the corner with a vase of flowers, and a washbasin in the one corner. There was a communal bathroom, but the windows had bars across as did each room in the house. There were armed guards in and around the house at all times and at night the doors were all locked and if we needed to use the toilet, we would have to summon one of the guards who would escort us there and back. The doors of each of the rooms had a peephole in so at any time the guards could check on us. We were given a bath and some fresh clothes to wear. I say clothes but these were more like bathrobe-type gowns. We were to wear these as they could slip off easily without any fumbling which is what the customers, as they called them, would want. We were not permitted to wear normal clothes as we were not allowed to leave the house anyway. It was in every sense a prison. I hated it and I would have rather taken my chances of survival in the camp than have to submit to some man I had never met before.

I asked to be taken back to the camp, that I did not want to do this work, but I was slapped around the face by one of the Latvian soldiers who hit me, then spat on me, while shouting, 'Ungrateful bitch! You are going nowhere and you will do as you are told or I will take you outside in the road and shoot you, do you understand?' I did not want to test his patience as I am sure he would have carried out his threat had I continued to argue with him. One of his friends smirked at me then said, 'I look forward to fucking you,' before walking out of the room.

We were given a period of settling-in time which was just a few days. After that the first soldiers who were on recreation time from the front came to the house. We were ordered downstairs into this big room at the back where we were viewed like cattle at an auction and the men then picked which one of us they wanted. I was hoping they'd leave me alone and that somehow I would get away without being picked but I was wrong. One of them pointed to me and must have said, 'I want her.' I think he spoke in German; I was not sure as my German was not that good. We then had to take these men back to our individual rooms where they would have sex with us. They smiled gleefully clutching small packets of condoms in their hands as we took them upstairs, followed by the guards who would keep an eye on things to make sure there was no trouble from anyone.

The worst part for me was that I had never had intercourse before. I was not remotely ready for what was to happen, but we had been instructed to just lie down on our backs and open our legs, no other sexual positions were to be used. I don't really want to go into details about what happened next, but it was painful and humiliating. This man who must have been in his mid-twenties did what he did with me and afterwards, totally oblivious to my discomfort, sat there on the bed with his feet up smoking a cigarette and smiling away. We were given forty minutes to an hour to endure this humiliation. When the German left, I noticed there was some coital bleeding, I felt physically ill and cried. One of the guards must have heard me as he opened the door and shouted through in Latvian, *'Jasanas apklust un savac sevi kopa!'* ('Fucking shut up and pull yourself together!'). I washed my face in the basin and dried myself and had to put on some more rouge and lipstick which we were given.

When German soldiers were on R&R from the front, they came to us all the time; sometimes one would visit twice a day if he became infatuated. It was sick, no other word for it. We were subjected to unpleasant physical inspections even though we were using birth control to ensure there were no sexually transmitted diseases or unwanted pregnancies. Yes, we received our rewards in the form of better food, we were fed hot meals every day, given packets of cigarettes if we smoked, bars of German chocolate and makeup. It was up to the soldiers if they wanted to give us more items. I tried my best to pretend I was happy and to keep smiling through the humiliation of being forced to give my body to the soldiers. Not all of the German soldiers were bad. I had the one young German soldier pick me and when we got to my room, he refused to have sex with me and told me he just wanted some female company, just to be held. He visited me a few times and always brought food and any items he felt I might find useful. The last time he visited me he asked me how I came to be here. I had to whisper in case the guard was listening outside the room. The only way I could tell him was to get him into the bed with me naked and lie on top of me so as it looked like he was having sex with me. It was in this way I told him, and before he left, he promised he would do his best to get word to my parents that I was alive and not too far away; that's all he was able to do and even then, he was risking his own life.

It would not be until after the liberation that I would find out whether this young German had managed to get a message to my parents. By early 1944 we knew that the Germans were going to lose the war. There had been desertions among the Latvian guards who were tasked with guarding the house. Another clue was the fact that no more Germans were visiting us; they were now too busy fighting for their lives against the Russians who were on an all-out offensive to recapture Latvia. We knew the Russians were close when we heard the first artillery shells land not far from the house. We were told to go down into the cellar. The bombardment of Russian artillery steadily increased and the one morning the Germans and those Latvians fighting on their side were gone; they had just fled.

Suddenly we felt a great sense of joy. The Germans had gone, there was no sign of them anywhere. I recall hours before the first Russians arrived it went deathly quiet; there was not a sound of anything going on outside. For the first time since arriving at that place we called 'The House' we went outside and walked around. When the Russians arrived, we explained what had been going on there. I told them I had been sent here after being interned at Kaiserwald. The problem was there had been so many collaborators amongst the Latvians that the Russians were suspicious of everyone. We were all questioned at length and the Russians soon realized that we were telling them the truth, paperwork found inside the house also confirmed we had been brought here from the camp. The Russian soldiers gave us some clothing and after looking around the house for anything of use, they left it to us. I was desperate to go home to my parents, in fact so much so that I began walking. I was stopped by one of the Russians who had processed our information and he explained it would not be safe for any of us walking alone. He then asked me where my home was; in fact, I showed him on the map, and he told me that if I could wait another day he would drive there as he had to go back that way with some supplies.

Going home was so emotional: my mother and father cried and cried and wouldn't let me go; they hugged me like a baby. They told me that they had given me up for dead until some young German came to their house one evening and informed them I was still alive, and I was well, as he had spoken with me. My parents had all these questions that I was horrified of giving them answers to, as I was unsure how they would react. In the end I had to tell them that their daughter had been used as a prostitute by the Germans and those Latvian traitors who had joined them, in one of their army brothels. It broke their hearts but I told them everything that had happened. I discovered that thousands of women had been forced into prostitution all over Europe by the Germans and those forces loyal to them.

I never discovered the identity of the young German soldier who had tried to help me by telling my parents I was alive. It is likely he was killed in the fighting as the bodies of dead German soldiers lay where they fell, everywhere, it was horrible. Most were thrown into unmarked graves as the Russians hated them and showed them no pity. That is my story and I speak for all the young girls and women who were taken away from their homes and sexually exploited by the Nazis.

Adding to this iniquity, the notion that German soldiers did not have sex with young Jewish female concentration camp inmates is a blatant lie. During my thirty-six years of research, I have met and interviewed a number of Jewish women who were interned in concentration camps such as Ravensbrück and Auschwitz, and at least two had suffered repeated rapes by senior German officers at both camps. If such things went on at these two notorious Nazi camps, then it is likely to have occurred at many of the others too. It would seem, where sex was concerned, even the supposedly totally loyal SS were prepared to flout the racial hygiene regulations, which were a prerequisite for their duty as the Aryan supermen of the Third Reich.

Besides women being procured for the services of prostitution, pornography was also specially produced for German soldiers. Most of it came in the form of magazines containing photographs or art of scantily clad or naked girls, sometimes in provocative positions. Postcards also were produced, bearing similar photographic or arty images of naked girls. Few examples of this material have survived as many soldiers, for obvious reasons, would never have taken such material back home with them.

Wehrmacht soldier Jens Ehrler remembers the pornographic material which was made available only to soldiers considered of a suitable age:

> These printed German periodicals were delivered very discreetly and then distributed among the men. I remember some of the men would just thumb through the images and then hand the magazine to someone else to have a look at; others would stuff them inside their jackets where they could be viewed later, in a more private environment. It was clear in many cases the soldiers felt that these periodicals were not perverse enough. They were considered okay to have a look at for the sake of a quick hand job. Young soldiers, like the 16- and 17-year-olds we had joining us late in the war, were permitted to kill and witness death and destruction, yet our officers did not want these young men seeing anything pornographic; it was ridiculous. I can remember seeing one of our officers thumping one young lad fresh out of the Hitler Youth around the ear once. The lad's only crime was to be caught having a crafty wank over one of these magazines. Our officers didn't really like this material as they felt it was a distraction that would benefit our enemy far more than it would us. In fact, once the magazines had been read, they were often torn up and used for toilet paper, so they did have their uses.

Chapter 15

Hermann Göring: Mr Toad of the Third Reich

As a former First World War fighter ace with the fledgling German Air Force, Hermann Göring once cut a handsome and dashing figure, yet even before the end of the war he had become perhaps the most berated individual within Hitler's inner circle.

Born on 12 January 1893, Hermann Wilhelm Göring became one of the most instantly recognizable figures in Adolf Hitler's Third Reich. Having commanded the fighter wing Jagdgeschwader 1, formerly led by the greatly feared top-scoring German ace of the First World War, Baron Manfred von Richthofen (the 'Red Baron'), Göring was a highly skilled aviator and marksman in the air. He finished the war as an ace pilot with twenty-two victories to his credit. Like many Germans in the wake of the defeat of 1918, Göring became bitter and resentful and when the Nazi Party first appeared on the discontented streets of Weimar Germany, he became one its earliest and most loyal supporters. Göring had met Adolf Hitler, who would become the leader of the National Socialist German Workers Party or Nazi Party, in 1921, and joined the party himself in late 1922. One of the Nazi Party's early followers, a former chemist in Munich named Gunther Hirschberg, recalled:

> The two [Göring and Hitler] levitated toward one another almost naturally; it was one of those unavoidable catastrophes. Both shared antisemitic views, blaming Jews for Germany's ill fortune of 1918 and the years beyond, and both had a strong desire to re-militarize Germany, rebuild her strength, her people, and take back what had been robbed from her by the Jews and traitors, as they called them. It was obvious the two men had struck up a very close friendship that one knew would last a long time. You also sensed that somewhere along the line one or the other would become a scapegoat; in the end it was Göring who would have to suffer that humiliation as he gradually fell out of favour.

Göring's loyalty to Hitler was without question. During the ill-fated Beer Hall Putsch of 1923 – the unsuccessful attempt to overthrow the government – Göring was one of those wounded, suffering a gunshot wound to his groin. Following this injury, he became severely addicted to morphine which he took to deaden the pain, and this may have played a part in his later downfall. Göring twice underwent lengthy treatment for his morphine addiction in a Swedish hospital and although he emerged relatively clean of his addiction, his dependency on morphine would continue to blight the greater part of his life. His unbending loyalty aside, Göring was a ruthlessly efficient organizer. Hitler recognized these qualities and Göring soon gravitated to the role of the second highest figure in the Third Reich, after Hitler himself. Göring was responsible for the creation in 1933 of the Geheime Staatspolizei, the Gestapo – the state secret police of Nazi Germany. Under Göring's direction the Gestapo rapidly flourished, becoming a ruthlessly efficient and greatly feared organization.

In 1936, Göring was entrusted with mobilizing all areas of the German economy toward war. In this context numerous government agencies were brought under his personal control. In 1939, Hitler designated Göring as his successor and his deputy, in all of his offices. The zenith of Hermann Göring's career came with his appointment to Reichsmarschall, a rank created especially for him, which gave him seniority over all the officers within the German armed forces. When Germany invaded Poland in September of 1939 it was the Luftwaffe under Göring's direction that conquered the Poles in just thirty-five days. The invasions of the Low Countries and France followed rapidly. In each of these campaigns the Luftwaffe was the spearhead, claiming most of the glory for breaking the enemy's will to fight.

However, Göring's fall from grace can be traced to the Luftwaffe's disastrous campaign against the British in the Battle of Britain. Göring had boasted to Hitler that his Luftwaffe would conquer the Royal Air Force in a matter of weeks. As fighting over the English Channel progressed throughout the long hot summer of 1940, it soon became evident that, despite the numerical and technical superiority of the Luftwaffe, the objective of securing air superiority over southern England could not be achieved. It was around this point that Hitler first began to doubt Göring's ability to live up to his boasts. Things became even more difficult for Göring from 1941, when it became all too clear that the Luftwaffe was unable to prevent Allied bombers from bombing German cities. Following the invasion of the Soviet Union, also in 1941, which opened up a second front in Hitler's war, the relationship between Hitler and Göring deteriorated further.

Göring had given Hitler his personal assurance that the Luftwaffe could supply the trapped German forces in Stalingrad with the resources they required to continue fighting. It was a delusional boast, and Göring's standing with both Hitler and the German people rapidly declined. Göring was sidelined, often the subject of cruel jokes and ridicule from Hitler, Goebbels and Bormann. Prior to the midwar years Göring had been steadily withdrawing from military and political affairs, devoting his attentions instead to the acquisition of property, plundered artworks, and jewellery, much of which had been confiscated from the homes of Jewish people, who became concentration camp victims. Around this time Göring became increasingly melancholy; he ate too much rich food, and drank too much alcohol, and as a result he began to gain weight. It was also around this time that his addiction to morphine and other drugs resurfaced.

Göring would only have one child, a daughter born on 2 June 1938 to his second wife, Emmy Sonnemann. The child's name was Edda Carin Wilhelmine Göring. Göring certainly was no adulterer and had been faithful to both the women in his life, a rare trait for a figure of the inner circle. His first wife, Carin, had died tragically of heart failure on 17 October 1931, just four days prior to her forty-third birthday. Carin's death devastated Göring and it was said he never fully got over the death of his beloved first wife. Göring's fall from grace with the Führer, his ballooning weight and renewed drug addiction soon took its toll on Göring's libido. Göring was a man possessed of a very low sex drive, especially since being injured by the bullet to his groin which had almost castrated him, during the failed Putsch of 1923.

Compared with other members of the Nazi inner circle who had multiple children and half a dozen lovers on the side, Göring appeared the odd man out and was thus ridiculed by the others. Martin Bormann, Joseph Goebbels and Heinrich Himmler were all scathing about him, who they viewed as being inept, lazy and piggish. Göring's lack of interest in taking lovers caused questions about his sexual orientation. Michael Schildt recalled:

> Yes, some pretty unpleasant things were said of Göring by the others behind his back of course, never to his face. Though I think at the time he wouldn't have cared anyway, but he knew people like Bormann and Goebbels were making snide remarks about him; even Hitler joined in in the ridicule. Hitler once whispered under his breath during a meal with guests and members of the inner circle, 'Look at him over there, he looks just like a pig.' Göring's physician was also partially to blame; far from keeping things in medical confidence he had handed Göring's medical details, at Hitler's insistence, to Hitler and Himmler. There were rumours that Göring had not had sexual intercourse with his wife for some considerable time, that the bullet he received in 1923 had almost castrated him. He was consumed with other desires but not those of the flesh.
>
> Göring preferred to lose himself in fine art, sculptures, jewels, drugs and alcohol. These things were his pleasure, his escape from reality. Emmy remained loyal to him throughout. Of course, she knew how his feelings had been hurt by being sidelined and accused of gross incompetence and nicknamed 'Fatty Göring', amongst other derogatory titles. Yes, she knew all these things and kept a discreet distance from her husband's declining mental and physical health. She was there if he needed a shoulder to cry on but I'm sure Göring had too much personal pride to shed tears in front of anyone. Göring had given his wife a daughter and she did not want for anything at all, and that, it would appear, was enough for her; she was there for him if needed but he tended to shut himself away a lot of the time. I heard that Emmy may have had a lover who visited in her husband's absence to provide her with sex, but it was highly unlikely, in my opinion, as I don't think Emmy was like that. One thing you can say for the Görings is that they were devoted enough not to need other lovers in their marriage. You couldn't say the same for the others who were out for fucking anything in a skirt that stopped and smiled at them. No, Göring turned out to be the smartest, most clean living and most intelligent of the lot of them, as was apparent at his trial for his part in the Holocaust at the end of the war.

Chapter 16

The Dr Goebbels Guide to Good Sex

After Hitler, Himmler and Göring, Paul Joseph Goebbels is perhaps one of the Third Reich's most infamous faces. Goebbels, the *Reichsminister* of Public Enlightenment and Propaganda from 1933 to 1945, was a man who demonstrated unquestionable loyalty and devotion to Adolf Hitler and National Socialism, to the end. Such was Goebbels' devotion that as the war reached its inevitable conclusion, he and his long-suffering wife, Magda, would murder their six young children before killing themselves.

Goebbels was an interesting character, a man of superior intellect and intelligence with oratory skills to match those of Hitler. Devious and clever as a fox, Goebbels was also a virulent antisemitic, which was plainly evident in almost every public speech he made to the German people. Goebbels masterminded the development of progressively harsher levels of discrimination against Germany's Jewish population, through racist propaganda that was designed to stir up hatred of all Jewish people in Germany – although it was rumoured that his own grandmother was of Jewish ancestry. Goebbels also possessed a virulent hatred of gypsy people, homosexuals, lesbians and coloureds. In his role as propaganda minister, he was both extremely gifted yet ruthless, and was an instrumental figure in both the Holocaust and the near-total destruction of Germany through his calling for 'total war' in a speech made at the Berlin Sportpalast on 18 February 1943.

Throughout his youth Goebbels suffered from poor health, including an extended bout of inflammation of the lungs. His most unflattering feature was a birth defect known as clubfoot, his right foot being thicker and shorter than the left. Goebbels was so self-conscious about this deformity that he underwent corrective surgery just prior to his enrolment in grammar school. The surgery proved unsuccessful, leaving Goebbels with a noticeable limp and having to wear a metal brace with a special shoe. This deformity prevented Goebbels from entering the German military at the outbreak of the First World War.

Goebbels, like many of the future inner circle of the Third Reich, felt despondent and betrayed by Germany's defeat in the First World War. Antisemitism, racism and nationalism were the logical paths that led many of these individuals to blame the Jews for Germany's post-1918 misery. Goebbels' association with Adolf Hitler and the Nazi Party began in 1924 and Goebbels would become one of Adolf Hitler's most committed servants, right until the end. When Hitler gained absolute power of Germany in 1934 Goebbels was tasked with selling Nazi Party values and future political policies to the masses, which he did with some considerable skill. The charming, charismatic Goebbels became indispensable to Hitler despite his constant philandering which was one of Hitler's greatest frustrations with him. Had Hitler not possessed such huge affection for the Goebbels family unit and the abilities of his propaganda minister, Goebbels may well have suffered a similar fate to that of Ernst Röhm. In February 1931, Goebbels became romantically involved with the woman who became known as the first lady of the Third Reich, Johanna Maria Magdalena Ritschel, Magda for short. The relationship was said to have been fraught with petty jealousies, on Goebbels' side. Goebbels was jealous of Hitler's affection for the beautiful Magda Ritschel, so much so that Magda decided they should marry without further delay, on 19 December 1931, with Adolf Hitler acting as witness to their wedding. Magda already had a son by her first husband, and she and Goebbels would produce another six children throughout their stormy, precarious marriage. Only her firstborn child, Harald, would survive the war.

Goebbels' insecurity may have stemmed from his physical impediments. Clubfoot aside, he also had a noticeably oversized head which seemed out of proportion to the rest of his physique. These physical issues go a long way to explaining his constant infatuations with other women, despite being married to Magda who did everything within her power to keep him happy. His stature as Reich propaganda minister served only to aggravate what was already an extreme form of emophilia, formerly known as emotional promiscuity, a common affliction in both men and women. Goebbels was the proverbial child in a sweet shop where young and attractive women were concerned, and it mattered not that either he or the focus of his desire were married; it was an emotional and sexual predation without any of the bounds of morality. Goebbels' sexual appetite was unrivalled in comparison to the other leading figures of the Nazi inner circle, having more notches on his bedpost than even the wily Bormann. We can see from this that Goebbels undoubtedly suffered with a compulsive sexual behaviour disorder, as quite apart from his womanizing, he was a regular client at the Third Reich's most infamous brothel, Salon Kitty, which still stands today on the Giesebrechtstrasse, Charlottenburg, a wealthy district of Berlin.

Wilhelmina Metzel, the great-grandmother of Rainier Pohl, was a beautiful young woman who had drifted in and out of prostitution purely through having fallen upon hard times. Wilhelmina was arrested, after an altercation with another woman on the Kurfürstenstrasse, by the Berlin Sittenpolizei (vice squad) and taken to their headquarters in Berlin where she was issued with an ultimatum: either work for the state or face prosecution, with the possibility of being sent to one of the concentration camps. Wilhelmina was aware of Salon Kitty, that it was a prestigious brothel reserved for the highest echelons of the Third Reich leadership and visiting foreign dignitaries. The women procured for Salon Kitty enjoyed a comfortable life. They were provided with consistent healthcare, comfortable rooms, meals, drinks, cigarettes and clothing, while additional luxuries were frequently bestowed on them by the clientele.

What many were initially unaware of was that Salon Kitty was bugged. Every room was fitted with bugging equipment and all conversations which took place in the rooms with the women were recorded. In a sense, Salon Kitty was operating covertly to ascertain the loyalty of those who visited – and the girls who worked there were the bait provided. Wilhelmina was 20 years old at this time and has admitted in her writings after the war that she was a favourite of the loathsome Joseph Goebbels. Wilhelmina wrote:

> He enters the establishment with an air of regality, yet he is small and walks with a limp. The girls who work here with me call him 'Imp with a limp' behind his back. Goebbels likes to watch two girls have sex on the bed before him, so another girl always joins me when he is here with me. He is much like an entomologist, only Goebbels collects vaginas instead

of bugs and flies. He brings the finest champagne and yes, he shares the bottle with us, to lighten the mood no doubt. He is not the least bit nervous or conscientious of his physical problems, particularly his foot. He sits watching me and the other girl kiss and caress for some minutes before removing his clothes and joining us on the bed. He enjoys fellatio, both of us taking it in turns to take him in our mouths. He is neither big nor small but average in size. As I go down on him, I ask myself, 'Does Magda do the same for him?' He pours a little of his glass of champagne over both of our breasts and giggles like a schoolboy as he licks it off; he sucks our nipples much like a puppy on a bitch, then it is down to business. He has full sex with us both, one at a time; he prefers missionary to any other position. I watch as he mounts the other girl first. He makes love to her, yet his eyes are firmly on me as he does the deed. His face is a contortion of pleasure, almost amusing yet one cannot laugh out loud, only to ourselves in our minds. Why is he not looking at her, I think to myself? She is beautiful and he should be looking into her eyes not mine. He saves his precious seed for me, without stopping to put on a fresh condom he literally drags me toward him; he is as clumsy as a toad, yet he knows his art well. He enters me within seconds and continues thrusting. He stares into my eyes, grunting and moaning like a pig in agony. Within a few minutes it is over. When he has done with us there are cordial handshakes and farewell my Frauleins until the next time we meet. He leaves us a second bottle of champagne as an extra perk for our services, then it is back home to Magda and the children. Does dearest Magda know that he comes here to have sex with us?

Goebbels enjoyed casual sex with a great many women. Many were starstruck at the thought of the Reich propaganda minister taking an interest in them, so they were easy pickings in many respects. Yet once used they were cast aside as just another sexual conquest who should be grateful that he ever gave them his attention.

In 1936, following a meeting with the Czech actress Lida Baarova, the pair began what has been described as an intense and passionate love affair, a love affair which almost destroyed the Goebbels' marriage, enraged Hitler, and provoked one of the worst scandals to date in the Third Reich. Goebbels informed Hitler that he was prepared to relinquish all his offices of state, leave Magda and marry Miss Baarova. Hitler was beside himself with rage over this insane proposal and intervened directly in the looming marital crisis. Magda had visited Hitler and had broken down in tears over the affair in his presence. It was a crisis which placed even Hitler in a difficult situation. He adored the Goebbels and their six young children who spent much time around the Führer, often referring to him as 'Uncle Adolf'. As a brilliant manipulator of the German people, Goebbels was indispensable to the Führer, besides, many members of the Third Reich viewed the Goebbels family as the prime example of family life to which any clean-living, devoted German family should aspire. Hitler himself confronted Goebbels, telling him he would never accept his resignation and then seeing to it personally that the two-year affair came to a swift end, never to be repeated. Miss Baarova herself became ostracized and labelled a harlot and it became impossible for her to remain and work in Germany. Her affair with Goebbels was something for which she would have to pay, for the rest of her life.

This near-miss in the calamity that was the Goebbels' marriage was by no means the end of Goebbels' philandering ways. Goebbels had secret boltholes all over the Reich where he could take women for casual sex; he even had a lakeside villa north of Berlin where he entertained many of his illicit female guests. The few women who have come forward and spoken about their dalliances with the *Reichsminister* for Propaganda have revealed a familiar pattern. A young woman named Vera Hirsch, who worked as a secretary attached to the offices of the propaganda ministry, from 1942 to 1943 until she vacated her position to give birth to her first child, recalled:

If there was ever a new female face joining the office staff, Goebbels would be immediately intrigued by them, especially if they were young and pretty. He liked the young and pretty ones as he was aware of their vulnerability and their receptivity to his infamous charm. He would charm them with conversation, and you could see what he was thinking. It was almost as if he fell in love with certain women without even consciously thinking about it or the consequences of his own actions. I know that he took several young girls from the propaganda ministry offices out for meals and things like that, and I know for a fact that he screwed most of them. Some of these girls were little more than besotted teenagers; it was quite disgusting when one looks back on it all now. I remember hearing that Goebbels often threatened suicide over some of the girls he seduced if they wanted to break things off with him. The mental states of these poor girls must have been in as precarious a position as the hymens he intended to break. What a stupid, immature man he was, especially as he had six young children, and a seventh, an elder son who had left home to serve in the military. What is more maddening is the fact that there were many Germans born with deformities such as his, who were euthanized as unfit Aryans. It appeared odd that he, the Quasimodo of the Third Reich, escaped this fate, quaffed champagne and abortion en croûte at the Führer's table, whilst others perished. There was a rumour that Goebbels had got one of his young conquests pregnant and that she had the child, and that Goebbels was never informed of its birth. By all intents he or she could still be alive today, unaware of who his or her father was.

It is difficult to understand what drives individuals such as Goebbels to seek extramarital sex with women who, in most respects, are complete strangers, when they have such adoring wives waiting for them at home. Yet this is an age-old affliction in many relationships, which is perhaps as prevalent in society today as it was back then. Did Goebbels somehow view sex with his wife Magda as a dull and obligatory act of face-to-face coition, which somehow lacked the excitement of the sex provided by the girls of Salon Kitty, or those females with whom he instigated passionate sexual affairs? Did the physical traumas of his youth, which may have instilled a sense of inadequacy in the mind of an otherwise hugely gifted individual, have some influence on his behaviour as an adult? Did sex and falling in love somehow compensate for all his physical failings, along with the playground bullying he must have endured as a result of his disability?

The answers are not always clear. The likes of Goebbels, even today, provide psychologists with a smorgasbord of suggestions as to the reasons for both the evil and lust he espoused.

Chapter 17

A Hard-on for Death

Reinhard Tristan Eugen Heydrich, born on 7 March 1904, in Halle an der Saale in Prussia, was without doubt one of the darkest, most sinister figures within the Third Reich. A man whom many regard, above all others, as the physical embodiment of evil itself, Reinhard Heydrich was the man Hitler referred to as 'the man with the iron heart'.

Heydrich was a cold, emotionless, vain, possessive, ambitious and totally ruthless personality, who was secretly despised by many of his associates. He was the founding figure in the Sicherheitsdienst (Security Service/ SD), an intelligence agency created purely to seek out and neutralize resistance to the Nazi state. In this guise Heydrich was complicit in the arrest, deportation and murder of non-conformist elements in the Third Reich and its occupied territories. Heydrich assisted in the organization of Kristallnacht (the Night of Broken Glass), a coordinated series of brutal attacks against Jews throughout Germany and Austria on 9 and 10 November 1938, and he was also an instrumental figure in the operations of the Einsatzgruppen (Task Forces), who operated in the wake of the Waffen-SS and the Heer. The Einsatzgruppen were responsible for the murder of over two million people through mass shootings, beatings and gassings, including 1.3 million Jews. Heydrich was also involved in the execution of the 'Final Solution to the Jewish Question' and chaired the now infamous Wannsee Conference on 20 January 1942, where discussions were held on how best to implement the murder of six million Jews. It has to be said that Heydrich set about these tasks with great enthusiasm, totally devoid of all human empathy.

It is difficult to grasp that a man born under the usually placid, romantic, emotional birth sign of Pisces could become such a monster. Heydrich came from a wealthy, secure yet nationalistically minded family, who were liked and respected within their community. His father was a composer and opera singer, and two of Heydrich's forenames were taken from operatic pieces composed by his father.

Heydrich was not quite a womanizer on the same level as other members of the Hitler inner circle, yet he certainly sought and enjoyed the company of women other than his equally charming Nazi wife, Lina. In December 1930 Heydrich attended a rowing club ball at which he met Lina von Osten. They both had Nazi Party affiliations and found much in common with one another. They became romantically involved and soon announced their engagement. Early in 1931 Heydrich was charged with 'conduct unbecoming of an officer and a gentleman', for what was in effect a breach of promise, already having been engaged to marry another young woman whom he had known for some six months prior to his engagement to Von Osten.

As a result of this poor conduct Admiral Erich Raeder dismissed Heydrich from the navy, which he had joined in 1922. One wonders, had Heydrich remained with the navy, whether his path through the mechanics of the Third Reich would have been different from the course it took. Heydrich joined the SS on 14 July 1931, yet it would be SS chief, Heinrich Himmler, who would ultimately be responsible for elevating Heydrich to his ultimate position of infamy, with the blood of millions on his hands.

Encouraged by his wife, Lina, Heydrich attended an interview with Heinrich Himmler. When Himmler interrogated Heydrich about his personal ideas of how to design and develop an SS intelligence service, Himmler was surprised by Heydrich's proposal – but he was so impressed that he hired him with immediate effect. Heydrich set about his tasks with his usual ruthless efficiency, and he was the kind of imposing personality that few dared to cross. Konrad Frisch, who was on Heydrich's staff with the SD for six months in 1941, and who resided in the USA, gave this vivid description of his former boss:

> Yes, he was a true Aryan in most respects, culturally, religiously and in the manner by which he pursued his beliefs and duties to the Reich. I had heard about him even before I joined his staff as part of my promotion package in 1941. Meeting him for the first time I found him a tall imposing figure with a thin face, chiselled cheekbones and prominent nose. He had an air about him which commanded respect, which was duly given. He spoke

with a voice unfitting of his frame: it was quite high pitched, unusual for a man of his physical stature. He was an energetic, keen sportsman too. He was accomplished at fencing, swimming, boxing and running, yet was also skilled with a violin in his hand or at the keys of a piano, which came as a surprise to many of us.

I noticed his competitiveness – he could never come second to anyone in any of his disciplines; failure was unacceptable and was construed as weakness; it was inept and contemptuous. Many of the junior officers feared him. I didn't despite the power he commanded, yet I respected him as I had to, as one of his officers. I can't say we were exactly friends, but I carried out my duties to the exception and he noticed this. I was first introduced to Heydrich in Berlin in 1941 when he arrived to conduct some business in the city and to visit Hitler. I travelled around with him more in the role of assistant than bodyguard, as he didn't believe he required officers to serve as his guards, especially in the Reich capital where everyone recognized him. Whenever he visited Berlin, he would always pay several visits to Salon Kitty. These visits were carried out under the guise of Reich security duties, though it was obvious he was indulging in other pleasures. I recall the routine very well for these visits to the salon, which was operating both as an intelligence-gathering post and a brothel at the same time. There would be me and another officer who would accompany him; we wore civilian attire for these little trips. I remember us entering Salon Kitty for the first time, and walking down some steps into the basement of the building through a door. I was shocked to see a small staff of listeners with all this electrical equipment linked to listening and recording devices that recorded all conversations that took place in each of the rooms. Whenever we arrived, we found it amusing, as the listeners would often pass us their headphones and you would hear grunting and gasping noises and the shrieks of pleasure of females coming through the speakers. Yes, it was amusing.

Heydrich would order all the other clients to leave the building, whether they had finished with their women or not. Once everyone had left the premises, he would personally see to it that all bugging, listening and recording equipment was switched off and disconnected. Heydrich showed me how this was all done and once it was done, he instructed me to 'Keep your eyes on all of this equipment all of the time. Should anyone attempt to reconnect any of the equipment, without me personally being here to authorize such actions, you are to shoot them without hesitation, under my orders. Is this understood?' He smirked as he said this, so I am sure he was joking, but he could have been serious at the same time, I don't know and I never found out, thankfully. Of course, the two of us acknowledged his instructions while the operators nervously stood down and began reading newspapers or books. I think they were left feeling a little uneasy at his reference to shooting them if they tried any funny business. Heydrich would then leave the basement and head off into the main building where he would choose one of the girls and have sex with her.

When he returned, he would be like a master rewarding his dogs for good behaviour and he would tell us, 'Go on, go up there and have some fun. You have thirty to forty minutes; don't be any longer.' We would leave our sidearms with him in the listening room and we would be off up those stairs like a shot. The girls there were the best whores in the Third Reich. They were beautiful, healthy and clean and it was one of the perks of our job. What we didn't know was that as soon as we shot off up the stairs to have our way with one of the girls, all the listening and recording equipment was reactivated. I didn't realize this until much later on, but as I never said anything much beyond 'hello' and 'goodbye' it did not concern me too much. I was never stupid enough to indulge in small talk anyway.

Wilhelmina Metzel wrote of Heydrich's visits to Salon Kitty and while she was never forced to entertain him, Heydrich had expressed an insatiable lust for a young, dark haired, 18-year-old former Berlin streetworker whom the other girls had nicknamed 'Mitzie'. Wilhelmina continues:

Mitzie was just a child really and the product of a poor upbringing and an abusive father. She worked in the same areas of Berlin where we all did at the time. She was arrested and given the same ultimatum, of either working here or being put before the courts and sent to a concentration camp. Mitzie had this lovely dark hair worn in a kind of a bob style; she had an oval-shaped face and brown eyes with beautiful full lips. She looked like a classy burlesque dancer, and she looked much younger than 18 and I think that is why a lot of the clients who came to the salon wanted to have sex with her. Of course, it was through Mitzie that we learned what Heydrich was like in the physical sense.

Mitzie told us that Heydrich was tall, yet he was no Tarzan specimen, that his physique was more of a wiry nature than bulging with muscles. Mitzie told us that Heydrich was cold sexually; he would walk into the room with those beady eyes which she said made her feel cold. There would be no conversation, just a hint of a smile then he would remove his clothes push the girl down and have intercourse with her. Mitzie said that sex with Heydrich was painful and that he hurt her by restraining her as they had sex and he would thrust too hard for it to be pleasurable for her. She said Heydrich would alternate from demanding fellatio to intercourse then he would tell her to turn around where he would have sex with her from behind. She said that Heydrich had a substantial-sized penis and what made it so uncomfortable was the fact that it felt so hard. She said he would bruise her internally, that's how it felt, and she would often bleed after intercourse with him.

Apart from the actual intercourse, he was what she described as a 'rough biter'; he would bite her neck, shoulders and breasts as if he were chewing a piece of steak or something. With Heydrich it was all about domination, holding you down and gratifying himself. He made love with all the finesse of a rapist. He left you in pain, like a man who had a hard-on for death. When he orgasmed inside her, she said he let out more of a growl, like an animal, rather than a gasp of delight, and he would bury his face in her breasts as if trying to stifle any noise. When he had finished, he would get dressed and as he did so he would look at himself in the mirror at different angles, preening his hair and running his hands down his face. When he left, he walked out, and his only words were either 'good morning' or 'good afternoon' and that was it, he was gone.

Mitzie said that being in this man's company was as about as appetizing as eating one's own earwax and begging for seconds, yet he made you feel obliged, that you should somehow be grateful for his company and the discomfort which he inflicted upon you.

Heydrich never showed any humanity, empathy or morality of purpose: he was just a monster. Had it not been for the Nazis and the power they bestowed upon him in the SS and SD, his character would have remained unremarkable.

For a man who had a hard-on for death, being assassinated by Czech commandos, about whom he had sneered 'were too cowardly and too weak to pose any threat to me,' is wonderfully ironic. In a sense Heydrich was a victim of his own arrogance and vanity.

On 27 May 1942 Reinhard Heydrich was assassinated in Prague, in a daring operation carried out by soldiers of the Czechoslovak army in exile in Britain. These brave Czechs were trained and equipped by the British Special Operations Executive (SOE). The intention was to shoot Heydrich dead on his commute with his driver from his home in Panenske Brezany, nine miles north of central Prague. The car in which Heydrich was passenger was an open-topped Mercedes, which would have to slow right down as it reached a curve in the road near a junction. It was here that the waiting Czech agents sprang into action. Jozef Gabcik stepped forward with a British-issue 9mm-calibre Sten submachine-gun which he had concealed with his coat. Aiming the weapon at Heydrich he squeezed the trigger, only for the weapon to jam at the critical moment. It was at this point that Jan Kubis, who had gone unnoticed by Heydrich and his chauffeur, threw a modified anti-tank grenade at the car. As Heydrich was by this time standing up with his pistol in hand, shouting at his driver to halt, the grenade exploded against the rear wheel. Heydrich was not killed instantly in the blast, but died a lingering death due to blood poisoning. The sepsis was caused by small metal fragments and horsehair fibres from the vehicle's upholstery, which had blown out from the core of the grenade explosion and embedded themselves in Heydrich's diaphragm, spleen and lungs. Heydrich expired at 4.30 am on 4 June 1942. There were few people to mourn his loss, apart from his family, his closest associates in the SS and SD, and of course Hitler and Himmler. Wilhelmina wrote of Heydrich's demise in her diary:

> We rarely receive any news outside of our goldfish bowl of an existence. Yet, Heydrich's death was national news that could not be kept quiet; quite the contrary, everyone soon heard of it and even we learned the wonderful news that this rape fetishist was dead. I only hope he died in agony, able to feel every moment of pain, and when his soul left his body, that it was promptly dragged to the dreadful underworld from where it emanated.

Mitzie's scorn for Heydrich mirrored that of many others who had secretly despised the Nazi devil incarnate and she viewed the reports of his death as an ode to his 'sandpaper vagina' jibe, a cruel remark, highly insensitive yet typical of the misogynistic bastard that he was. Later in a private moment, she lay reflecting in her own mental retaliation: had only she been a beast with equal ferocity, capable of utilizing urticating vaginal hair, she would bind his wrists with silk before delivering a paralysing bite into his spine, and then dragging him away into some dark yet moist and warm burrow, slowly to consume him.

The true epitaph for Heydrich's demise lies in the Nazis' vengeful slaughter of the Czech people which followed, in retaliation for his assassination. For the man described as having had a hard-on for death, his demise was less than heroic.

Chapter 18

The Man Who Made Love With His Boots On

Martin Ludwig Bormann, born on 17 June 1900 in Wegeleben, Prussia, was the dark horse of the Third Reich. Suspicious and as wary as a weasel, he disliked being photographed or filmed, preferring to remain in the background whenever official news cameras rolled. Bormann would not even allow Eva Braun to film him on the few occasions she recorded footage of life at the Berghof when important Nazis and their families gathered there. Yet his rise to power was due in part to this anonymity.

By his very nature Bormann was a committed workaholic and a highly skilled organizer, in all aspects of the tasks allotted to him. He rose rapidly through the ranks from a lowly Nazi Party official to the head of the Nazi Party Chancellery. In this way he was able to acquire immense personal power. Once accepted into the inner circle of the Nazi hierarchy, Bormann accompanied Hitler virtually everywhere he went, providing briefings and summaries of events and requests. From 12 August 1935 Bormann effectively took over the duties of Rudolf Hess, under the title of head of the Nazi Party Chancellery. Following the ill-fated flight of Rudolf Hess to England on 10 May 1941, with a peace proposal for the British government, Bormann acted quickly to cement his personal position in the regime, soon making himself indispensable to the Führer. He was as complicit as the other leading Nazis in the persecution of Jews, political opponents and minority groups in the Reich territories. In fact, Bormann was also one of the leading proponents for the continued persecution of the Christian orders in Germany. The quiet demeanour of the man nicknamed 'Brown Eminence' was a character trait that led many to underestimate him.

Bormann was known to have a quick temper and was certainly not a man to be taken for granted, and he was loathed by many in Hitler's inner circle. Much of the hatred toward Bormann came from the fact that access to the Führer always had to go through him, and in this context, Bormann enjoyed a high degree of exclusivity over the other figures in the inner circle. He was also a serial womanizer and had his fair share of illicit affairs, yet at least he made attempts to be discreet. However, on more than one occasion Bormann was caught literally with his pants down. One of his staff walked in on him while he was engaged in a sexual act with a woman. He did not notice the intrusion, but the member of staff, before making a stealthy retreat, noticed Bormann's legs, his trousers rolled down to his ankles, and still wearing his boots. It was not the done thing to repeat what one had seen with people such as Bormann – he was a dangerous man if crossed. Bormann was also known to visit the Salon Kitty, and whenever he arrived, he insisted the staff allow him to enter through the back entrance of the building. He would enter almost like a weasel sniffing the air, ready to bolt at the slightest disturbance. Wilhelmina Metzel recalled this about the man who made love with his boots on:

> He was intensely wary, suspicious and paranoid whenever he visited the salon. My only surprise was that he was actually capable of having sex with one of the girls while in such an alert state of mind. I prayed that he didn't ever choose me; the mere thought of having an overweight old oaf like him bouncing around on top of me filled me with revulsion. At least Goebbels brought fine champagne; Bormann just brought his lust and that piggy face of his.

Bormann's most high-profile sexual affair was with the German actress Manja Behrens. The two had met at one of the many high-society balls attended by prominent Nazis. On this occasion it was Bormann who instigated the affair, pursuing the young actress relentlessly like a dog might a hare. Under pressure Behrens agreed to meet Bormann so they could have sex, knowing full well that he was a married man with young children. Behrens also understood that she was involved with a man who was very close to, and highly valued by, the Führer; thus it was dangerous territory.

What developed was a passionate yet very covert affair which involved much sneaking around for both parties and the bribing of friends to loan the couple various apartments where they could at least have sex without the threat of being compromised. Some months into the affair Bormann, possibly struggling with guilt, revealed to his wife, Gerda, that he had fallen in love with his mistress. Just as Magda Goebbels had tolerated her husband's affairs, Gerda Bormann rather surprisingly suggested she and her husband establish a polygamous household with Manja joining them. Mrs Bormann suggested that they could alternate the duty of childbearing between them, ensuring that at least one of Bormann's women would be available for sex at all times.

Whether this suggestion was a clever bluff on the part of a quick-thinking wife frightened of losing her husband to another woman, or a serious proposition, is not known. Gerda suggested that a contract of sorts be drafted, granting the mistress the same rights as the lawfully wedded wife. It has also been said that Gerda proposed a new law should be created in Nazi Germany that would enable all healthy, red-blooded males of valuable breeding stock to be permitted to have two wives under the same roof. In the event Bormann's dream of being able to bed two women at his leisure fell through and no contract was ever drafted. Manja Behrens soon disappeared into obscurity, having taken a job at a munitions factory where she began working fifteen-hour shifts. Despite Bormann having pledged undying love for Miss Behrens, he soon forgot about her and their affair was never rekindled. Bormann settled back into more or less the same dull insipid routine as before, taking advantage of any woman prepared to have sex with him.

As the Reich crumbled to the backdrop of heavy Russian artillery fire in April and May 1945, unwilling to commit suicide like Goebbels and many others, Bormann bolted from the Führerbunker in Berlin. The proverbial rat leaving the sinking ship of fascism, he fled into the night, never to be seen again. His death has been shrouded in mystery and the subject of much conjecture ever since.

Chapter 19

Rape and Sexual Abuse in the Concentration Camps

Accounts of rape and other sexual abuses of inmates interred in the various Nazi concentration camps came as no surprise to me at all. I had been given such accounts many years ago when I first began researching and interviewing. Back then this was primarily with the intention of creating a personal archive of Second World War stories, long before any of my books became a reality. At the time, the notion that Jewish inmates in particular were singled out to be used as prostitutes, or for other sexual abuses in the Nazi camp system, was widely rejected. It was generally accepted that any Nazi worth his or her salt would never willingly indulge in any form of physical or sexual activity, particularly with Jews. Breaking the Nazi racial hygiene regulations would have been one of the most serious contraventions of Nazi laws. Then I began hearing accounts of young Jewish girls being used as prostitutes by Nazis running the concentration camps, but such stories were dismissed as fabrication. I could never understand why this attitude toward this particular topic prevailed for as long as it did.

Of course, since those days many female former concentration camp inmates have very bravely come forward to reveal just these kinds of accounts of rape and abuse, which I had documented many years previous, in recently produced television documentaries. Since then, it has become accepted that we actually know very little of the level of rape and sexual abuse perpetrated against Jewish women and girls in the Nazi concentration camp system.

I believe I was one of the first to give this issue any serious form of literary consideration in my fourth book, *Women of the Third Reich: From Camp Guards to Combatants* (Pen & Sword Books, 2019). It was in this book that I decided to include Celina Earhart's account of her rape ordeals while a prisoner at Auschwitz. Celina was a 17-year-old Jewish girl when she was sent to Auschwitz. She was a very attractive young girl and was passed fit and selected for labour in the camp. Other members of Celina's family – her grandparents – were not so lucky. They were placed in the line leading straight to the gas chamber. That was the last time Celina ever saw her grandparents, trudging down that barbed-wire enclosed route to certain death. Despite the extreme emotional trauma, this period of her life prompted Celina to speak again of her ordeal on arrival at Auschwitz, and the rape and abuse which soon followed her incarceration:

> We had already lost our home along with the confiscation of all of our personal property. We had been stripped of everything which we had. When we arrived at that place [Auschwitz] we had nothing at all but the clothes we were wearing. We were unloaded like animals from cattle trucks, guards were shouting at us, 'Move, faster, faster!' We were ordered to remove all of our clothes, yet it was the middle of February, and I remember it was a freezing cold day when we arrived. We had to stand there naked in the freezing cold until this inspection had been carried out. They [the Germans] were in no hurry at all and gave no consideration to our health standing naked in the freezing weather. They seemed to be enjoying it all with their thick winter coats on and their flasks of hot coffee which were brought out to those carrying out the inspections.
>
> It was supposedly doctors doing the inspections; they would put a stethoscope to our chests order us to breathe in and then out, move our arms up above our heads then back down again and shout at us to go and join this line or that line. All the old people including my grandparents all ended up in a line with young children, and the last time I saw them was as they were ordered to move quickly down this corridor of barbed wire. They turned a corner and that was it, they were gone, and I never saw them again. That line was the one leading straight to the gas chamber. Old people and young children were of no use to the camp. We didn't know at that time that all these people were on their way to be murdered.
>
> I was given a uniform which was filthy, it was heavily soiled with faeces and what looked like dried blood. It was the jacket and trousers made up from blue and white striped material that we all had to wear. On the breast there was the Star of David which we all had to wear on our clothing. I was sent to work in a chemical workshop which was very unpleasant work; the chemicals, including paint, gave off fumes which often hurt your lungs and burned your skin. I had only been in the camp for what must have been three weeks when they came for me in the early hours of the morning. I was blindfolded and taken to a shower block where I was thrown some soap, the first soap I had ever seen since my arrival at the camp. Water was

switched on and I was ordered to wash myself thoroughly. I recall seeing how dirty the water was as it rolled off my body. When I was clean, I was told to dry myself before being given an inspection. Two of them talked amongst themselves before ordering me to change into these clothes they had brought for me. I was frightened as I had no idea what was going on or what this was all about. I thought that maybe they were going to release me. At the time I had no idea at all that I was going to be used for their sexual gratification. I was always of the opinion the Nazis hated us Jews, that to them we were vermin to be wiped out; I never imagined that this would ever happen to me.

I recall the fear, yes, I was very frightened, and my heart was pounding in my chest. I was taken into a kind of office where there was a bed against the wall. There were three of them in the room with me; one of them was an officer, I knew this from his uniform so he must have been important. They had bottles of alcohol and clearly, they had been drinking. They made remarks on how good my body looked considering I was a Jew. One of them then just walked forward, grabbed me and lifted me up onto a table which was in the room. I was pushed back, and I saw him putting a condom on and knew straightaway what they were going to do with me. I was pushed back onto the table and raped. When he had finished the other two then took it in turns to rape me too. When they had finished having their fun with me, I was ordered to put my normal uniform back on and was taken back to my block where I was simply told to keep quiet before being pushed through the door. No one dared say a word. Though some of the other women saw this, no one dared ask me what had happened or where I had been.

It was several weeks later when they came for me again, in the night. I was taken and made to wash with soap and put on this dress they had provided for me. In the same room this time it was just one man, but this man was much older than the last ones. I guessed his age about 60 as he was balding and what hair he did have was silvery. He was wearing a suit and not a military uniform but from his manner I suspected he was military. He took off his clothes and ordered me to pleasure him. It was disgusting as I had never done anything like this before and it made me feel sick, but I knew if I failed to please this ogre bad things might happen to me. I thought to myself, 'You could be in the gas chamber in the morning.' It just seemed to go on and on before he told me to lie down on the single bed in the room. As I lay down, he then lay down on top of me and began to gratify himself upon my body. His sweat ran down and dripped from off his head into my eyes and my mouth. Again, it seemed to go on forever until he finished. When he got off me, I got up off the bed and started to dress but I didn't get very far as he barked at me, 'No, no, lie back down as you were a moment ago.'

I thought he was going to start all over again, but he stood in the corner of the room lighting a cigar. He took a few puffs and exhaled the smoke, blowing smoke rings. Then he walked across to me, opened my legs, fumbling around. I thought he was putting his fingers in me but then he stepped away, laughing like a big fat child, and said, 'Do you know, I have always wanted to do that.' He had pushed the unlit end of the cigar into me. The cigar had gone out, so he lit it again and continued his stupid laughter. He then left the room, and two uniformed guards came in and ordered me to get dressed. Before I was taken back to my block I was told to sit down and eat some of this German cake they brought in, along with some coffee. Why they did this I don't know. Did they feel a sense of guilt? I will never know why they did this.

After the war my experiences were kept quiet. My mother and father survived Auschwitz too, though they would remain physically damaged from their experiences. They would have no talk of what happened and forbade me to ever talk about it. My parents also said that, 'If you tell anyone about it, no one is ever going to believe you. Germans using dirty Jews for their pleasure, we would be mocked and ridiculed, Celina.' So, I never told anyone about it, not until now. Now feels the right time for me to talk about it. My parents were lucky to have survived, I know that much of their story. My father died before my mother, but before she died, we once sat down and talked about the war and our imprisonment. My mother revealed to me that the Germans had once beat father very badly, not about his body but around his testicles, and prodded him there with sticks too. They damaged him there and that is why my parents were unable to have any more children. What made this news worse was that it was a woman guard who carried out this assault. Who she was, we didn't ever find out, but I hope she is rotting in hell for what she did.

Piotr Ivanovici, a Polish Jew, was also a victim of regular sexual assaults while interred at Auschwitz in 1944. Whilst it was extremely difficult for Piotr to discuss the things the Germans did to him, he felt very strongly that the outside world should be reminded of the suffering of all Nazi concentration camp victims and the sexual abuse both men and women were subjected to on a daily basis. Piotr recalled:

It is physically painful to talk about, the things they did to me and others. Why did they hate us so much that they wanted to inflict such pain upon us? There were times I would rather have been taken outside and shot like a dog than have to face the pain and humiliation of what they did to some of us each day. The guards would come and harass us regularly with excuses such as we were not working fast enough or being productive enough. We would be forced to strip naked, and they would laugh at us, saying, 'Oh, look at his, isn't he small!' referring to our penis sizes. It was just humiliating and degrading. If that was not bad enough, they would strike us around the private parts as if it were some game. Women guards were among the worst; they made us kneel down in a line on all fours once and one of them walked along with a stick in her hand prodding each of us in the anus. It was not a light prod either, it was forceful to the point where the end of the stick entered your anus. They sodomized us with their sticks. It was just a disgusting thing to do. If you moved or flinched from the pain the guards would beat you and that woman would come up and kick you with her boots or stamp her heels on your fingers.

This woman was given many nicknames: 'The Beautiful Beast' and 'The Hyena of Auschwitz'. This woman was caught and executed after the war and her name was Irma Grese. She enjoyed inflicting pain on our genitals, she was a sexual sadist and did worse things to the poor women under her charge. Many of us left Auschwitz with nothing to our name, many of our families gone and many of us permanently disabled from what they did to us. I can never forgive them, ever.

It is never an easy or pleasant thing to see an elderly man cry about things that were done to him so many years ago, but this is how vivid those memories are. They are like yesterday, and the nightmares too, they never go away. Victims of the Nazi concentration camps were like animals arriving for slaughter, thoroughly dehumanized once inside the camps, and there could be no salvation from the evil embrace holding them captive. The concentration camps were not only places of torture, misery, disease and death, but also of rape and sexual abuse. These places were, and still are, if you care to visit them, an assault on the senses. They reek of evil, death and suffering even after the passing of many decades since 1945.

Individuals responsible for the day-to-day running of the camps came from a variety of backgrounds. Generally, many of the female guards, as with the males, were not necessarily the brightest and it was relatively easy for one to enrol as a camp guard in Nazi Germany. Most of them were individuals with less than glowing educational credentials and therefore the basic entry level (Algemeine) SS tasks such as camp guards suited many of them. It gave them a uniform, a sense of power and purpose, yet it also instilled a ruthlessness which they were obliged to maintain. Some were forced into the camp system, and it was these individuals who would later corroborate what former inmates like Piotr Ivanovici and Celina Earhart have told me.

It is fitting that Piotr received his survivor's medal, the Auschwitz Cross, from the Polish government, in 1991. It was a decoration which meant much to him personally and he wore it every time he attended memorial services for those murdered during the Holocaust. Inscribed on the back of this highly poignant decoration are the words 'People's Republic of Poland to Prisoners of Nazi Concentration Camps'. Piotr died peacefully at his home near Gdynia, in Poland, in 1994.

Celina Earhart received her decoration later that same year, 1991. I recall her showing me the cross not with any sense of pride but a sense of deep sadness. When she took the decoration out of its box, she held it carefully in her trembling hand before handing it to me to look at. It was the first time I had ever handled one of these decorations and it was a humbling experience. I handed the decoration back to Celina and her eyes filled with tears as she placed it back in its red and gold box. Then she said, 'This is not just for me, I am just one of so many. This is for all those who went into that dreadful place yet did not come out of it. It is a symbol of both pain and survival, of coming out of a terrible dark storm and into a beautiful rainbow.' Celina's words seemed a fitting close to what was our final meeting.

Chapter 20

Lebensborn: A Biological Call to Arms

It should come as no surprise at all that the *Lebensborn* or Fount of Life programme, introduced in Nazi Germany on 12 December 1935, was proposed and initiated by the chief of the SS, Heinrich Himmler. The *Lebensborn* programme was implemented in an attempt to increase the birth rate of Aryan children of those German citizens classified as both racially pure and healthy, in accordance with the accepted Nazi racial health and hygiene laws. Those considered non-Aryan were of course excluded from the programme for obvious reasons. On 13 September 1936 Himmler drafted the following document to be distributed to all members of the SS:

> The organization 'Lebensborn e.V' serves the SS leaders in the selection and adoption of qualified children. The organization 'Lebensborn e.V' is under my personal direction, is part of the Race and Settlement Central Bureau of the SS, and has the following obligations:
>
> 1. Support racially, biologically and hereditarily valuable families with many children.
> 2. Placement and care of racially, biologically and hereditarily valuable pregnant women, who, after thorough examination of their and the progenitor's families by the Race and Settlement Central Bureau of the SS, can be expected to produce equally valuable children.
> 3. Care for the children.
> 4. Care for the children's mothers.
>
> It is the honourable duty of all leaders of the Central Bureau to become members of the organization 'Lebensborn e.V'. The application for admission must be filed prior to 23 September 1936.
>
> *Reichsführer der SS* Heinrich Himmler.

Initially the *Lebensborn* programme operated as a welfare institution for the wives of SS officers. The organization ran facilities such as maternity homes incorporating a full package of care right up until the moment of birth and some weeks afterwards. The programme also catered for unmarried women who became pregnant or had already given birth and were in need of aid, provided that both the female and male met the required classification of being 'racially valuable'.

Himmler had investigated the feasibility of the concept of *Lebensborn* well in advance of its implementation and was one of the leading proponents of race and eugenics. The main principle of *Lebensborn* was somehow to accelerate the Nazi gene pool and produce, by factory farming methods, racially pure, healthy Aryan children. Its legacy would be the spawning of a generation of Germans who would be born without a past, effectively, and no defined family roots as such.

Nazi Germany was a machine of conquest, and conquest is an endeavour that is costly in lives; lost lives needed to be replaced, therefore the most valued resources were the males, the warriors, fighters and conquerors, for Hitler's proposed thousand-year Reich. This was at least part of the logic behind *Lebensborn*.

Once again it was largely Germany's youth who would fall victim to the insanity of their leaders, particularly the young males and females who possessed the Nordic traits of blond hair and blue eyes. It was this physiological model that drove Himmler's obsession with creating an Aryan German race. The Nazis encouraged what they termed their 'special children', those born with blond hair and blue eyes, to understand and be proud of and committed to the procreation of offspring that would inherit the same genetic qualities as themselves. This, it was said, could only be achieved through the copulation of males and females with the same Aryan German attributes.

As the fortunes of the war began to turn against Germany's favour, so the *Lebensborn* programme was accelerated. Yet what was the Third Reich's leadership hoping to achieve by this? In many respects, it would appear this was done purely in an effort to deliberately sabotage a whole generation of Germans, as there seems little other logic in carrying out such an action.

Kirsten Eckermann has a unique perspective on this. She was there at the time and was a member of the girls' Hitler Youth, the BDM:

Yes, *Lebensborn* began purely as an exclusive baby-making club for SS personnel and their wives. At its inception they wanted only the blond-haired, blue-eyed couples with pure German ancestry, yet as the war progressed the whole programme appeared to change. The authorities began to appeal even to the members of the Hitler Youth to do their biological duty toward ensuring the Aryanization of Germany's future people. Yes, girls as young as 15 were encouraged to have children out of wedlock with a male with the same characteristics of blond hair and blue eyes. I know many girls who volunteered for this; their parents tried to step in to stop things but were threatened by the authorities that should any harm come to the girl for making her decision there would be very serious consequences, so many parents had to just sit back and watch their daughters become pregnant, sometimes by males many years their senior. When the time came, the girls went into their local *Lebensborn* clinic, gave birth, received their aftercare and once fit enough were encouraged to repeat the process again if they wished. Many of these girls were just far too brainwashed and naïve to understand what they were getting themselves into, that in some degree they were being sexually exploited.

Through *Lebensborn* there was yet more opportunity for some males in our society to sexually exploit naïve young women, under what was state-sanctioned promiscuity. I was propositioned myself on several occasions. I would have young men come up to me, ask me my name and then ask, 'Are you interested in fucking?' My answer was usually, 'Fuck off!' They didn't like girls telling them to fuck off or calling them wankers or things like that. I was not exactly a pure blonde, but my hair was fair and my eyes blue and that meant I was fair game for the Aryan thing. They would tell you in the BDM that you should be fucking hard and having lots of children, as many children as your body can procure for Führer and fatherland, they would say. They would tell you, 'It will be okay; we will talk to your parents on your behalf so as they understand, and you shall have no trouble. When the time comes you will receive the best of care and the child will be taken out of your hands so you will have no worries.' In a sense it was a biological call to arms, and I refused to take part when I was asked. What was the point of it all, really?'

The males certainly received greater pleasure as willing participants in the programme than did the females, it would seem. Jochen Hunnes recalled:

I was 20 years of age and I served in the Waffen-SS Leibstandarte, the Hitler Bodyguard as they called them. Even as an unmarried member of the SS I was told I had a role to play in the continuity of our Aryan principles. If you had the pure German blood, which I had as my family could trace its ancestry three generations back as being pure German, and you had the right look, the blond hair and the blue eyes, it mattered not if you were married or unmarried, there was always a girl or a woman of the same appearance who would be willing to have sex with you as part of the *Lebensborn* programme. If you got her pregnant it was like, 'Right, well done, now here you go, here's another girl.' For a young man this was good, and many offered their services as a result. Most didn't care that they would never again see the women they had sex with, or see the babies that would result from their couplings; for many it was just another duty although a more enjoyable one than the normal aspects of soldiering. We nicknamed it 'biological soldiery'. I know for a fact that when a male child was born it was cause for great celebration – another fighter, a useful asset, had been born. Yet if it was a girl there was far less interest; it was a case of, 'Oh, well, it's a female; put her in with the others.' Looking back, it was nothing to be proud of at all and condemned many babies to what was in reality a soulless existence. I remember when Himmler talked privately among fellow members of the SS, he spoke jokingly about the females, and he once remarked cheerfully, 'Taking a female's virginity is much like pulling the wings off a butterfly. By doing so you destroy the very thing that makes them so beautiful, so precious.'

Dr Riefer Kranse worked as paediatrician at a *Lebensborn* facility outside Berlin He recalled that, by early 1944, the whole programme had evolved into what he termed 'an immoral miscellany':

It was sad. At first it was all very carefully managed as a breeding programme. However, it collapsed into chaos as the war went on and pretty soon there were these sorry-looking young girls being admitted to our clinics all over the Reich. Clearly some should never have ended up pregnant, as they were far too young to be able to deal with the psychological problems of nurturing a child within, feeding and nourishing it for all those months, then going through the agony of birth in some soulless environment, without their family around them, and then not even being able to hold the infant they had given birth to. The babies were taken away as soon as the umbilical cord was severed, that's where their association with that baby ended.

I expressed my concerns at the ages of some of the girls coming into the clinics, and I served at more than one, and encountered many 15-, 16- and 17-year-olds. The youngest I ever came across was a 14-year-old girl. She had told one of the nurses that at least two young men had made love to her. I can't say whether it was a small mercy or not that this poor young girl gave birth to a dead child. It was stillborn; she still had to go through with the birth, yet when it finally came into the world a sickly colour, totally silent and void of all signs of life, the umbilical cord was cut and the corpse was tossed into a bag and taken to the incinerator. There would be no mourning, no funeral, and no grave; the dead baby was merely an object of no further use.

It was at that point I completely lost the ability to continue with my work any longer. Some call it a mental or nervous breakdown, but I was told simply to go home and rest and come back when I felt better. I never went back, and that vision of the young girl and the stillborn infant still haunt me to this day. Yes, I feel thoroughly ashamed of having been a part of that organization. If I could turn back the clock and change it all I would, but I can't.

Charlotte Schreiber was 15 in 1944 and had been a member of the BDM for two years. She vividly remembers how the whole of the Hitler Youth movement was called on to assist in the furtherance of the German Reich:

It was interpreted as 'furtherance', ensuring that those born during the Nazi era would be the ultimate Germans and pass on their genes in the future. They would have Aryan Nazi blood flowing through their veins, and I guess they summarized that the political ideology would somehow also be there naturally. It was madness, during the last two years of the war, the Nazis were basically encouraging young girls to be promiscuous with their bodies, to have sex and if they got pregnant it didn't matter, as the *Lebensborn* homes would take these unwanted children. So, it was like go away, do your duty as a German mother, fulfil your role. Yes, I had a friend who slept with a boy and he got her in the family way, as they call it. Her parents were furious, her father wanted to shoot him and disown her, but her mother almost committed suicide over it. It caused that family no end of pain. The authorities insisted the girl go into one of the *Lebensborn* maternity clinics, and so she did, and she had a perfectly healthy baby. She was never shown the child and it was taken away so quickly she never even saw its face or discovered its sex. Afterwards she was told to go home, that others were waiting for attention. Only then did she understand that she had been used, not only sexually but biologically too.

The big problem was and still is, young girls have a certain vulnerability; they have to be protected from themselves sometimes. The boys or men who were seeking sexual intercourse with young girls and women under the guise of *Lebensborn* were entirely false. Once they'd got what they wanted they were off to the next one and so on and so on. It wasn't just the young girls falling prey, there were older women who were having sex, getting pregnant and then giving up their babies to these homes.

Sometimes Mothers Crosses, the awards given out to German mothers, seemed more important than one's morality.

Ursula Siben fell pregnant by accident in the summer of 1942. She has only the bitterest memories of the *Lebensborn* programme:

> Yes, I was one of those stupid girls. I was 18 years old at the time and I had been seeing my boyfriend for over a year; we had even discussed getting married the following spring and I had no reason to think that anything was going to change at that time; we were both very happy and very in much in love, or so I thought. We used to go into the forest whenever we could; we were both working in the munitions industry and we valued our time off together greatly. We had made love before, but we always used birth control as having sex without it was unthinkable back then. I don't know how it happened but we both got carried away and ended up making love without using birth control.
>
> The stupid thing was, as he was making love to me, all the time that little voice in my head was screaming. 'Ursula, the birth control, goddammit!' I couldn't help it as it felt so good, so different that I couldn't have stopped him. He whispered how much he loved me as he ejaculated inside me. I can just remember thinking, 'Oh, fuck Ursula, you better hope you get away with this one!' We continued on as normal but then I missed a period and knew straightaway I was in big trouble. I told my mother and she was not too bad; she just insisted that we move our planned spring wedding forward and have only a simple ceremony. I broke the news to my boyfriend that he was going to be a daddy, and that we would have to bring our planned wedding forward. He seemed happy but uncharacteristically quiet. I asked if there was a problem and he told me there wasn't, that he was very happy at the news. We arranged to meet to discuss things about how we were going to get married but he vanished. Yes, he ran away, and I didn't know where he went and he never got in touch with me again. I found out some years later that his parents had told him to go and hide at his grandparents' house.
>
> It left me in a terrible predicament. There was no way I could have the baby at home with me, and there was no way I could afford to rent a place of my own; there was nowhere I could go to remain with the baby when it was born. It was my parents who made the decision to donate my baby for adoption through a *Lebensborn* home. At the time I agreed with them as there was no other way out of this for me. When I was due, I went into the clinic and three days later I gave birth to a daughter. I saw the baby for just a few minutes, as I asked them if I could just hold the baby for a moment. I was given those precious few minutes and then the baby was taken away.

When I felt better four days after the birth, I begged them to let me have the baby back, once I had sorted somewhere to live, that I could care for the baby myself, I just needed some time.

Do you know what they did? They took me down a long corridor that led out into this huge room, which was just full of cots containing crying infants, from newborns to those several weeks and several months old. There must have been 200 babies in there and the noise was deafening. It reminded me of a farm, only this farm was full of little screaming humans instead of animals. The SS nurse who accompanied me turned and said, 'If you can find your child you can have her, but chances are she is not here any longer; little girls are quick to find homes.' I can remember feeling a sense of panic. I looked into random cots, but all the babies looked the same. I can recall becoming so upset that they had to sedate me.

When I next woke up, I was back home in my own bed. My parents refused to talk any further about what had happened, and in time it was forgotten, yet I have never got over the feeling of shame and guilt. Somewhere out there I have a daughter. Does she have any children herself, is she okay, did she have a happy childhood? These are all the things I will never ever know. There were no records left after the war, the SS had been outlawed and you could not access any of those records that had survived anyway; they were all taken away by the Allied authorities. I was not the only one. Today there are organizations and help for those of us who went through the *Lebensborn* clinics. When I think to myself quietly, I feel angry, I feel angry at how we as young girls were used by our own society, how dishonourable some areas of that society were. Until Hitler, Himmler and the Nazis there had never been anything like *Lebensborn*; there had been some mild promiscuity as there is in all societies, yet nothing as bad as it was under the Nazis. *Lebensborn* for many young girls was more a fountain of death than it ever was life.

I have to carry the guilt for my part, even though my circumstances were different. I wanted to keep my baby and I would have done, yet they made the decision I was not to ever have that chance. I have only myself to blame for being young, naïve and very stupid.

Chapter 21

Sex in Psychological Warfare

Sex and pornography as a weapon of mass distraction were exploited by both the Allies and Nazi Germany in the Second World War. Whereas the Allies had sought to target mainly individuals within the Third Reich's leadership (as already discussed with the obscene anti-Hitler propaganda), Nazi Germany felt their brand of sexual/emotional warfare would be better employed if used directly against the masses of Allied troops themselves.

However, rather than having a seriously detrimental effect on the morale of Allied troops, whose wives and girlfriends back home would undoubtedly have been occupying much of their thoughts as they battled their way toward Germany, the highly pornographic material produced by the Germans spawned something of a collecting culture amongst the Allied troops, who actually found it all very amusing, and somewhat stimulating, in equal measure. The messages conveyed by the pornographic images were the typical examples of attempting to mobilize the Allied troops into some form of emotional mutiny, or to distract them from the job at hand, by convincing them that their wives or girlfriends back home were cheating on them, that other males were keeping their wives or girlfriends sexually fulfilled in their absence. The material may have had some limited effect upon the minds of younger, less mature soldiers or freshmen, arriving in the theatre of war in the wake of the Normandy landings, but for the most part the material was greeted with a degree of surprise and outright amusement.

The material was distributed in the form of leaflets which could be dropped from aircraft, or printed flyers left in strategic locations on the ground, where the Germans knew the Allied forces would discover them. John H. Thorberry Jnr, who served with a US mechanized unit, recalled:

> It was normal for us to search any buildings we encountered during the advance into Germany. These buildings were always checked for any

enemy who might be hiding in them and for any booby traps that if left might kill or injure members of units coming up behind us. It was normal to fire a few bursts from the .50 cals into any building first, to be sure they were empty of enemy forces, then we would go in and scout the building.

I remember this one was just full of these cartoon-like pornographic images with messages printed in English on them. The messages had things like, 'Who is looking after your girl or your wife while you are here?' The images depicted bare-breasted or naked American girls, surrounded by gangs of young men plying them with alcohol, with the intention of taking them home afterwards. Others portrayed the women making love with other men and were very graphic indeed. It was a bit of a joke really and we didn't take it seriously at all; you had to be a bit emotionally weak to be bothered by that stuff, and the things we had seen and done up to that point, well, nothing bothered us, especially this filthy propaganda stuff. It made good toilet paper though. I know some of the guys would keep it on their person, probably jerking off over it later [he laughs] and some guys collected this stuff as souvenirs, but no, I used it mostly as toilet paper. I had a wife back home and felt I'd be better off saving all of my energy for her when I got back home [he laughs].

It is certainly true that the pornographic material used by the Nazis in an attempt to unhinge the Allied troops, particularly late in the war, was of such a graphic nature it proved a useful stimulus for any normal red-blooded male who required some light relief.

The question remains: why did Nazi Germany devote perhaps more effort than the Allies to the use of pornography as a part of their psychological warfare strategy? The answer is quite simple: the Germans have always enjoyed a relative openness with regard to the subject of sex. In Germany being naked, especially around others, was not construed as lewd behaviour. On the contrary, naturism was not only traditionally embraced by Germans as a fundamental part of health, fitness and physical and mental wellbeing, but was an activity pursued by many other European countries. The Nazis in particular understood that those in the West had slightly different views toward being naked in the great outdoors, where the masses swam and sunbathed together in harmony. Thus, the Nazis envisioned that while the English were slightly prudish, the Americans on the other hand possessed excessive sexual appetites, which pornographic propaganda could usefully exploit.

Of course, these theories were completely wrong. Yet the Germans were convinced, maybe by studies involving their own young people, that young enemy soldiers in a state of hyperactive bodily development had a more or less continuous sexual fixation and an associated appetite for sex. Some German physicians were even convinced that sexual deprivation arising from being in the theatre of war was a major motive for soldiers who considered committing suicide. One physician argued (in a medical paper) that highly arousing, non-aggressive erotic stimuli could be a mediator of aggressive behaviour by males toward other males, under certain unique conditions. Whatever the considerations were for using pornographic material against enemy morale, it is pretty clear that it was devised to nullify motivation and might even be deployed to drive wedges between the Allied powers. The Nazis were experts in the divide and conquer theory, aimed at souring relations between British and American soldiers, and between the soldiers and people called civilian 'slackers' back home.

A good example of this German pornographic ingenuity in the psychological warfare sense was that recorded by Sefton Delmer, a reporter with the French Army who would later become an official of the British wartime propaganda agency. Delmer recalled a visit to the French front back in 1939, where he was shown a German-produced leaflet comprising a thin piece of paper showing a French soldier doing his duty at the front. However, if one held the picture up to the light, the scene underwent a shocking transformation. In place of the brave French soldier, one now saw in explicit, salacious detail a British 'Tommy' fornicating with a woman identified in the caption as the French soldier's fiancée. Where the British troops were concerned, the Germans focused their attentions against their American allies by playing on the 'oversexed, overpaid and over here' reputation gained by American troops based in England. One example of a German-produced leaflet showed a burly American sergeant in bed with an English girl, emblazoned with the words, 'You Americans are so different.' On the reverse was a brief message, blatantly to the point, which read, 'The Yanks are putting up tents in merry old England. They've got lots of money and loads of time to chase after your women.'

Nazi propagandists also attempted to take advantage of alleged latent antisemitic feelings amongst the Allies. One particular airdropped leaflet created by the Germans early in the war shows a nude blonde girl holding a copy of *The Times* newspaper. The girl is wearing a British Army turtle helmet and gazing into a full-length mirror. Her image, as reflected in the mirror, is that of a dark-haired, obviously Jewish woman. She is in an ape-like crouching posture with a sinister smirk upon her face. In her hand, the image of the newspaper is reversed and now reads *Semite* in the mirror. Of all the pieces of German sexualized propaganda produced in the war, this was without doubt one of the most imaginative. Whilst bearing a sexual image it was also sending a message that the British were fighting a war for the Jews. If the Nazi propaganda machine felt that both British and American troops were that inept, that they would become psychologically and physically crippled by these leaflets, that they would somehow lose their desire to fight, then they were soon proved very wrong. And, as a soldier of the 35th Infantry Division recalled, in February of 1945:

> We received these pornographic leaflets through an artillery bombardment. When the bombardment had finished, we collected up all these leaflets as they began to blow away in the wind. One guy immediately took a shit and wiped his arse on one of the leaflets; he didn't even look at it, toilet paper was such a luxury, and we thanked the Germans for giving us such an abundant supply with which to wipe our arses.

Even Sir Arthur Harris, chief of RAF Bomber Command, waded into the arguments about these obscene German leaflets when he remarked, 'My personal opinion is that the only thing achieved by the dropping of leaflets was largely to supply the continent's requirements for toilet paper for the five long years of the war.'

Today pornographic and/or sexually orientated psychological propaganda is still in limited, often covert, use. Sexually derogatory images have been used as recently as the Iraq and Afghan campaigns. Yet today many might find such material amusing, especially as part of their daily social media exchanges.

Chapter 22

Fit zum Ficken! (Fit to Fuck!)

The terms *Luftwaffenhelfer* (air force assistants) and *Flakhelfer* (Flak-helper) were applied to any member of the auxiliary staff of the Luftwaffe during the Second World War. Most were young people and were viewed merely as students conscripted as child soldiers, forced to abandon their school education to aid in the German war effort. Following the implementation of the decree *Kriegshilfseinsatz der Jugend bei der Luftwaffe* (Youth War Assistance Service in the Air Force) in 1942, whole school classes of male students born in 1926 and 1927 were called up for military service under the supervision of personnel from both the Hitler Youth and the Luftwaffe. This decree was later extended to cover people born in the years 1928 and 1929 and included females.

The deployment of young people in the service of the Luftwaffe was not purely military and limited continuing school education was permitted for as long as it was seen as feasible. By August 1944 some 450,000 young women had been enrolled as helpers in the Luftwaffe auxiliary anti-aircraft defence. Most of the young girls entering the service did so through the Bund Deutscher Mädel. The females first had to become members of the Wehrmacht before they could enrol as *Luftwaffenhelfers* or *Flakhelfers*. Officially, of course, it was strictly forbidden for females to perform 'armed duties' within the military. Yet the females, like the males, had to be trained to use and carry weapons in order to defend themselves.

This is a grey area often open to contention among historians. Scholars do not always agree about the true extent of the armed mobilization of German females in the critical last phase of the war in Europe. This needs little explanation here; I have documented this issue in great detail in my previous books, so will not waste space repeating already published territory here. What is interesting is how the young girls and women were received by their male counterparts, in the course of their Luftwaffe duties, and whether or not any romantic interaction took place between them. Perhaps this question was best answered by Arnold Hibzicht, a 20-year-old Flak gunner stationed with a unit to the eastern Berlin suburb of Brandenburg. Arnold recalled:

> I had joined up at the age of 18 in late 1943 and by 1944 more young people than ever were being called up to the military, due to the seriousness of the war situation by that year. We were in command of a 3cm Flak auto cannon with four barrels; it was deadly against low-flying attack aircraft, which were common in the skies above the city, particularly to the east. We encountered mostly Russian aircraft en route to bomb the central areas of Berlin, where we were stationed.
>
> You couldn't help but notice many girls entering the Luftwaffe service as helpers, as they called them. We young men didn't mind having them with us at all, as they provided some nice distraction from the gloom of the whole situation at the time. The girls were employed in a variety of tasks, things as menial as bringing us food and drinks if any were available, message carrying and operating searchlights for the guns at night-time. In most respects they were in as much, if not more, danger than we males were. I remember four new female faces turning up at our post in late 1944 and I became friendly with a woman whose name was Erica.
>
> We were standing around a fire we had made to keep warm and that's how we got talking. Erica was 18 years of age and from the Spandau district of Berlin. It was a cold yet still night and we were both placed on watch duty; things were strangely quiet in the air that night, and no warnings had come through to us, so we stood there rubbing our hands before the flames to try and warm them, and we talked about all kinds of things, parents, home, things we wanted to eat when all this was over, and where we wanted to go in life after the war, all sorts of things. Me and Erica began to spend a lot of time with one another, and I suppose it was obvious that I liked her, and she liked me. Yes, I fancied her a lot from the moment I saw her. I found her face, her brown eyes, and her blond hair very attractive indeed. Yes, she was a very pretty girl, and I was falling in love with her. We were often on watch duties together and it was during one of these that we shared our first kiss, and it was very nice.
>
> When we were excused duty, we would go off on walks whenever we could. I suppose after a short while of just kissing we were both wanting more of one another. We were just two normal young people after all, quite natural to have these feelings. I remember there was this abandoned, sandbagged army observation post in one of the fields where we walked, so we went to see if it was comfortable and dry inside. We had a look and yes,

it was dry, and out of the cold and far more comfortable than trying to be intimate out in the elements, so we both went inside. The army guys had made this place quite a little home-from-home and we were very surprised to find even the bunks were intact, with blankets and pillows.

Erica was worried that the army guys might come back and discover us in there and we could end up in trouble with our superiors. I was so excited I made exceptional efforts to reassure her that they wouldn't be coming back anytime soon and we would be alright. As we kissed her nervousness seemed to abate and Erica became more relaxed in the comfort of my arms. I began to explore her body with my hands but she squealed and pulled back. So I asked her what was wrong, and she replied, 'Nothing is wrong Arnold, but your hands are bloody cold!' We had these thick trench coats on, which made every movement awkward, then woollen jumpers underneath and shirts underneath those – it was a real pain you could say, with much clumsy fumbling. Given the chill air within and the fact that the blanket on the bunk was a little on the damp side, this wasn't quite a five-star hotel; but it was better than nothing and in the dry.

We undressed each other and quickly got onto the bunk, pulling our trench coats over the top of us. I was so excited I forgot all about the chill air as I ran my fingers down Erica's beautiful body. She moaned quite loudly with pleasure, so I began kissing her to stifle the noise, despite knowing there was no one around to hear us. It was not long before I was doing what the older men used to joke about, calling it 'riding the mare'. It was not my first time, nor was it Erica's, but this felt different; there was an intensity between us, we weren't just having sex, a quick fuck as they say, this was making love. I had fallen for Erica and would have been happy to have waited longer had she so wished. We changed around a couple of times, and she finished our little session on top of me which was very nice, as it was the first time any girl had ridden me. Yes, it was very erotic and for that time we forgot about the war going on around us. Afterwards we lay in each other's arms talking about the war. Erica told me, 'I'm glad we did this, as we could both die tomorrow, next week, or even next month, who knows?' For her youthfulness there was much maturity in her conversation, and I found that very attractive about her too. We decided we would stay there for the night as it was getting dark. We made love again later, then fell sound asleep. It was very pleasant indeed.

We were both startled awake in the early morning daylight as a voice from within the post roared, 'What in god's name are you two doing here? Where are you from, what are you doing here, and shouldn't you both be on duty?' Our tired eyes desperately fought to focus on this tall figure wearing a cap standing before us in the doorway. All I can recall thinking is, 'Oh fucking hell! It's an officer.' We both leapt up from the bunk, desperately fighting to cover our modesty and feeling very embarrassed. Sure enough, we had been compromised by an army officer who demanded to see our *Ausweisses*. We fumbled in the pockets of our trench coats, produced the papers for him, and he barked again, 'And what are you supposed to do when in the presence of one of your superiors?' We both quickly saluted him standing as rigidly to attention as was possible, whilst attempting to keep our naked bodies concealed from his view. Erica, with wonderful presence of mind, then calmly addressed the officer, saying, 'Sir, we are on leave from our duties, we are in love and wish to be married as soon as possible and just wanted some time to ourselves, sir.' The officer immediately produced a torch and proceeded to shine it in our faces so he could have a good look at us. I think Erica's good looks and apologies saved our skins, though we had done nothing wrong other than being in what might have been his observation post. He stood looking at us for a moment, flickered a hint of a smile before saying, 'Well, you best get dressed both of you, I will give you both ten minutes, you shall leave, and we shall forget you were ever here.' We stood to attention again, both saying, 'Yes sir' at the same time, and adding a 'Heil Hitler'. The officer saluted, gave us a 'Heil Hitler', smirked at us, shaking his head and walked out through the door making sure to pull the curtain across as we caught a glimpse of other soldiers milling about outside.

When we walked out of the bunker there were around eight German soldiers outside, all of them were smirking at us and we both understood what was going through their minds and the way they looked at Erica said it all. We trudged back across the fields, hand-in-hand, as we had to report for evening duty. As we walked, I said to Erica, 'What was that about being in love and wishing to get married?' She replied, 'Well, it did the trick didn't it, he was calm after I explained, and I saved your sorry arse didn't I?' We both laughed about it all the way back, but as we walked I felt a grinding sensation in the pit of my stomach. I really was in love with Erica, I thought she was great, and if they separated us now, I knew I would be devastated. I hoped that maybe me and Erica really would get married as soon as we were able to.

The following weekend after our little incident at the observation post Erica went home to see her family for a couple of days. When she returned, she presented me with a photograph of herself and on the back she had inscribed for me a little message which basically said 'a friendly reminder from your Erica'. The photo was beautiful, and I placed it inside my pocket with my *Ausweiss* as a treasured item. The fact that she had written 'from your Erica' told me that she was going nowhere though we had never discussed marriage as we were still fighting a war. She did tell me once that if anything were to happen to her, I was to promise her that I wouldn't be upset and would carry on in life. It was strange, two young people having to make such sentiments as that. I swallowed hard, promised her that I would do as she wished. I told her I loved her, and she told me she loved me too, very much, but at the moment we should focus on our duties and not get distracted by things that could wait until the war was won. The problem was, we were losing the war by that time, nothing was certain and there was a lot of fear. It was in the February of 1945 that our role as Flak gunners changed. We were told to prepare to use our guns in the ground role, to shoot at the Soviet soldiers and their tanks as they approached, that this would be our primary task when the Soviets came, because they were getting close.

All the girls including my beloved Erica were called together and told they should prepare to evacuate the position and the area as it would not be safe for females once the Soviets attacked. Erica didn't want to leave; my last vision of her was her crying and begging for them to let her stay there with me. I had to tell her, 'Go, I will come and find you when all this is over.' I told her I loved her more than anything else in the world and to go and be safe. We had a few minutes in which to embrace, kiss and console one another and then I watched her leave, still crying, with the others. I felt devastated, I wanted to go with her but any man attempting to leave their post from now onwards would be shot dead for cowardice and desertion of duties; that's what we were told. We had to stay there and await the coming onslaught, and all I could think of was my Erica, I had to survive and see her again.

When the enemy did come, we stood little chance of holding them off for long. The 3cm cannon was exceptionally powerful but was not always capable of stopping a tank. We aimed for their tracks most of the time, blew their tracks off the wheels and then let the other members of the Hitler Youth, armed with *Panzerfausts*, finish them off. We were rapidly outflanked and surrounded and the Soviets soon overran our position. They shot two of my comrades dead, but the rest of us were taken prisoner. They told us we would never see Germany again that we would be taken to Russia in order to receive sentence for the crimes we had committed against the Soviet people. The Soviets searched us, took our documents off us; they found the photograph I carried of Erica and threw it on the floor. Luckily, I was able to pick it up and conceal it on myself, so I didn't lose it again. We were taken back through the territory from which the Soviets had come. It was miles and miles of dead bodies, burning vehicles and houses. We were put into a kind of camp, just dirt surrounded by barbed wire and armed Soviet women guards who showed us no pity. From there we were put on trains and sent us to Russia. I did not return from Russia until 1956, that's eleven long years I spent there.

I saw many die as we were made to carry out hard labour in freezing conditions with very little food or water. The only thing which kept me alive was seeing Erica again, that is all that mattered to me. When I returned home with other German prisoners, I immediately began my efforts to find Erica. It took me two months, but I eventually found her at an address in Spandau in a block of flats. I went excitedly and called on the door of her address but was met with a scene of utter emotional dejection. Yes, Erica opened the door of the apartment yet there were two little children either side of her. She couldn't talk to me there and then and asked me to meet her at the local park where she would explain everything. She looked upset and after telling me to meet her at the park the next afternoon she shut the door. When we met there was no romance on Erica's part. She said she had thought I had been killed, as she tried to find me, but no one could give her any information and she did not have my parents' address, to contact them and ask them if they had any information. My parents could have told her I had been taken prisoner, but I understood she could not have waited all those years for me.

She had moved on, met someone else and the two little children were the product of her marriage with her husband. I took out the photo of her I had carried with me all those years, and it made her smile and it made tears well up in her eyes. We agreed it was probably best we did not contact each other again, that there could be nothing between us now as too much had happened. I offered her the photo, but she told me, 'No, you keep it, it's something with which to remember me by, from a time when we were both young.'

At that we both got up off the bench and walked in different directions and I never saw her again. I still have that photo and even after the passing of all these years, whenever I look at it, I get a pang of pain in my guts, of what might have been, had I not became a prisoner of war of the Soviets.

Luise Butschelle was just 17 when she received notice to report for duty as a *Flakhelfer*. Luise recalled:

I was issued with an ill-fitting uniform, boots and this cap we had to wear bearing an eagle and swastika emblem on it. I knew a lot of the girls who were called up for service in our district but there were a lot of boys too, some of whom were strangers to me, people I had not seen before. I didn't really want to be doing this work as it was the job of the army and air force to defend us, not our job. We were not soldiers; we were just young people. They taught me how to fire a pistol and I was issued with a pistol for self-defence only. I was attached to a makeshift Luftwaffe airstrip outside Berlin and there were twenty of us girls in all, assigned to various duties which included cooking and ensuring the tents we lived in were kept clean and tidy. The airstrip was nothing really, just a stretch of field which cows had once grazed in.

It was during my time there that I often saw this handsome young man who began smiling at me each morning he saw me, then later he would wave to me too. Eventually I plucked up the courage to stop him and talk to him. He told me his name was Heinz and I think he was shocked that I had stopped him to ask him his name. After a few weeks we were catching any moment we could; we would sneak off into nearby fields if the weather was fine and spend time making love there or just cuddling and talking, whatever we wanted to do we did. We were young people full of energy so why not; that's how we felt back then, live for the moment not the next day or week or even month. Yes, a lot of us were having a lot of sex, it was a good relief from the tensions created by the war.

We were very lucky to have been in the west and be captured by the American and British soldiers. They treated us very well and once the war was over and we had been processed, we were free to go and were released. Me and Heinz went and lived with my parents once we had married, in 1947, and from there, we rented a small house once Heinz began working in local agriculture. The farms were desperate for fit, healthy, young men to help get things back on their feet again. I fell pregnant just two months after moving into the house near the farm where Heinz worked, and just our luck I gave birth to twins, two girls.

I can't speak for everyone but me and Heinz count ourselves very fortunate; had either of us not been called up we would never have met.

Dieter Rischmann served with the crew of an 8.8cm Flak anti-aircraft gun based outside Berlin and has recalled what he remembers as 'a parade of pretty faces' from the Hitler Youth who arrived to be trained on range-finding equipment with his unit:

Oh yes, some of them were real beauties, very petite yet attractive in their smart uniforms. We were normal red-blooded young men and of course we were attracted to them as we got to know them. Of course, we wanted some romance with them, and I took a shine to one of them, a girl named Debra; yes, she was very pretty and my favourite. I made a point of letting her know my feelings for her and was overjoyed when she reciprocated those feelings. So, we began our romance.

What was it like? Well, it was just like any other romance where two people are attracted to one another; there is nothing odd about that, is there? Yes, she was a virgin, and she did not consent to sexual activity until she had got to know me properly and when we first had sexual intercourse, she insisted on me using a contraceptive every time as she had no desire to add fuel to the Third Reich's 'baby boom' as she called it. We had sex any time we could, and we once did it in the back of a Luftwaffe truck, which was pretty adventurous back then, I can tell you. Yes, we had some fun me and this lovely girl, but it petered out slowly and we lost interest and we then went after others who took our fancy. They were great times in some respects; if it wasn't for all the death and destruction surrounding us it would have been even better.

Dieter also recalled a particular incident where he witnessed a lover's tiff between a female *Flakhelfer* and her rogue boyfriend:

It wasn't amusing really, as this young man the girl had been having a relationship with had been seeing one or two others at the same time as her too. It all came to a head (excuse the expression) one evening when he came running out of one of the huts still fastening his trousers as he was running. This girl was chasing after him and she shouted after him, 'You fucking little rat! I will kill you when I get hold of you!' She actually picked up a heavy steel shell casing which stood by the door to the hut and threw it at him. It missed his head by inches, and he continued running from her like a scared rabbit.

Oh yes, we stood there and howled with laughter at him, wondering what this rogue had done to receive such treatment from his girlfriend. We discovered a little later that his girlfriend had been giving him oral sex when she noticed he had some unwanted guests crawling around the hair of his private parts, and understandably she was very hurt and angry.

An officer heard the commotion and came out to see what was going on so we beat a hasty retreat into one of the other huts and watched from the window. The officer shouted at the pair, 'What the hell do you think you are doing? Stop this nonsense immediately and explain yourselves.' He marched them both into his office where the young man then had the unenviable task of explaining himself. It must have been very embarrassing for him, and for her too. Both were sent to the medic for treatment and the young man weas sent packing in disgrace, but where they sent him, I cannot recall.

The next day a special parade was ordered, and this officer gave us a lecture on our sexual activities. It was difficult to keep a straight face as he said, 'This is not a sexual Olympics, this is a military unit. If you put more effort into your shooting as you do with fucking, then we'd have won this bloody war by now. You are no good to me if all you are is *Fit zum Ficken* [fit to fuck] and from now on, I want no repeat of yesterday's antics. Is that clear? Anyone breaking the rules in future will be subject to court martial. Now, do I make myself perfectly clear?' We all said, 'Yes sir!' After berating us further and warning us of drawing attention to our personal lives, he said, 'Now pull yourselves together and fuck off out of my sight.' Needless to say, we scurried back into our huts like cockroaches in a kitchen once the light is turned on. We did laugh about it though, as it was amusing.

During the final weeks of the war the whole of the Hitler Youth organization was ordered to join the fight against Germany's invaders. German schoolchildren were not exempt from reporting for military duty under the emergency decree and all were allocated roles. As the total collapse began and command and communication broke down completely, many Hitler Youth groups began to operate off their own initiative, fighting in groups known as Werewolves. John McCrory, who served with a US armoured regiment in Europe throughout the campaign against Germany recalled what he termed 'the Butterfly Effect':

We captured and disarmed many young kids along the way, some of whom had eyes full of hatred for us, others more relief that it was all over. Some of the females we encountered were as young as 10 years of age, others older, generally 17 or 18. Dealing with these young people wasn't particularly difficult. We would take their weapons from them and search them to ensure they were not carrying anything hidden, and then they would be questioned. I think the females intrigued us as they became very friendly with us once disarmed and away from their male counterparts. I think it was the males who more or less forced them into fighting against us. There were groups of females and always a male who seemed to be in charge of them, leading them if you like. These males were often given a thumping just to remind them that we were now in control and any screwing around with us would be met with violence. That seemed to do the trick.

I think all of us came away from Germany with certain memories that stood out. One of the memories I have, which I reflect upon often, was one of the German girls I met. I was only a kid myself really, at 19 years of age, so I guess I could relate to them in a sense. I remember we were looking forward to driving all the way into Berlin but for political reasons it seems the Russians were given that honour, so we were that dog holed up in the backyard on the chain, waiting for any scraps thrown our way. So, we had time on our hands to get to know certain individuals in our area. I met this girl named Lottie, her proper name being Charlotte. She was the archetypal German girl in every respect, blond hair tied up in plaits, big blue eyes, high cheekbones, just pretty as hell she was. It was somewhat soothing just having her smile at you, a friendly face in an enemy country, yet just weeks ago she was among a group firing Panzerfaust rockets at us from inside farm buildings. It was crazy. What had changed? I think we just discovered that despite the geographical differences and different languages we were not that different really; once they saw that, it just became normal if you like.

Lottie's English left much to be desired, and most of what she knew was typically the swear words, things like bollocks, fuck off, etc. Sometimes I would get one of our lads who could speak German to ask her different things. She explained she hadn't been interested in fighting, but the Hitler Youth males went around all the homes in her village threatening the parents with guns that if their kids didn't join them, that they'd all be shot as traitors. Such cases were common all over Germany and threatening people to take up arms or be executed just disgusted me. Lottie was 17, so two years younger than me, but I spent a lot of time with her. All the other guys had girls they liked and holed up where we were for a while, we had time on our hands. I was aware she was younger than me and I respected that.

Lottie would bring us things like eggs and small pieces of pork meat which went down very well. Where she got them from? No questions were ever asked. I couldn't help falling for Lottie despite the warnings about getting too attached to local girls we might meet. With Lottie it just happened naturally; we shared a few kisses and things just evolved from there really. Any spare time I got I would sneak off to spend it with Lottie. I couldn't stop looking at her and her smile kinda made even the gloomiest day bright in an instant. It was wonderful going out walking with this beautiful German girl. Yes, we did become intimate, but I'd rather not go into the details as it's personal. The stick-in-the-mud came with Montgomery [the British commander] who began issuing all these dictates about non-fraternization with Germans. Maybe he suddenly had nothing else to do with the war as good as won, but it pissed us off greatly and most of us just thought, 'Fuck him. Who is he to tell us what we should and shouldn't do.' It was like he was saying the Germans were our eternal enemy. Well, he was wrong there, wasn't he? We were still in the services of the US military, and we knew the time would come when we would be going back home.

Before we had to move off, I took Lottie's address and promised to write to her and return to see her as soon as I could. In return she promised to wait for me to come back to her. We both kept our promises to each other, and we were later married and yes, we had a great life together. But the attitude of certain guys in our unit annoyed me, especially when we were on the boat back home, and you'd hear guys talking and they'd say typically dumb things like, 'Yes, those German girls were so fit for fucking,' like sex was the only thing they cared about. The German girls certainly weren't promiscuous from my experience, and I met many during my time over there. Sex wasn't a big deal with them like it was in some societies. I mean they understood it, what it was all about, but it wasn't high on their recreational pursuits from what I could see.

Under the Nazis sex was reduced to a duty in some respects. Apart from the Hitler thing which had been drilled into them for years they were well brought up, with good manners and always took pride in the way they looked. Once the Nazis were gone, they had nothing more to fear, and they could be themselves again. Maybe under Hitler they'd had a duty to obligate themselves to the males of their society for the production of future soldiers, and be housewives to support them, but once Hitler was dead, that was it. They were free of that mentality and free of the chains binding them to that dreadful political regime.

Richard Smythe served with the Worcestershire Regiment in Germany. He remembers some of the German girls he met:

Most of the girls we saw were mostly auxiliaries attached to the Luftwaffe and their uniforms were the only clothing they had at the time. There was initial hostility, but this soon gave way to friendly chit chat and things, and they soon understood that things were very different for us both, as people. We had never had to live under a dictatorship while they had. Not all had supported Hitler and a great many were forced into doing things they never wanted to do, under the threat of death or being sent to one of the concentration camps. I remember one young girl, still in her teens I would have thought, who was caught trying to lay landmines in the path of our vehicles. When questioned she told her interrogators, 'They told me if I didn't do what they said, they'd go and shoot my parents. What was I supposed to do? I love my parents.'

I just remember thinking to myself, 'Jesus Christ, how could someone this pretty become so terrifying?' This young lady was a stunner, she really was, and it brought home to me just how used and exploited these girls really were. It was terrible and you had to have been there to fully understand all of this shit, believe me.

Chapter 23

Adolf and Eva: A Consummation of Death

The material which appears below was written in one of two personal diaries which belonged to an Austrian woman named Klara Busch. It was submitted for inclusion in this work by her daughter, Ingrid Pittmann, an acquaintance of Giselle Junghman whom I had interviewed many years ago while gathering research material for what would become my first book, *Hitler's Girls: Doves Amongst Eagles* (Pen & Sword Books, 2017).

Although Ingrid Pittmann gave me a very detailed summary of the content of her mother's writings, it was some three months after I had made my initial contact with her that I received the fully translated material. Ingrid herself had taken the time to do the translation for me, via email. Of course, as happens with any such material, there will be the usual chorus of disbelief from those whose study shelves are still crammed with the kind of recycled history books which many of us had rammed down our throats at middle school in Britain in the 1970s.

Klara Busch's writings are beautifully eloquent and an extremely rare document comprising a record of her private conversations with Eva Braun's youngest sister, Margarete, which have never been revealed, previously, in any form. The two women had become good friends during the years of the war. Klara had been introduced to Margarete Braun through her husband, Friedrich, who had served alongside Hermann Fegelein, Margarete's husband. Both men were serving with the same SS headquarters staff and soon became familiar with each other.

It was no secret that Fegelein was not popular with other officers and staff in the SS. Many of Fegelein's colleagues suspected that his marriage to Margarete, which took place on 3 June 1944, was purely for political reasons and possibly to advance his military career, but his close proximity to the Braun family and Hitler afforded him a high degree of protection from his critics. Fegelein had also made efforts to cement a friendly relationship with Hitler's private secretary, Martin Bormann. Despite Fegelein being a serial womanizer, Eva Braun was happy to have her brother-in-law among Hitler's entourage. The two would dance and flirt openly with one another at social functions, at which Hitler always remained detached from Eva.

In Margarete's opinion, many historians of the day were not fully explicit with the truth when they wrote about her sister, Eva, or Eva's husband, Adolf Hitler. Ingrid had read my first three published books and felt that the material in her possession, material that originally had belonged to her mother, might complement many of the themes that I was writing about.

Ingrid explained that her mother had spent much time typing up what was effectively a memoir, to serve as the basis for her own manuscript. Klara's manuscript would never be completed and remained in a study drawer until her death in the late 1980s. When the material was forwarded to me, I was unsure what it might reveal, if it would reveal anything new at all. To say I was pleasantly surprised would be an understatement. The original draft was littered with spelling errors and had not been edited, at all. Once translated it all had to be edited into a readable, coherent form, suitable for inclusion in a book. The following material is the result of that endeavour. Nothing has been cut or censored from the original transcripts and I leave it to the readers to to decide whether the content is relevant to the rest of this book.

Klara had given her manuscript, the memoir of her conversations with Margarete Braun, the working title of *Love and Lies in the Third Reich*. It seemed an appropriate contribution with which to bring this particular book to a close.

Saturday, 19 June 1954, I took a seat at a table outside Lorenzo's, a street café which was once in operation in Munich's busy metropolis. Lorenzo's was owned and run by an Italian immigrant family that had been in Munich since the late 1930s. I had originally suggested to Margarete that we meet up in Paris, yet the characteristic rudeness of the French, something we had both experienced on previous trips there, put us off this idea, so, ironically, Munich the former Nazi heartland it was. Margarete did not take much persuading either; we both craved much more than some second-rate lice ridden basement room of some Parisian hotel, where one ran the risk of drinking more rat's urine than wine from their glasses.

Whenever in Munich with my husband we would always come to dine at Lorenzo's and enjoy the coffee which we both felt suited our palates, unlike the motor oil served up in many other such outlets at the time.

From our visits to this establishment over the war years and beyond we were on first name terms with the Lorenzo family. Mrs Lorenzo was a short yet quite large woman, her legs and ankles used to resemble those of some grand piano, and she was possessed of a typical fiery Italian temperament. It was always an amusing scene at this place, Mrs Lorenzo would constantly berate her husband, in her native tongue of course, while at the same time keeping an ever-watchful eye over her two beautiful young daughters. The two tall slender girls with their Hispanic-looking complexions, dark brown eyes and jet-black hair which tumbled beyond their shoulders served food and beverages to the customers throughout the day. The al fresco style of the establishment may have insinuated a relaxed almost decadent atmosphere, yet Mrs Lorenzo made it seemingly impossible for her two daughters to engage in any worthwhile conversation particularly with any male patrons. I often recall seeing the eldest girl, whose name was Loretta, who was around 19 years of age at the time, sitting on the steps behind the main building with her head in her hands in floods of tears. Her mother would be standing over her with her hands on her hips gibbering away in Italian. I used to think to myself, girl you need to get away from all of this, what kind of life are you ever going to have here?

It brought back the memories of Eva Braun and how she must have felt at times, a young woman who had everything yet nothing, often described as infantile, a little girl trapped in a woman's body, a proverbial bird in a gilded cage. I had come here today specifically to meet Eva Braun's youngest of two sisters whom I had been introduced to in 1944. I had originally met Margarete Braun through my husband, an established member of the SS on Adolf Hitler's personal staff, and we became very good friends, as did all the women who enjoyed the privileges of Hitler's inner circle. We were all considered as his form of surrogate family. I had accompanied my husband to the Berghof on a few occasions; it was in every sense a kind of club, but not a club that just anyone could join – you had to either be one of the inner circle as it is often referred, on the Führer's personal staff or married to someone who was; no one else was permitted unless on important state business of course.

As I sat sipping from the dwarfish espresso cup with these memories flooding back of what were for us golden days of conquest, I felt a tinge of sadness. I felt tears begin to well up in my eyes, so much so I took the sunglasses out of my handbag placed them over my eyes, then lit a cigarette. As I drew on my cigarette. I looked about the street, it was a picture of normality, then I thought of the Berghof, which was now just a ruin, a ghost of sorts which would haunt all those who had indulged in its one-time opulence. As I scanned the busy street around me, I was shaken from my melancholy reminiscences by the sight of Margarete as she excitedly bobbed and weaved through the maze of people. I stood up, put out my cigarette and we hugged and greeted one another with a kiss.

Margarete looked fabulous and fresh and after congratulating her on her recent marriage to Kurt Berlinghoff, her second husband, we sat down, ordered our lunch and two cups of black coffee. It had been a long time since we had last seen one another; we had much to talk about and began by discussing the immediate aftermath of the war and what we had both been up to over the past nine or so years. Most of our lunch conversation was merely small talk, neither of us felt comfortable discussing the Nazi era in such close proximity to the other patrons. None of them recognized who Margarete was, but after we had eaten and finished our coffees Margarete suggested we go to the house she shared with her husband, on the Agnes-Bernauer Strasse in the city, where we could talk without our privacy being compromised by any listening ears. I went and settled our bill with Mrs Lorenzo who wished me a *buon pomeriggio* [good afternoon] as we left.

We leapt onto a tram which took us the short distance to the Agnes-Bernauer Strasse, where we jumped off then walked arm in arm excitedly down the street to Margarete's house. She unlocked the door and we walked in, and I was amazed at how nice her home was. It was very stylish and both Margarete and Kurt had obviously a strong love for anything art deco. Margarete took me into her living room, where I sat down on this rather large, very plush green velvet-covered sofa. A large and very impressive bronze lamp stood on a marble-topped table at the side of the sofa. The lamp was an antique and in the form of a naked girl with her arms reaching up to the heavens and disappearing into the lamp shade. The pose of this inanimate young lady with her full breasts. athletically lithe, evenly proportioned torso and long slender legs once again brought back the memories of Eva that I had neatly stored within my catalogue of memories.

Of course, I knew Eva only a little, as I only saw her and briefly engaged in conversation with her at special social gatherings. She was never free in the same sense that me and Margarete were; we used to go out and walk and things, but Eva could never do that. Margarete poured us both a large glass of brandy, something that I wasn't really used to drinking of an afternoon, but I took it anyway and thanked her. I took a sip and placed the intimidatingly full glass on the coffee table before me. Margarete began our conversation with the words, 'My god, where did it all go so terribly wrong? My beautiful sister is dead, my first husband, who was a good husband to me despite vengeful spite to the contrary, is dead also, my parents and my other sister, Ilse, are all heartbroken, even after the passing of these nine years. I know it is going to hurt for an eternity. I am not sure I can cope with that, you know.'

It was at this point they began to go over the events of Adolf Hitler first meeting Margarete's sister Eva, when Eva was just 17 years old and Adolf Hitler 40 years old. As recorded by Klara, Margarete continued:

It is commonly known how my sister met Hitler. At the time Eva was working as a model and photographic assistant for Hitler's personal photographer, Heinrich Hoffmann. Hoffmann was a brilliant photographer and Eva was incredibly lucky to have gained the privilege of working alongside him. In fact, Eva was very proud of the work she did with Hoffmann, and she enjoyed working as a saleswoman in Hoffman's shop. Hoffmann had many young German girls aspiring to be models and most of them were rejected by him. He had an eye for the right subject and Eva was of course one of what he termed his 'jewels'. Eva was naturally photogenic, in the sense one could feel her personality through the photographs taken of her, she was playful almost childish but vulnerable at times too. Eva possessed a physical aesthetic, she was tall, lithe, blonde and beautiful. Hitler had seen some of Hoffman's work and he showed a particular interest in those photographs of Eva.

This is how Eva and Hitler met, though their romance, if you can call it a romance, did not really start for another two years after their first meeting. It was more a gradual romance and I recall our father's initial horror about their relationship when Eva finally broke the news to us. Our father was not happy with what he felt was an excessive age gap between his daughter and a man he once referred to as 'an ogre'. Eva was besotted with Hitler, and I know that she really loved him and in those early days when their romance began, she moved into a house in Munich that Hitler had personally provided for her use. At this Munich house Hitler would visit Eva on a regular basis, where the two of them could make love in total privacy, this was of course before he became consumed with his total obsession in the role of Führer and as father to his people. It was at this place in Munich where Hitler would visit my sister and the two of them would share a bed in that house. Hitler had taken my sister's virginity long before this secret semi-cohabitation began with her. Their sex life was as normal as any other couple, their lovemaking was regular and vigorous. There was certainly nothing wrong with Hitler's genitals either. The rumours of him having just one testicle and deformed genitals was rubbish, but people will insist otherwise, they can never face the truth as the distortions of history prove far more fascinating than the reality. The picture of an evil ogre with warts, ugly genitals and all manner of ailments suited the anti-German propaganda machine perfectly.

Hitler was a lot older than Eva and obviously more experienced than she was at sex. I recall saying to her once, 'My dear Eva, really what are you doing with that old man?' She raised her eyebrows, flashed that almost childlike smile and replied, 'If only you knew, dear sister.' As sisters do, we talked frequently about our personal lives and experiences, often comparing them. When we talked about sex it was obvious that Hitler was the dominant one in the bedroom department. She said that Hitler was tactically romantic; what she meant by that was that Hitler would always insist on taking the lead with her and being in control of her during sex. She explained he would never let her sit astride him to pleasure him, he didn't like the idea of any woman being in the dominating position of being on top during lovemaking. She did tell me it wasn't as if she didn't try but every time he would pull her down onto her back assuming the dominant missionary stance. She didn't appear to be bothered by this as males back then were regarded as being in charge; it was expected of them to be dominant as real men should be.

In some respects, Hitler was an odd character in how he viewed his own physicality. He was not one of those men taken to standing before a mirror admiring himself even in private. When relaxing at home he would never sit around in short trousers and a vest like many men. He was possessed of a shyness almost but yes, in most other respects as a couple they did all of the usual things that any normal couple would do. During sex Hitler enjoyed the elements of foreplay. Eva revealed that Hitler particularly enjoyed fellatio being performed upon him, yet she did not find it the most pleasurable experience for obvious reasons, yet even during fellatio Hitler would never lie prostrate in a state of submission for her, he would always insist on standing before her while she would be totally naked kneeling down in front of him. Hitler also enjoyed performing cunnilingus on Eva; yes, we talked about these things a lot as sisters do, so it really was nothing out of the normal for us. I remember saying to Eva how I could never kiss a man with a moustache, as I felt they, like beards, harboured bacteria and were unhygienic. Yet Eva argued, saying that that famous, meticulously trimmed moustache provided wonderful extra stimulation during their oral sex.

As for Hitler's sexual performance, Eva couldn't really compare him with anyone else as he was her first real sexual partner and the man who had taken her virginity. When they first began having full sexual intercourse, as with any lovers, they were doing it as frequently as they could. Hitler, ever mindful of his duties to the people of his future Reich, used contraception when making love to Eva. Yet Eva admitted to me that on more than one occasion, Hitler did not stop intercourse with her to put on a contraceptive. It seemed there were times when Hitler was so consumed with passion, he simply chose to go all the way minus birth control. He never even withdrew at the point of no return, yet Eva never got pregnant and maybe this was a blessing.

From all that Eva told me it was pretty clear that Hitler's sexual preferences were more or less normal, much the same as any relationship. Apart from his insistence on dominance, there were nothing one could say that was odd with their sexual relationship. Of course, there were these persisting rumours that no one dared repeat about Hitler enjoying sadomasochistic sex acts. This came about largely as a result of psychological profiling carried out by the Allied Office of Strategic Services [OSS] in 1943 and Hitler's later state of mind. They made assumptions from this, I think, and these were not true. It is feasible if Hitler was in possession of such perverted desires, he may have indulged in them with the other women who had figured in his life, including his young niece, Geli Rabaul. It is true that incest figured largely in Hitler's life as he himself was conceived through incest, Hitler's mother and father being uncle and niece with a substantial age gap between them. Eva distanced herself from any talk of Geli Rabaul and would never mention her name at all. Hitler did keep photographs of Geli, refusing to keep them somewhere more discreet. Eva and Hitler argued over this many times and the arguments were often quite heated, but Hitler was stubborn, refusing to hide the photos of Geli. Did this in some way insinuate that Hitler was still in love with his dead niece? Eva felt he kept these photos more out of a sense of guilt over her death, but only Hitler knew the answers and he would refuse to discuss such things with Eva. This caused her to get depressed at times; she felt cheated on. Hitler had a selfish side, he could be rude, arrogant and moody and Eva could never have changed that about him. She somehow felt threatened and insecure over the women Hitler had enjoyed before her, so it was not just a grudge or anything with Geli Rabaul; Eva suffered bouts of jealousy as do many other normal women. There were many unfounded rumours that Geli was at the time of her suicide pregnant with Hitler's child; others argue she had been made pregnant by a Jew. There were those who believe Hitler had Geli killed, but this is hogwash. Either way I don't know anything about Geli, and Eva would never talk of her or mention her name to me, and I respected that.

Eva knew all too well that thousands of women all over the Reich had desires and fantasies over the man she was in love with. The women of the inner circle all despised Eva, especially Magda Goebbels. Magda

Goebbels hated Eva secretly because Eva was prettier than what she was and yes, she possessed the one thing she and the other inner circle women wished they had – the Führer. Eva didn't like Magda Goebbels anyway; Eva viewed her as rather pathetic, allowing her husband to go around screwing anything in a skirt he fancied. Eva understood Frau Goebbels was as insecure as maybe she was. Without her husband, what was she and what did she have? Eva would say, 'Are we [me and other women] really so different from each other?' Eva's reaction to it all was mixed; some days it bothered her, other days it didn't. She said to me once, 'The difference is they, as his adoring subjects, have the fantasy, the thoughts in their minds, yet I have the real thing.' Yes, women like Magda Goebbels believed that Eva was dumb, that she was unintelligent and for that reason she believed that perhaps she [Magda] best presented an image fitting for the First Lady of the Third Reich, not Eva. Hitler liked Magda, he made no mistake of his fondness for her and liked having her at his side. In fact, I am sure Hitler was in love with Magda too. It is my belief that had things been different, Hitler and Magda Goebbels may have become intimate with one another, maybe even a couple. The only thing that probably prevented Hitler having sex with Magda Goebbels was the fact that he loved her husband, Joseph, equally, as much as he did her. Joseph Goebbels was indispensable to Hitler right up until the end; he was the only one of the inner circle that stuck with Hitler and didn't betray him, so much so he and Magda killed their little brood then themselves. To do that takes devotion far beyond anything else, does it not?

I think Hitler also developed feelings for Traudl Junge, his youngest secretary. Traudl was pretty and blonde and similar to Eva in looks. Traudl was very nice, and she was not bitchy like the others and shared the same dislike for Frau Goebbels too, yet Traudl was more discreet with her likes and dislikes. I asked her many years ago, during our short correspondence via letter, about Hitler possibly having feelings for her, to which she replied: 'I know that he had feelings for me, but I am also sure that the feelings he had for me were entirely professional, more fatherly than anything else. I certainly didn't feel any intimacy could have existed between us, and no, I certainly would have not reciprocated any such feelings. I liked him as a boss, a good boss, that was all it was.'

I know without any fear or doubt that Eva never would have participated in any form of sadomasochistic or dirty sexual behaviour, as many were led to believe from obscene propaganda brought about by the Allied forces or Hitler's political enemies. She would never have allowed any man to urinate or defecate upon her or inflict pain upon her during sexual intercourse, as some have suggested occurred between them. Eva may have appeared very sweet, quiet and submissive, but she could be very strong willed indeed and was never afraid to argue with Hitler or say no to something she was unhappy about; she had a fiery temper at times, and they rowed like any other couple. Eva was also obsessive with her personal hygiene and that of those around her and there was no way she would have allowed even the Führer himself to defecate or urinate upon her in any context; it's just a totally laughable and untrue scenario. Eva certainly would not have done it to him either, no matter how much he might have pestered her to do so. It was something that was not in my sister's nature or character to have indulged in and these stupid stories really annoy me intensely to the point where I am shaking with fury. Do these people think they knew my sister better than me?

Eva understood to a degree that she would have to keep to the shadows, as Hitler's political career and service to the German people always had to come first. For the most part she could deal with this, though she would get upset when she would see photographs in the press of Hitler attending functions with other women. People have said that Eva was unintelligent and lacked the intellect to attend important social functions in the Third Reich. Eva was not unintelligent at all, but she possessed a childlike sense of humour which Hitler may have found embarrassing in public, therefore he never took her out to any of the big state functions. She would remain where she belonged – in that gilded cage where she had everything, yet nothing. Her loneliness and what she interpreted as rejection caused her to become depressed and do silly things and yes, she attempted suicide because she could not tolerate it any longer. Hitler would talk to her in private, reassuring her that he would marry her once he had reached his ultimate goal (whatever that was). It was enough to calm her down and he did make efforts to pay her more attention and spend more time with her for a while.

I always sensed when my sister was down which is why I spent as much time with her as I could at the Berghof; we had some wonderful times there. When I was with her, it was like she had an ally of sorts, as she knew I was not afraid to speak my mind to Hitler. I once argued with him over my smoking habit. He asked me not to smoke and I refused. He didn't like cigarettes or smoking at all and expected guests to refrain from their habit while he was present.

There were times where I was told her doctor had given orders for her to rest and visitors were to be kept away for the time being. This was obviously when she was down and melancholy. I wish I could have taken her hand and dragged her away from it all, but where could we have gone? And Eva would have only gone back to him anyway. As the years passed, even when Hitler was home with Eva, he would spend too much time fretting over political matters to the point where he became paranoid about even his most trusted officers secretly colluding against him.

Hitler became so consumed with this paranoia of the world about him that his intake of various medications concocted by his personal physician increased. Eva was not happy about the amount of drugs Hitler was being given by his doctor, Herr Theodor Morell, but Hitler trusted his doctor and would have nobody interfere in his personal medical matters. Eva revealed to me that all of the medication Hitler was taking had made him impotent, that he was incapable of making love to her, especially by mid-1944. She told me that she was unable to arouse him sexually despite what she termed as 'trying everything'. It was then she revealed that Hitler liked the idea of her masturbating herself; she felt unsure about this at first as I think she found it a little embarrassing, yet she did oblige him on the very few occasions he asked this of her. I don't see this is anything abnormal in a relationship though, lots of couples enjoy watching each other play. Yet despite trying all she could on her part, Hitler was still unable at this stage to have penetrative sex. Hitler was aware of his manly failings, and this made him even more irritable and aggressive than he already was. Doctor Morell gave him these pharmaceutical cocktails which contained various amounts of the drug Coramine [nikethamide]. It was hoped this would help his failing libido, yet apparently it didn't.

To Hitler the greatest thrill of all was of that of addressing the masses; even sexual intercourse with Eva could not compare to that. That is what Hitler enjoyed the most – he was totally consumed by the adoration the masses had for him, and after giving speeches he would often be highly emotional and exhausted. Eva could do little to shake him out of his melancholy as Germany's fortunes declined; he couldn't comprehend that he was losing, that he had somehow failed. He would say to Eva in private conversation that he felt he had given the German people the tools they needed to secure victory and that, somehow, they had failed to use them properly. He would just shut Eva out totally as he would do with most people close to him; he wouldn't allow himself to be consoled and be told that everything would be alright, because he knew it wasn't alright.

I am certain that toward the end the weight of the defeats in Russia, the Allied landings at Normandy, the onset of Parkinson's Disease coupled with all that poison Morell was pumping into him, led to a form of psychosis and loss of capability to grasp reality. He became ever more suspicious of those around him, and me and his staff would see less and less of him. Despite the fact that Hitler had lost interest in all aspects of sex, there was no question that Eva would ever have left him as she genuinely loved him, despite that love she yearned for never being fully reciprocated. She did her best to support a man that had become paranoid and delusional to the extreme, but that was Eva's way. She could have had affairs as she noted several opportunities with names I shall not mention here. She admitted almost having sex with the one admirer but in her own words, 'I came so close and yearned for it so much, yet I came to my senses before the act took place.' Eva had many admirers among the Hitler staff, yet many were just too afraid to risk doing anything other than dance with her. I admit I was a terrible flirt, along with my sister. But as Eva was the Führer's woman, had she ever betrayed him, I think he would have killed her and the culprit responsible too, I have no doubt about that. Hitler was violently possessive with all of his women, this we understand, he wanted them all to himself, all of the time and if he wasn't with them, they had to be caged in some way. Eva's greatest failing was allowing this to happen to her, she could have said no right from the start, but she was so young and naïve at that time. Our father did try to warn her that all that glitters is not gold, but then he understood the privileges of having a close association with the most powerful man in Germany and possibly Europe, at that time, we as a family were all to blame, but Eva was in love, and nothing was ever going to alter that.

The ghost of my sister haunts me daily, you know, those last days at the Berghof, in July of 1944, before Hitler bade farewell to leave for his military headquarters. There were no more parties held at the Berghof after that and it was soon abandoned. On 19 January 1945 I accompanied Eva to the Reich Chancellery in Berlin. The state of the city was shocking; it was a very depressing atmosphere there, so much so we left there on 9 February and we went to Berchtesgaden. While we were there, I tried to persuade Eva to stay with me, but she was adamant she would return to Berlin to be at Hitler's side. Hitler had tried to persuade Eva to leave Germany before it was too late, but she refused. Eva asked me to take charge of all of her business and personal correspondence which I did, and I can assure you none of it exists anymore as I destroyed it all in order to prevent some media circus taking place if the material was ever discovered. I held Eva in my arms and cried like a baby begging her not to go. I had that sense that I would never see her again. Can you imagine what that's like, saying farewell to one of your family when they still had so many years ahead of them?

I remained behind at the Berghof, and it was there I received the news that my husband had been arrested for desertion of duty. I know poor old Fegelein was far from perfect. I knew of the rumours that he had been unfaithful to me on several occasions. His fate lay in the balance as Hitler considered sending him to help defend the city of Berlin. Heinrich Himmler's treachery had put Hitler into a rage and he ordered that Himmler be arrested and my husband shot. I was pregnant with our first child at the time but neither this nor the fact that I was Eva's sister could influence Hitler's decision. Had I been there I would have petitioned vigorously for my husband's life, but I could do nothing.

I heard of my sister's wedding on the 29 April and that, despite the terrible gloom that hung over the Reich Chancellery, Eva threw a party before Russian shells began to land all around, bringing the proceedings to a swift end. I know she was trying so hard to be happy yet some of those with her were crying for her. The next news I am told of is the death of my sister, and that Hitler is also dead, both having committed suicide in the confines of the Führerbunker below the Reich Chancellery.

Yes, I have cried and cried for my beautiful sister; every night I go to bed, when I close my eyes, I see her face, I hear her voice and I feel her sadness. Why did it have to be her, that is the question not only me, but the whole family asked ourselves. I wish we had done more; we could have left the country before things had gone too far between my sister and Hitler. It was fine at the beginning but then it became a nightmare. After my husband's execution I knew if I said or did the wrong thing, even though Hitler was my brother-in-law, there could be no guarantee of my safety: he would have had me killed too, without so much as a second thought. My only consolation at that time was on 5 May 1945, while still at the Obersalzberg residence, I gave birth to my daughter whom I named Eva Barbara in memory of my beloved sister.

Sadly, Eva Barbara committed suicide in 1975 following the loss of her boyfriend the previous year in a fatal car accident. Margarete died on 10 October 1987 at Steingaden, Bavaria, at 72 years of age.

Hitler agreed to marry Eva Braun only when Germany was in the throes of total destruction, and all was lost. Their wedding, if one can call it a wedding, took place in the Führerbunker beneath the Reich Chancellery in Berlin on 29 April 1945, to the backdrop of exploding Russian artillery shells. The witnesses present at the wedding were Martin Bormann and Joseph Goebbels. Hitler, who appeared a shadow of his former self, hunched over, grey faced and shaking with the onset of Parkinson's Disease, hosted what can best be described as a sparse wedding breakfast with his new bride. There would be no consummation of the marriage as Adolf Hitler and Eva Braun had entered into a death pact. Neither would be leaving the Führerbunker alive and during the last hours Eva wrote a final letter to her sister, Margarete, and bade farewell to the members of staff who had served them so loyally over the past eleven years. Eva was resigned to her fate yet appeared happy and upbeat. Traudl Junge, Hitler's youngest secretary who had become a close friend to Eva, recalled:

> My last vision of Eva was like a haunting image. She looked lovely and she clasped my hands within hers and I couldn't help but be overcome with the emotion of it all. She was saying farewell to me forever and I knew I would never see her again. She wiped away some of the tears from my eyes then she said to me, 'Oh my dear Traudl, don't cry and don't be sad for me; you have been such a wonderful friend.' She took me in her arms and hugged me and we kissed one another. There were a few personal items of hers which she wanted me to have; she bequeathed them to me and then she turned and left the room. I broke down and cried for some minutes.
>
> It could never have ended any other way, under the circumstances. Eva told me, 'I could never be captured by the Soviets; what they would do with me would be unthinkable.' She was right, had she given herself up what would they have done to her? Would they have defiled her as they had done with many of the German women they encountered? What would they have done with her afterwards; would they simply have executed her? These were just some of the thoughts that had been going through Eva's mind during her last hours of life.

Adolf Hitler and Eva Braun committed suicide at approximately 3.30 am on 30 April 1945. Eva took a cyanide capsule while Hitler had shot himself through the right temple with a sidearm. Their bodies were taken into the rear garden of the Reich Chancellery, doused with petrol and set alight. It was an inglorious end to one of history's most bizarre couplings.

Having taken Berlin, Stalin had dispatched his troops to scour the grounds of the Reich Chancellery with the intention of recovering the remains of Adolf Hitler. Had they been discovered in any recognizable context they would no doubt have suffered the same indignity as the corpse of Joseph Goebbels, which became a grim exhibit for the Allied press. Hitler and Eva would not be lying in White Thassos marble graves of monolithic proportion, surrounded by floodlights and razor wire, with their obituaries lit in neon, as most neo-Nazis would have had them.

Yet even all these years later people remain fascinated by what some refer to as a 'necrocoital relationship' as opposed to a romance. Revelations of coprophilia and sadomasochism which followed in the wake of the deaths of Hitler and Eva Braun have helped to perpetuate the Hitler myth and encourage various fictions regarding their sex life. It seems that even today there are those who persist with attempts to profit from theories with no conclusively proven foundation. Recent so-called documentaries that profess the supposed sexual perversions enjoyed by Adolf Hitler, based no doubt upon concoctions created by his social, cultural and political enemies, serve no useful purpose whatsoever. Hitler is by no means unique in receiving this form of historically incorrect attention; dictators, who have come and gone before and since Hitler, have been privy to much the same treatment. Some people may enjoy this kind of television which is consistent with the times in which we are living. In my previous books I have touched, if only briefly, on both the lighter and darker elements of human sexuality, as part of the lives of the people I have interviewed. Sex is a natural function of everyday life, and without it none of us would be here.

Chapter 24

An Exclusive Club

The untimely departure of Adolf Hitler and Eva Braun from the funeral pyre of the Third Reich brought an end to a supposedly necrocoital political and social relationship that had lasted twelve long years, and had brought Germany to ruin. Hitler had placed a pistol to his temple and blasted himself into the nether void, fully aware that many of his once most-trusted accomplices had abandoned him. They were pursuing cheap attempts to save their own skins; they had not been the faithful disciples he had thought them to be; and like many of the goals he had pursued throughout his life, he had yet again failed.

As the corpses of Hitler and Braun were carried up the stairway from the Führerbunker below the Reich Chancellery, the mood became increasingly sombre. The bodies were taken into the Chancellery gardens, where they were doused with petrol and set alight. The background choir of Russian artillery shells provided a fitting dirge for a man and a regime which had resulted in the deaths of millions. As the bodies burned and thick black smoke rose from the flames. the pyre emitted an acrid stench, an incense of evil that drifted toward the greying, angry heavens above.

In the Führerbunker deep underground the mood was fittingly solemn. Those still present in the grey concrete tomb by now were resigned to their fate. Many of the occupants were blind drunk and people who would never have dared light a cigarette with the Führer in occupancy were now openly chain-smoking whilst pondering their own fates. In these last hours of hopelessness, the alcohol helped nullify both reality and pain. While many continued their drinking and smoking, some burst into song, mostly rousing, patriotic verses from 'the good old days'. Couples began pairing off and disappearing into darkened side rooms along dimly lit corridors, clutching bottles.

Juanita Koertzer, whose boyfriend was an SS soldier who had served with the Liebstandarte SS Adolf Hitler, was present in the Führerbunker together with the wives of many military personnel. Juanita recalled the deterioration of the situation in the Führerbunker, both socially and morally:

> I was 19 years old, old enough to grasp the reality of the situation. Law and order began to break down rapidly, particularly after Hitler, Eva and the Goebbels family had killed themselves. The atmosphere in the concrete tomb which was the bunker was horrible; it was thick with tobacco smoke, the air stank of piss, vomit and sweat, the walls were damp and slimy to the touch and the dull yellow lights kept flickering. I was scared they would go out at any moment and we would be trapped in the subterranean pitch blackness. I quite understood why many of those in the bunker had taken alcohol, of which there was lots, and just got blind drunk. The reality of what was going on was just too unbearable for many to comprehend. I walked along a dimly lit passageway, down some stairs and found an empty office with paperwork strewn all over the place; there on a desk was a half-bottle of champagne. Clearly it had been looted from the Goebbels' personal stash; I knew that from the brand. I wiped the end of the bottle and took several large swigs, it tasted superb, certainly not the rat's piss I had tasted before.
>
> I wasn't alone for long; a drunken soldier burst through the door and came staggering in. He had a bottle in one hand and blood on his lips. He hadn't noticed his lips had been cut; the top of the bottle was broken and the jagged edges had cut him. He began leering at me and babbling on about how we should take this opportunity to celebrate one last time, that wouldn't I rather have a German soldier on my belly than a Russian one, all those kinds of things. He removed his jacket and just took me and pushed me backwards onto this desk that was in the room. He had his full weight on me and was pulling away at my underwear. I was shouting out *'Nein! Nein!'* at the top of my voice, yet he continued his assault undeterred. I scratched at him as I had quite long nails, but this had no effect on him at all; he was clearly out of control on alcohol and probably Pervitin too, and he was intent upon raping me there and then. He had pushed up my skirt and with one hand had grabbed both my wrists, holding them tight so it was difficult for me to fight him off. I could see his trousers and pants were down and that he was erect and capable of penetrating me if I could not fight him off soon. He had torn my underwear and pulled it aside and had almost got me when another soldier burst into the room, pulled him off me then began to punch him full force about the face, a few times. This other soldier just shouted at him, 'What the fucking hell do you think you are doing? You are a disgrace, look at the state of you!'

I just ran out of the room and left them to it, but I can recall hearing the dull thud of kicks and groans of pain as I ran out of the room. It was clear that there was nowhere safe in the Führerbunker and that next time I might not be so lucky. I went and sat down with some civilians and their children who had come to the bunker to seek safety. I hoped that by sitting with them I would not get molested again.

Erika Hefner, the mother of three children, was also present in the Führerbunker and recalled:

Sitting in the gloomy passageways with drunken soldiers, some of whom had passed out completely, with vomit pools at their feet, was not what I wanted my children to have to see. We walked along different passages as that bunker was bigger than what many think it was; there were many doorways and almost everyone I looked in had either groups of men and women getting drunk or clearly having sexual intercourse. They had abandoned all sense of morality and duty and were just having one last good time in there before the Russians came. I recall looking behind the door of one of the offices and there was a woman sprawled on the floor totally and utterly drunk and unconscious with one of the soldiers lying between her legs. Another young man was sitting in the corner of the room just watching them. Maybe it was his turn next, I don't know, nobody seemed to care anymore. Any officers present tried to bark orders of, 'Get out there and fight!' but – excuse my choice of language – were told to 'fuck off'. Nobody wanted to know, and everyone was now very scared, it was the end; sex and drunkenness were just dulling the pain of the inevitable.

Monika Schmitz who was 15 in 1945 and lived in Spandau, recalled:

I recall hearing things at the time, that the Führerbunker was the place to be; it was an exclusive club, it was safe in there, there were cigarettes, plenty of booze and everyone was fucking each other in there near the end, before deciding whether to blow their own brains out or make a run for it. The death of the Reich was hardly something one could drink or fuck to, was it? They should all have taken a weapon and helped fight like many of us ordinary people were doing out there at the time. It was a diabolical irony in many respects, their last stands were made with their cocks, not their rifles, and these were supposedly the leadership and fighting men, those we had been obliged to look up to as some kind of vanguard of our country. Of course, that was all shit, we found that out pretty quickly when the time for do-or-die actions came. I know some of them fled, never to be seen or heard of again and those who were caught would later say they were just doing their duty and following orders. Did Hitler order those cowering in the bowels of his bunker to drink, fuck and party? Somehow, I don't think so, but by that time he had clearly lost it mentally anyway.

Hitler's youngest secretary, Traudl Junge, who was present in the Führerbunker in the dying hours of the Third Reich, had said her personal farewells to both Adolf Hitler and Eva Braun, before their suicides. Junge recalled:

> There was very heavy drinking going on in the bunker, in some of the rooms. These were people resigned to the fact they might be killed soon when the Russians arrive. There were drunken soldiers staggering around and yes, I would not be surprised to hear that some women were offered certain comforts; it was such a melancholy atmosphere.

For those remaining in the Führerbunker it was indeed now a time to consider one's fate and what one should do. Nobody was interested in becoming a martyr for what was now considered a lost cause; a final bout of inebriation, a last fuck and then it was every man and woman for themselves. Classified figures in the Nazi hierarchy, such as Martin Bormann, would leave the Führerbunker and melt into the night, never to be seen again. Their fates remained unknown for decades after the war's end. Those who managed to avoid the hangman's noose and who made it into the afterlife of Hitler's Third Reich would enjoy almost celebrity status. After all, they were members of what many would refer to as an 'exclusive club'.

Chapter 25

Pipistrelle Whispers*

Gerta was separated from the violence and depravity raging in the world outside her walls by a mere six or so inches of ancient stonework. She lay in a soft, warm, twilight enclave, momentarily reflecting, visions of nymphs cavorting on endless achromic landscapes, for as far as the eye could behold, filled her thoughts as she slowly drifted into a slumber:

The forest man emerges from the thick dark forest into the clearing where a grand temple-like structure stands beyond finely manicured lawns. These lawns appear as if a single great carpet, bathed in the soft hues of the moonlight. He half-crouches in a posture suggesting half-man half-beast, his nose sniffing for sweet scents carried forward upon the midnight breeze, his yellow eyes transfixed by the only visible, tiny speck of light emanating from the structure before him. The light comes from the soft glow of candles from a chamber on the lower floors. A rush of excitement and adrenaline floods his whole body; within seconds he is sprinting across the cool lawns intent upon reaching the window, despite the threat of discovery and almost certain death.

He reaches the walls of the building, thick vines which embrace the structure aid his entry as he scales the short distance from the ground. At the open window he sits gazing in: on a bed of gold satin lies a sleeping beauty, one of the king's virgins, exclusively for his own use and denied to all other males in the kingdom. She lies sleeping face down, her head resting upon her arms, her features partly obscured by a tumble of locks of golden hair. On each of her upper arms she wears a silver armlet signifying that she belongs to the king himself. With spiderlike stealth the forest man makes his move toward the sleeping woman. Her left leg already drawn up, her knee resting against the soft pancake of flesh of her breasts, his manhood hardens; maddened by desire he carefully positions himself over the sleeping woman. A gentle push against her visible opening, she stirs

---

* An old German term for erotic/vampiristic dreams.

momentarily before continuing her sleep, another gentle push and by now she is aroused to the fact that another man, other than her king, is using her,

She gazes wearily over her shoulder at the figure of the man taking her, shaking her head in denial as the forest man continues to enter her, yet she does not cry out; instead her fingers grasp her pillow with a strangler's grip, holding it to her mouth, her moans stifled within its fabric. The forest man continues for some minutes before she feels his body become as taut as a hangman's noose, his thrusting faster and with a greater urgency. Unable to vocalize his pleasure, what emanates from his throat is a series of short swine-like, guttural grunts. As he finishes in her he remains quite still for some minutes, allowing his fluids to drain fully in her. Withdrawing, he backs away toward the window from where he entered. Before leaping to the ground below he takes one final look back at the woman who is now soundly asleep again. Like a cat scorned by its owner, he leaps to the ground and sprints back toward the forest. Dawn is breaking over the mountains in the distance.

The birdsong is soon interrupted by shouting and a commotion from outside. Gerta climbs wearily out of her bed and parts the curtains to see what all the noise outside is about. The Gestapo are at work, busily breaking down a door to a home across the street. She watches as they rush inside, accompanied by soldiers. They emerge seconds later; two naked young men are literally thrown out of the house onto the street where they are savagely kicked and beaten. One of the soldiers forcefully prods the testicles of one of the young men with the muzzle of his rifle. A lorry pulls up and the soldiers shout at the men, 'Get up you filthy bastards! Come on, get up quickly. If you think things are harsh now, you wait until later.' The men are bundled, bloodied and bruised, into the back of the truck. The soldiers follow them in and one pulls down a canvas cover and the lorry lurches off on its way. Gerta's eyes began to fill with tears. She knows one of the young men; he is 21 years of age, a very nice boy. She never sees him again – his final place of rest is likely the smouldering ashpits of Auschwitz-Birkenau in Poland.

The dreadful legacy of the Third Reich's funeral pyre has been the subject of thousands upon thousands of texts since 1945, yet it has always been deemed politically incorrect to portray German members of that particular generation as victims. I was determined to cover all sides of the Third Reich story, in all its ugly detail, starting with my first book,

Hitler's Girls: Doves Amongst Eagles, plus many of the books I have written since.

As Germany fell, both men and monsters stalked the streets under the supposed banner of liberation. Some behaved as disciplined soldiers should behave, yet many did not. The great terror for German people was that the Red Army would be first to claim Berlin, and they did so with an uncompromising sexual brutality. It is also worth mentioning that many Polish soldiers fought alongside Russian troops during the battle for Berlin, many of whom were just as eager for vengeance. The blood lust was certainly justified in the hearts of many Westerners at the time, especially those who had seen the concentration camps and murder factories such as Auschwitz. At the time, an English priest remarked, 'German women deserved to be raped.'

With the passing of so many years, many people have begun to question and re-evaluate the morality of the liberators, particularly as it concerned children, young girls and women being taken and raped, as a part of the bounty of victory, as the legitimate spoils of war. I had thought that no sane individual could possibly agree with this particular entitlement, but you may be surprised to learn that there are people out there who defend it, who appear to condone and support the mass rape of females, from little girls as young as 8 to elderly women of 80, by members of the Red Army who stormed into Berlin. This was seen at the time as being an acceptable punishment.

American General George S. Patton, upon hearing the news that the Red Army had taken Berlin, was visibly dismayed. He was not a man to hide his opinions and was vehemently anti-Russian; he once described Russians not as European but as Asiatic people, hence their ill-discipline and fondness for savagery. Of course, if you had witnessed the slaughter of your family, the burning of your home and the total annihilation of your community, and survived, to return and fight the very enemy who had done this, then you may feel that the savagery displayed by factions of the Red Army was in respects justified. However, if you choose to adopt this attitude as part of the ethos of warfare, you are likely to end up hurting the wrong people. The Russian people suffered intolerable cruelty and brutality under the Nazis; some 19 million Russian civilians perished as a result of Nazi aggression, and 8.6 million Red Army soldiers gave their lives fighting for freedom in the war. Yet this does not and should not ever be considered a reason to condone the act of rape in war. Asiatic races in particular, throughout their histories, have often expressed their acceptance of rape, sexual violence and/or sexual slavery, as a means of humiliating their enemies – females in particular. The Romans, Vikings and many other cultures of the ancient world all used rape and sexual violence in an almost ritualistic fashion following a victory. Yet the Second World War was a far cry from the ancient world – it was the twentieth century, a time where it was hoped that man was finally abandoning the notion that savagery was acceptable, at all. Ultimately, in Germany's case, it was Hitler, Himmler, Goebbels et al. who were to blame for what occurred during the death throes of the Third Reich.

Many German women have since spoken out bravely about their rape ordeals at the hands of the Red Army, and these accounts have been well documented in my previous books. One of the German women with whom I spoke recalled the ordeal of her rape at the age of just 11:

> I had never willingly supported what the Nazis were doing in Germany. I was a child and as such had little choice in the political and social direction our country took at that time. At the end of it all there was no joy for me and many others, as those who had arrived under the banner of liberation abused us as much as the Nazis had done, if not worse. No Nazi had ever raped me but those sent in to to remove the evil did so without any hesitation at all. Two of them took me away from my mother and took it in turns with me. All I can tell you is that it hurt, it was the worst pain I have ever had to endure, then there was the humiliation afterwards; as a child that is incredibly difficult, if impossible, to understand and come to terms with. As an 11-year-old child, I did not even know what sexual intercourse was back then. All that I knew is that they were doing something serious to me, something which was hurting me so much down below I thought I was going to die.
>
> Well, I didn't die, and it didn't destroy me as a human being. I went on to fall in love, get married and luckily have children. There was some concern early in my teens that I may not have been able to have children due to the rape, but I proved them wrong. I later began to understand what had happened to me and why, and I found it in my heart to forgive them for what they did to me. If it made them feel better for the slaughter of their families and of their people then that is fine. Ultimately, we all face our judgement day, and I can depart this earth with a clear conscience which is more than they may have done, as they may well be dead now, I don't know.

> In war sex is as much a weapon as is a rifle or a bayonet. Just think about that for a moment and you will understand that what I'm saying is correct.

An estimated 90,000 rapes were recorded in Berlin during the Soviet invasion and subsequent occupation. This figure is conservative and provides a record of cases of women who came forward for medical assistance, or reported their ordeals later to Allied military medical staff. The actual figure is believed to be well in excess of 100,000 rapes. In Vienna as many as 70,000 to 100,000 rapes were perpetrated by Red Army soldiers. In Hungary 50,000 to 200,000 rapes were recorded, and there were thousands more in Romania, Bulgaria, Poland, Czechoslovakia and Yugoslavia. There are also proven accounts of Red Army soldiers raping the emaciated, pyjama-clad victims of concentration camps.

Professor of Modern History Richard Evans has stated: 'Rape was often accompanied by torture and mutilation and frequently ended in the victim being shot or bludgeoned to death. The raging violence was undiscriminating.'

All of this sexual depravity was of course sanctioned by the Soviet leader, Joseph Stalin, a dictator who would bring as much if not more death and suffering to his own people than Hitler had done. The rapes also spawned a huge number of unwanted pregnancies that resulted in either backstreet butchery or babies being born, only to be abandoned by their mothers, often dying somewhere in a gutter. These unfortunate, unwanted children grew up with no knowledge of their background other than that they were the product of rape. They were frequently consigned to some postwar religious order who reminded them every single day of their childhood, of their worthlessness. Does this bleak reality bring about a change of heart for those who say that all German females deserved to be raped? I doubt it. This is all too often a deliberately overlooked subject. The mass rape of German women was one of the most wretched and shameful episodes of the war. Rape and/or sexual abuse was not a necessity for securing victory; this appalling behaviour served only to show the world, albeit at a much later date, what depravity so-called human beings are capable of, in the name of vengeance.

Once the nightmare of National Socialism was at an end, all that had been destroyed would be rebuilt in time, ironically, with the assistance of former enemies. Germany's partition into the socially and politically opposed ideologies of East and West, communist and capitalist, were of little concern to German citizens living in the relative freedom of Western Germany.

Gerta continues:

> I count myself very lucky. I had married young like a good German girl should. At least that's what they told us all under Adolf Hitler. The young man I married was also lucky; he came back from his war after being captured by the British. The last time we had had intercourse was several years previous. It was very nice and we had begun to experiment as ordered by the state, purely for childbearing reasons. Some of the things we did caused us much amusement and we laughed. This was due in part to our tough physical regimen in the Hitler Youth. My young husband was supremely fit and I was as supple and flexible as a gymnast. We tried intercourse where I placed my ankles over his shoulders; we found it hard not to laugh at first; it seemed ridiculous to us both although we greatly enjoyed it. I remember saying, as we manoeuvred ourselves to accomplish this position, 'My god, Friedrich, if you push your thing into me any deeper it will pop out of my belly button!' With the war now over and Friedrich back home safely, we could fall in love all over again but as free young people. This time I was more relaxed than before. I sat in the bath and poured champagne over my breasts and invited him to lick it off me. Of course, he wasted little time in joining me and doing so. Yes, we felt released of our political chains and all the obligations which came with them.

Many of the victors craved their demobilization, to return home to normality, their wives, familiar surroundings, clean sheets, fluffy pillows, patchwork blankets and the luxury of pipistrelle whispers in the evening after spending some much-needed time making love.

It was a very different story for German women. Many of them were pregnant as a result of rape and many would never see their husbands or boyfriends who were lying dead and mutilated on the battlefields, where their enemy had left them to rot. Other men died from their wounds, were summarily executed, or were simply marched off to the Soviet Gulags to be worked to death. Some were lucky enough to return home many years later, but more of them died under the hospitality of the Russians than returned home to Germany.

In 2013, the artist Jerzy Szumczyk, a student of the Gdansk Academy of Fine Arts in Poland, created a controversial sculpture which he titled *Komm Frau* (Come Here Woman). The sculpture appeared on the Gdansk Avenue of Victory as a tribute to all the German girls and women who had been raped by soldiers of the Red Army, as the war neared its end in Europe, particularly in the east during 1944 and 1945. The statue evoked powerful emotions; it depicted a pregnant German woman being raped by a Russian soldier as he holds a pistol to her head. The statue was soon removed by the authorities from its position on the Avenue of Victory. Jerzy justified both the creation of the work and its placement. He had felt compelled to make a stand on this now historical issue. It was an entirely honourable gesture with no malice intended, made by a man who certainly never wished his work to become some form of political statement or expression aimed at sympathy for the Nazis.

This is an intensely difficult subject for many reasons. As I have already mentioned, there are those who even today feel that innocent German girls and women who lived under the Third Reich deserved to be raped. They are of the attitude that they were guilty by association, regardless of their political allegiances or their ages. In my personal view, anyone who condones the act of rape, in any context, is every bit as twisted and evil as the perpetrator.

Chapter 26

Nazi Fetishism in the Twenty-first Century

Third Reich Nazi uniforms, badges and items of clothing often described as 'fantasy' apparel, adorned with swastikas and SS symbols, have a niche following in the sub-cultural world of sex and sexual fetishism today. This is of course unique; one cannot say the same for Communist Russian or Imperial Japanese iconography, two equally murderously oppressive regimes, yet history appears to have conveniently forgiven them their crimes.

Nazism in pornography is nothing new either., If you were a young adult in 1970s Britain you would have been well aware of the appeal possessed by Nazism, particularly in printed pornography of the day. There were 'men's magazines' produced in Britain and Europe that regularly featured sexy girls wearing Nazi uniforms. Far from being construed as morally or visually offensive, there was no 'shock horror' reaction to such content in the glossy pages of these publications. These magazines were widely available and placed strategically out of reach of youngsters, on the top shelves at most newsagents of the time. The Nazism that was featured in 1970s pornography did not offend people in the same way it does today.

In 1965 the first videocassette recorders (VCRs) or home video recorders, were produced. Some seven years later, in 1972, the first videocassettes of movies were produced, effectively bringing the cinema into private homes. Naturally, the porn industry was keen to capitalize on this revolution in home entertainment technology, and by the mid-1970s there was a plethora of Second World War Nazi-themed sexploitation or soft porn movies. Most of these Nazi soft porn movies were made in Italy, the acting was highly questionable and the storylines weak, yet they proved highly popular at the time. These films weren't subject to any in-depth psychological or moral examination by those individuals or couples who either bought them or rented them out. They were merely for 'getting off' and they fulfilled that purpose. The list below details fourteen of the most notable titles in this now forgotten Nazi soft porn genre:

- *Ilsa, She Wolf of the SS* (Don Edmonds, 1975)
- *SS Hell Camp* (Luigi Batzella, 1977)
- *The Gestapo's Last Orgy* (Cesare Canevari, 1977)
- *Women's Camp 119* (Bruno Mattel, 1977)
- *SS Experiment Love Camp* (Sergio Garrone, 1976)
- *Salon Kitty* (Tinto Brass 1976)
- *Nazi Love Camp 27* (Mario Caiano, 1977)
- *SS Girls* (Bruno Mattel 1977)
- *The Night Porter* (Lilianna Cavani, 1974)
- *Salo, Or The 120 Days of Sodom* (Pier Paolo Pasolini, 1975)
- *Love Camp 7* (Lee Frost, 1969)
- *SS Nazi Convoy* (Jesus Franco, Pierre Chevalier, 1978)
- *SS Camp 5: Women's Hell* (Sergio Garrone, 1977)
- *Fraulein Devil* (Patrice Rhomm, 1977)

Much of the logic behind the production of these Nazified porn movies lies with the film producers themselves. It was easier to get violently sexual film content past the censors if it was presented as having some basis in historical fact, however vague this might have been. The filmmakers had no real interest whatsoever in being factually correct – the sole intention was to get each film past the censors and make a profit. The 'not shocked by anything' attitude of 1970s society, and film audiences in particular, meant audiences were suddenly craving more extreme, weirder and wilder psycho-sexual experiences.

Nazi soft porn films certainly pushed the boundaries of bad taste and tested the receptivity of not only the censors but their audiences too. Yet this genre of the soft porn film industry was a short-lived venture and by the 1980s had become redundant. This was down to more than just one factor. Some maturer audiences grew bored of the 'soft' nature of the actual sexual content of these films, despite scenes of torture and rape, but which were not perverse enough or didn't go far enough. Apart from the violence displayed in these films there was no penetrative sexual intercourse; scenes showed only what is called today 'dry humping' or merely going through the motions of the act. Society's taste for porn wasn't waning by any means, it was just evolving.

By the 1980s the softcore porn genre had been drowned almost completely by the arrival of low-budget hardcore porn films, made virtually all over Europe. Again, the Nazi theme was prevalent in many of the storylines where actual penetration was taking place, amongst other things, but again the use of Nazism in these films would be short-lived. The hardcore porn industry would continue to grow yet the swastikas, uniforms and Nazified themes would be replaced by a huge white bed upon which a good-looking couple would go through the entire repertoire of the Kama Sutra before reaching the grand finale.

Today Nazi fetishism and sexual fantasies still exist and there are those who cater for this. Where Nazi clothing is concerned some people wear the genuine article, or the 'fantasy' pieces out of political sympathy, or general adoration, and there are those who indulge both the real and 'fantasy' material in the sexual context. The lines between the two have blurred, especially in the current overtly politically correct times. Accordingly, this is a subject worthy of some examination with which to bring this volume to its conclusion. If one wishes to research the subject of Nazism and its association with sexual fetishism, one need not look that hard. There are of course websites which cater to those sympathetic to National Socialism as a political/racist entity, and those who see a sexual side to Nazism. For example, in the United States in particular, the White Power movement has grown beyond the supposed image of gun-toting, large, hairy men wearing flannel shirts, to petite schoolgirls and college students sporting nightwear adorned with SS skulls and eagle and swastika emblems of various design, many of which are 'fantasy' pieces. It is apparent that many of the young women posing in this attire with SS runes or skulls or eagle and swastika designs are the offspring of White Power-supporting families.

How one arrives at this prognosis is quite simple: no matter how deep my own personal interest in the Nazi era may have been as a youngster, there is no way my parents would have tolerated me bringing pillows, duvet covers or even nightwear adorned with swastikas or SS symbology into the house, even had I wanted to do so – which I most certainly did not, as I understood what these images represented, from an early age.

On the other hand, I would not have allowed my own children to do this either, had they followed my interest in the Third Reich era. So, one has to assume that these mostly young women have what amounts to a nurtured interest in Nazi iconography, in its political context, through parental influences. The images of these young women posing in their nightwear with Nazi iconography, as opposed to teddy bears and pink flowers, is certainly not strictly intended to portray a sexual image to the onlooker, but more of a political stance, though the individual interpretation as always lies in the eyes of the beholder, however he or she wishes to construe a particular image.

The commercial use of Nazi iconography is of course nothing new. We have already examined its widespread use by the 1970s porn industry, in both film and literature. When the punk rock explosion began in 1976, clothing designers profited handsomely from the creation of clothing adorned with the swastika, not out of any political affiliation but purely for the shock value, and to enhance the movement's anti-establishment stance. The swastika daubed on various pieces of clothing was specifically designed to alienate both society and the establishment, and to a degree it worked. Yet, this clothing was expensive, and most followers of this cult music phenomenon preferred to make their own, often adding swastikas with paint or marker pens. Either way the result was the same, instantaneous shock value and gasps of horror from passers-by on the street. Yet one cannot apportion blame to the punk movement alone, for its inadvertent role in commercializing Nazi iconography; one has to blame society itself for allowing and tolerating it to happen in the first place.

It is odd that even those who participate in fetishism associated with Nazism are often unable to fully explain their reasons for this. A young woman I interviewed but who did not wish to be named, said simply:

> I can't explain it, I mean I would never support the torture, prejudice or mass murder of anyone. I just like the look of Nazi uniforms and I bought a reproduction black Waffen-SS tunic and put it on. I don't know why but I felt strangely aroused by the imagery when I looked at myself in the full-length mirror, wearing the tunic and nothing else. Was it down to the visions of tall blond-haired, blue-eyed Nordic-looking young men I held in my mind? I don't know, maybe. My boyfriend first encouraged me to wear the tunic as part of our sexual routine. When I wore the tunic, he performed better than when I didn't wear the tunic, so we kept it going. It could be the same with any uniform: I could dress up as a nurse or a policewoman, but my boyfriend doesn't want that, he likes the Nazi uniforms. Since buying the repro tunic, I have added a visor cap and I bought a pair of repro boots too, which I sometimes wear during sex.

It's something we do in the privacy of our own home, we don't involve anyone else, and I certainly don't allow myself to be photographed, or post photographs of myself on social media like some do. If people think I'm a weirdo or I'm sick in the head, then they are entitled to think that, but then they don't know me, do they?

I asked her what her parents would think of her fetish for Nazi clothing, and her boyfriend's, if they ever found out about it. She replied: 'Well, they won't ever know. As I've already stated, we don't advertise the fact and what we do takes place in the bedroom of our own home, and when we've finished, the uniforms go into a wardrobe.'

Nazi fetishism was once very common in bondage, discipline, sadism and masochism (BDSM). Nazi-themed pornography formed the focal point of low-budget BDSM porn movies, which were an acquired taste even within the well-established porn movie genre. In recent years this has declined somewhat, yet the violence of Nazism still proves to be a popular fetish for people from all walks of life, race and religious denomination. It is said that today Nazi fetishism is most popular in Asian and gay pornographic material. Finding the evidence with which to dispute these facts is certainly not that difficult an endeavour. A middle-aged gentleman from a quiet town in the North of England gave his view of what many might call Nazi fetishism:

> There are all kinds of fetishes. Why is it so bad to have a fetish for Nazi stuff? No one complains about Japanese rising sun flags despite the Japanese being responsible for some of the most heinous of crimes committed in the war. What attracted me to the Nazi stuff was the combination of the smart look of their uniforms and the strong German accent. I liked the way the Nazi women wore their uniforms, their blonde hair in pigtails and I found the whole look was a huge turn-on. It took a long time to find a partner who shared this same fetish, but I met one through a dating website. We both dress up in Nazi uniforms when we have sex and we both enjoy it. We take turns in being dominant and we even talk to each other in German when we make love. We enjoy it yet we have no political interest in Nazism at all; it's just the look and a strange sexual allure for us.

I asked what was wrong with, for example, a British, American or Russian Second World War uniform – would any of these have the same effect? He replied:

No, not at all, those uniforms are just so unsexy and dull. I don't like the colours either – they look like cowshit to me. We both like it a bit rough too and the Nazi theme has that element of pain too, doesn't it? In previous relationships I would never have allowed a woman to use a whip on me, but with me and my partner now, we both use a whip as it comes with the Nazi theme. The whip is as natural as the high-leg leather jackboots and the uniform. I admit we often go to parties with other likeminded adults who have a sexual fetish for anything from the Nazi era. For us it's a way of life or rather our sex life, and we enjoy it greatly and we see nothing wrong with it.

A 21-year-old American student who gave her name as Anna explained her Nazi fetish in the following simple terms:

A lot of guys love a chick who throws on a T-shirt with a huge swastika on it, and does various poses for the camera. I have several T-shirts; one has a skull with the letters SS on it, the other has an eagle and swastika design. Guys don't want to see me wearing just plain white shirts when I post photos on my webpage. I'm not into cuddly bears or anything as I'm not a baby. Yes, I find the Nazi stuff very sexy, very strong and masculine and that is a turn-on for as many chicks as it is for guys. I make a lot of money from subscription fees for my photographs, so I'm happy to do them and if anyone is pissed about it that's their problem, not mine. I know a lot of Nazi cosplayers too [costume players, people who *practise dressing up*] but they are very exclusive and don't advertise on the normal worldwide web, and you just get shut down once they find you or if some dick reports you. I know a girl who is a close friend of mine who has a swastika tattoo on each of her breasts. She says the swastikas make her feel sexier and the guys she dates love them too.

A middle-aged woman who admitted having worked in the porn industry in the early 1990s recalled her Nazi fetishism:

Yes, I starred in a few short films shot in Europe, mostly where we all wore Nazi uniforms, put on gas masks and fucked each other. By the late 1990s it was getting very difficult to find reliable distributors for the films we made and suddenly they were considered in bad taste, even by porn industry standards. Things just suddenly changed, and we couldn't make any money from films which had Nazi themes in their storylines. It wasn't viable anymore to do them, so we moved on.

It was a shame as I really enjoyed the dressing up and I liked the look of the German Nazi uniforms and the guys who wore them. They were always handsome guys with blond hair and blue eyes who weren't necessarily German but who looked the part with their huge cocks and‑whips, boots and pistols. Yes, acting out those Nazi fantasies was once a lucrative industry but now a lot of people hate them and won't have any association with them. Trends in the porn industry have changed a lot. If you were caught making a Nazi porn film today, you'd get thrown in prison and labelled as a Nazi sympathizer. I think it's all a bit stupid and has gone a bit too far, but that's just my opinion.

A 21-year-old American student who gave her name as Helen, and who regularly posts images of herself on internet sites, gave the following explanation for her particular fetishism:

My family is traditionally of deep South ancestry. We have ancestors who fought on the Confederate side in the American Civil War. I make a lot of the shirts that I wear myself. Most of what I make are like nightshirts, but you can get other stuff from websites, stuff like bedcovers, pillows and cushions with the swastika or SS skulls printed on them. I don't put the nightshirts on to look sexy, necessarily, I'm not trying to turn anyone on – I am catching people's attention and trying to convey my views. The easiest way to gain the attention of males is to put on a shirt yet have nothing else on, leave the legs bare or something, just enough to catch their attention. The same applies to females but I wouldn't say what I do is really a lesbian aesthetic. So, I'm not a sexual fetishist where Nazi stuff is concerned; I am a political follower of an ideology I believe in. I believe in an Aryan race, that Aryans belong as a single world-ruling community within a single culture which does not allow itself to be polluted by outside cultures, races or anything else. The Nazis were the best example of that particular philosophy in my view. But as always you see only what you want to see in any supposed sexy image of a girl or a guy. It's what you yourself make of it, but for me it's definitely a political statement, yet if guys find it sexy it doesn't bother me at all' it should be a free world and everyone to their own ideas on how they live their lives.

Helen's narrative certainly proved interesting, so I asked her what she felt about Nazi genocide and murder, and what she felt about supporting a regime that had been responsible for the death and destruction of millions, including many Americans:

I wouldn't seek to go out and kill anyone and I don't condone mass murder of any kind, but I do believe if your own culture is threatened by one which is alien to you then you should be entitled to protect yourself and your fellow communities if that alien culture threatens that of your own. That's all I will say and who, if they are totally honest, says that I am wrong? Am I wrong or am I right? If someone thinks I am just some cute, dumb Nazi baby they can think again. I think those who get a sexual kick out of Nazi stuff are merely covering up for underlying political affiliations.

A young woman, a UK-based cosplayer, who quite understandably gave her name as 'X', explained her fetish for Nazi material:

Guys and girls love seeing me lying half naked on a Nazi flag or wearing a skimpy outfit with swastikas on. Why do they like it so much? I don't really know but I get a real kick out of the thought that maybe both guys and girls are getting off over my photographs. I am aware of trends, especially in cosplay, and there are a lot of Nazi fetishists out there from all over the world.

I asked where most of the interest in her images originated from, and she replied:

Most of the harder images which I do, I charge a subscription fee, and these images cannot be accessed in any other way and they cannot be downloaded either. I don't do these images for nothing, its sign up and subscription, where age verification has to be confirmed too. Most of the interest in my images comes from Asia or the USA; rarely do I get anyone logging in from Britain or Germany which is odd really, isn't it? I'm not ashamed of what I do. I am simply catering for a need; it's money. I'm not interested in the politics or bullshit which surrounds Nazi regalia; it's strictly a business component in my view. So, does that make me a fetishist or just another business-minded person, just like those who profit from selling Third Reich medals, uniforms and weapons etc?

With ever-tightening restrictions on content posted on the worldwide web it is becoming increasingly difficult for those wishing to share material which purports to glorify or sexualize Nazi era material. Restrictions are being increased even for the legitimate sale of historical artefacts connected with the Third Reich, artefacts such as those which have graced museum displays all over the world since the end of the war, and which are equally as important as any other area of world history. There is a real danger that this area of history might be legislated out of existence, and if this were ever to occur it would be a disastrous trend indeed. Of course, there will be those who would welcome this if it ever happened, but history is there specifically for us all to learn from, to assist in the prevention (wherever possible) of certain events repeating themselves in the future, the importance of which can never be reiterated strongly enough. If I can consider this venture a success, I can say this is my art, and, while deep in self-depreciation mode, I have reached for the cherry atop a dogshit trifle. I've tried my best, thank you and goodnight.

>   Neither voyeur/author
>   and his utilization of excrement
>   to paint the pretty picture of melancholy smiling.

Afterword

To admit I felt a degree of trepidation prior to embarking upon the synopsis for this particular work would be something of an understatement. First, I had to be convinced that it was both a good idea and commercially acceptable. I started work on the book almost immediately following approval of the synopsis by my publisher, and I found the process of writing it strangely neither enjoyable nor melancholic.

The ongoing COVID-19 pandemic and subsequent long period of furlough which followed meant that the book evolved rapidly. During its formulation, I couldn't help but harbour some momentary thoughts that I may have initiated some form of literary suicide. Yet with the book now complete, I am at that point of reflection at which all authors arrive following the completion of their latest work. I can say I have no regrets whatsoever at having written this book. On the contrary, I hope that whoever reads this work, even if they come to it with an already open mind, will learn something of the excessively contradictory nature of Adolf Hitler's Third Reich, especially its at times misogynistic attitude toward women and their sexuality.

I was also perhaps a little concerned that somehow this book might be misconstrued as being a crude attempt to produce a *Fifty Shades of the Third Reich*. Let's be honest, any book which focuses on sex as its primary topic of analysis is almost always subject to a high degree of scrutiny, curiosity, ridicule and hostility. But why? Sex today in its normal context, by which I mean that it takes place between consenting adults, whether they be heterosexual, gay or lesbian, is considered perfectly acceptable.

The line is crossed when sexual activity leads to perversion or the abuse, grooming or actual physical abuse of children and/or animals, and in many cases other adults. Sadly, those who seek such depravity reside in all areas of the human community. The basic mechanics of sexual grooming in particular have changed little over the years, but modern technology has made it easier for the deviant to pursue his or her prey, especially through the plethora of endless, ungoverned, online media.

The Third Reich was far from the culturally united regime which it professed to have been. For young people in particular, Hitler's rise to stately prominence heralded something of a dark age where sex was concerned. The Nazi distribution of power among those who stood to prosper from its abuse was extensive, even more so than has been previously thought, as this particular work has attempted to illustrate. Of late there have been many programmes that have had every opportunity to discuss some general analysis of what sex under the Third Reich was really like; sadly, so far all have fallen well short of their objective to reveal anything new or useful. Predictably, most of them focus on the supposed sexual perversions of Adolf Hitler, for which there is no actual unequivocal proof. There are those who would have delighted over this work had it revealed some imaginary scene where Adolf Hitler and Eva Braun banqueted on each other's faecal matter while sipping urine from champagne glasses as a prelude to a kinky sex session at the Berghof. I can only offer my apologies for having disappointed such readers. It was my hope that maybe something could be learned from those males and females, young and old, straight, gay or lesbian, Jewish and non-Jewish, who had fallen victim a very unfortunate set of circumstances and the sordid undercurrent of a regime that wore a falsified veneer of panache.

One of the defining features of many dictatorships, apart from the violence, prejudices, summary executions, puppet courts and the complete dismantling of everyday basic freedoms, is the exploitation of its subjects, from the very young to the very old. Generally, the forms of exploitation that thrive under these regimes include political, financial, social and sexual abuse.

Material used in the preparation of this book, as with all the first-hand material which I have amassed over some thirty-six years of research into the social and military history of the Third Reich, was by no means easy to acquire. I knew that visiting the Public Record Office at Kew, for example, would turn up very little if any of the kind of material required for this book. There was no textbook to refer to, no *Concise History of Fucking*, nor anywhere near enough printed material to grace this book with a glowing and extensive section on references, a bibliography or sources. Had this printed material been available, this book would have been just another patchwork of poached efforts and not something I could ever claim as my own.

The Third Reich was awash with victims of sexual abuse, some of whom were prepared to talk and others who found it far too distressing, even after all these years. It is their stories which are the focus of this work and therefore, I am eternally grateful to those individuals who gave their time to share their memories, no matter how painful they may have been, in order to make this work possible. This includes people who contributed their personal letters, anecdotes and diary entries.

The years following the demise of Nazism, particularly in West Germany, were relatively trouble free; many say the 1950s–1970s was Germany's golden era. As a race the Germans have never been shy of their sexuality nor embarrassed by naturism. Getting one's kit off and walking around or just sunbathing nude on a hot day was something many Germans were brought up to embrace from a young age. Being naked was never perceived as dirty, overtly sexual or a novelty in Germany, as it was by most Britons with their prudish morality.

Of course, this is nonsense. Far worse things than just being naked have gone on for many years behind many closed doors in England. Most resorts in Germany catered openly for those who preferred clothes and those who didn't, with never a red face nor a giggle to be seen or heard. Yet today, the world is a radically different place, a place where romance in particular appears to be well past its sell-by date, almost irrelevant in an age of penis cams, spermicidal soaps and cum-swapping parties which leave participants with more than just crumbs in their lunchboxes and an itchy crotch by the Sunday morning. Ann Summers (the British retail company selling sex toys and lingerie), once a real crown of thorns to the virgin blood-swigging, man-hating, trouser-wearing feminists, yet enjoyed by millions of sexually bored housewives all over the world, has been irrevocably overtaken by shag-meets, dogging and twenty-four-hour online pornography.

The structural integrity of love itself has been tested beyond all reasonable emotional limits, leading many to ask if the traditional concept of love still exists today. Marriage certificates may well be signed on toilet paper, for all they are worth today – 'to love honour and destroy' in many cases. The neon-lit streets of every major city in the world are awash with vice: prostitutes openly ply their trade, a live sex show will pull a bigger crowd than a movie premiere, and where punters are asked on entry if they want coke sprinkled on their Haribo cock rings.

The acts of having sex and making love which once were so distinctly different have now become blurred within the lascivious vomit splash of millennial society where unashamed promiscuity has become a rite of passage for some, as much as mindless violence is now a trivial pursuit for the bored. Yes, the once purely fictitious *Clockwork Orange* you all dreaded is here and yes, it's time you realized it before it chews you up and spits you out onto the concrete. Long gone are the days where grouse munchers and the illegitimate offspring of the bourgeois champagne-quaffing elite stared down with some disdain upon the red and inflamed anal clap of the sexual activities of us mere mortals. Today, both are tainted with the same heavily soiled toilet brush in what is the 'pie and custard' of world society. Yet sex today is perhaps more approachable as a subject and study area than it has ever previously been. In millennial society sex has become both big business and a proverbial thorn in the side of the human race, the reasons for which have already been noted. Sex today has found a niche in the commercial empires of the millennium; and by comparison with previous decades, there is far greater sexual freedom in society today than there has ever been. Today sex and sexuality have burst loudly, naked and full frontal, out of the privacy of the bedroom, brothel and empty conference room, and into the spotlight of social media, television advertising, glossy magazines and in the tawdry rash of weekday soaps so beloved of the ailing BBC. Yet there are those in power today, operating through various media, professing to support all manner of good causes, who have already decided that they alone possess some divine authority to be our moral consciences, that it is their individual right alone to protect us from our own history and that of the greater world about us, deciding for us what we should or shouldn't be saying, doing, watching or reading. These are the same seemingly invisible, faceless bureaucrats who cast their expensive suits and shirts onto the sticky floors of some backstreet 'Butter Sauna' while diamond-studded gold vibrators throb happily away in their rectal passages.

These are not necessarily individuals but sometimes corporate entities who have espoused a new cancer of apathetical thinking, particularly where any new literary works associated with the Nazi era are concerned.

It now seems any attempt to produce and promote (on a personal level) anything new about the Third Reich is automatically met with open hostility and accusations of having alienated the whole damned world. If social media giants, and Facebook is the primary offender, continue along these lines of prejudice and blatant censorship toward our world history, it will eventually destroy historical literature as we have always known and appreciated it. It also appears that today the now ancient if long-lost engineers of humanity itself have failed to account for the fragility that is truth.

Under the Hitler regime there were no choices, no democracy and no freedom of expression. Today we have reached that same impasse. In the field of modern historical literature, I too can say I have experienced them all – the trolls, the assassins of one's integrity, the fetishists, those who are clearly unhinged and those who make you feel as if you are attempting to educate the brainless, those who need to be constantly reminded of the intellectual property that is their own stupidity. At the same time many of the basic freedoms that good men and women gave their lives to protect are steadily being eroded in an electric fog of political correctness and cultural genocide. If this stance is permitted to continue unchallenged, then we will all be guilty of allowing the mistakes of the past to be repeated.

Tim Heath
July 2021

Bibliography

Herzog, Dagmar. *Sexuality in Europe: A Twentieth Century History*, Cambridge: Cambridge University Press 2011.
Kinsey, Alfred C., Pomeroy, Wardell B. & Martin, Clyde E. *Sexual Behaviour in the Human Male*, Philadelphia & London: W. B. Saunders Co. Ltd. 1948.
Kinsey, Alfred C., Pomeroy, Wardell B. & Martin, Clyde E. *Sexual Behaviour in the Human Female*, Philadelphia & London; W. B. Saunders Co. Ltd. 1953.
Maines, Rachel. *The Technology of Orgasm: "Hysteria," the Vibrator and Women's Satisfaction*, Baltimore: John Hopkins University Press 1999.
Marquis de Sade. *Philosophy in the Bedroom*, New York: Grove Press 1971.
Vermeil, Edmond. *Germany in the Twentieth Century: A Political and Cultural History of the Weimar Republic and The Third Reich*, New York: Praeger 1956.

Acknowledgements

The Deutscher Historiche Museum (DHM) Berlin, German Federal Archives, National Archives UK, The Wiener Library, The Imperial War Museum, Joshua H. Studding, Tula Kubiczek, Johannes Kriebst, Greta Streibaum, Herbert Lange, Hilde Gabel, Peter Bachmann Barwald, Kirsten Eckermann, Andrea Brecht, Katherina Briedenich, Berta Littmann, Celina Falk, Ursula Vogel, Theresa Moelle, Arnold Hilbre, Melitta and Balthasar Kramer, Klara Wyborny, Engela Losch, Rebecca Noetz, Walter and Ernst Reickart, Hildegard Kustin, Martin Wengel, Anna Dann, Jess Steiner, Ilse Baumann, Katrina Niekerk, Hilde Schwarz, Gabrielle Haefker, Alessa Goberg, Erica Gordon, Dana Busch, Elise Bettmann, Martin Schröder, Peter Rickmann, Arnulf Scriba, Kurt Uling, Ruth Goetz, Olga Kirschener, Selina Mayer, Jens Ehrler, Gunther Reissner, Helena Voight, Max Woessel, Diana Roehoff, Doris Grunnemayer, Martha Ozols, Wilhelmina Metzel, Vera Hirsch, Konrad Frisch, Jochen Hunnes, Dr Elizabeth Riefer-Kranse, Charlotte 'Lottie' Schreiber, Ursula Siben, Walter Gollob, Ernst Neissau, Martha Hutter, Gunther Hirschberg, Michael Schildt and Traudl Junge.

With special thanks to Ingrid Pittmann for the use of the memoir written by her mother, Klara Busch. All material either written or dictated in German, originally, was translated into English with the kind assistance of Hedra Klems.